South Dakota's Governors Residence Cookbook

A Culinary Legacy Celebrating the First Families of South Dakota

A product of typensave™ software.

Printed in the U.S.A. by

P.O. Box 2110 • Kearney, NE 68848
800-445-6621 • www.morriscookbooks.com

Foreword

The cliché "home is where the heart is" has been embraced by South Dakota's first families since becoming a state in 1889. South Dakota's first families made their home anywhere they could for the first 37 years of statehood. For the next 12 years, home was in a small yellow house on the east shore of Capitol Lake.

The original Governors Residence was constructed in 1936 with Workers Progress Administration (WPA) funds from the federal government. Because of infrastructure problems and outdated facilities, a new Governors Residence was completed in 2005.

South Dakota first families have shared food with each other, their cabinets and staff, extended families and friends, and in official state gatherings. In this cookbook, the first families, their extended families, cabinet, and staff share recipes from their families with the people of South Dakota. We extend our appreciation to everyone who contributed recipes and offer apologies to those whom we were unable to identify or contact. We encourage past and future first families, governor's staff, and cabinet to contribute recipes for future editions of this cookbook. For additional information, please contact the South Dakota Heritage Fund.

We also wish to acknowledge and thank the Department of Tourism and State Development for providing the photograph for the front and back cover of this cookbook and the State Archives for the use of their historical photos.

Proceeds from this cookbook and future cookbooks will be deposited in a fund with the South Dakota Community Foundation. The fund will be used exclusively to provide funding for future fixtures, furnishing, and furniture at the Governors Residence. We appreciate your support through the purchase of this cookbook and hope you will enjoy a celebration of good food, down home cooking, and the history of South Dakota's first families.

First Families of South Dakota

1889-1893	Governor Arthur C. and First Lady Margaret (Wylie) Mellette Children: Wylie, Anton, Charles, and Richard
1893-1897	Governor Charles H. and First Lady Martha (Frizzell) Sheldon Children: Ethel (Bayard), James B., and Charles H.
1897-1901	Governor Andrew E. and First Lady Martha Ann (Chappelle) Lee Children: Jessamine (Fox)
1901-1905	Governor Charles N. and First Lady Eunice Jeannette (Slye) Herreid Children: Grace and Roscoe
1905-1907	Governor Samuel H. and First Lady Mary Ellen (Masten) Elrod Children: Barbara (Knittel) and Arthur
1907-1909	Governor Coe I. and First Lady Lavinia Curtis (Robinson) Crawford Children: Robert Dean, Olive Curtis, Jeanette (Lusk)
1909-1913	Governor Robert S. and First Lady Florence (Albert) Vessey Children: Harry, Verna, Florence, Bernice, and Charles Robert Jr.
1913-1917	Governor Frank M. and First Lady Emilie (Beaver) Byrne Children: Carol, Francis, Malcolm, Joe, Emmons, and one son and one daughter who died in infancy
1917-1921	Governor Peter and First Lady Lydia (Anderson) Norbeck Children: Nellie (Wegner), Peter Harold, and Sally (Earle)

1921-1925	Governor William H. and First Lady Harriett (Russell) McMaster Children: William H. Jr. and Dorothy M. (Armstrong)
1925-1927	Governor Carl and First Lady Gertrude (Bertelsen) Gunderson Children: Helen Louise, Florence G. (Cooper), Carol G. (LaGrave), and Norris Elwood
1927-1931	Governor William J. and First Lady Sarah (Farrand) Bulow Children: Maurene, William J. Jr., Kathleen, and Calanthia Farrand
1931-1933	Governor Warren E. and First Lady Elizabeth Jane (Parliamant) Green Children: Maxwell, George, Mildred, and Edson
1933-1937	Governor Tom and First Lady Lorena (McLain) Berry Children: Baxter, Nell (Phipps), Faye (Jones), and Paul
1937-1939	Governor Leslie and First Lady Elizabeth (Ward) Jensen Children: Natalie and Karen
1939-1943	Governor Harlan J. and First Lady Vera Sarah (Cahalan) Bushfield Children: Mary Janeth, John Pearson, and Harlan J. Jr.
1943-1947	Governor Merrill Q. and First Lady Emily L. (Auld) Sharpe Children: Lorna May (Leedy)
1947-1951	Governor George T. and First Lady Madge Ellen (Turner) Mickelson Children: Janice (Carmody), Lavon (Meyers), Patricia (Adam), and George Speaker
1951-1955	Governor Sigrud and First Lady Vivian Dell (Walz) Anderson Children: Kristin Karen

1955-1959	Governor Joseph J. and June (Shakstad) Foss Children: Cheryl, Mary Joe, Joseph Frank, and Eric Peter
1959-1961	Governor Ralph and First Lady Lorna (Buntrock) Herseth Children: Karen (Wee), Connie (Stenseth), and R. Lars
1961-1965	Governor Archie M. and First Lady Florence Maxine (Dexter) Gubbrud Children: John Dexter and Maxine Louise
1965-1969	Governor Nils A. Boe Borghuld Boe, sister of Governor Boe, served as the official hostess during his two terms as governor.
1969-1971	Governor Frank L. and First Lady Patricia (Henley) Farrar Children: Jean Marie, Sally, Mary Susan, Anne Marie, and Robert John
1971-1978	Governor Richard F. and First Lady Nancy (Pankey) Kneip Children: Kevin, Kent, Keith, Kurt, Philip, Paul, Patrick, and Michael
1978	Governor Harvey and First Lady Ann Marie (Giegel) Wollman Children: Kristin
1979-1987	Governor William J. and First Lady Mary Dean (Thom) Janklow Children: Russell, Pamela (Derheim), and Shonna (Haugen)
1987-1993	Governor George S. and First Lady Linda (McCahren) Mickelson Children: Mark, Amy (Brecht), and David
1993-1995	Governor Walter Dale and First Lady Patricia (Kilber Caldwell) Miller Children: Nancy (Miller) Yahnke, Karey (Miller) Albers, Walter R. (Randy) Miller, Renee (Miller) Johansen, Cade Caldwell, and Rebecca (Caldwell) Bauer

1995-2003   Governor William J. and First Lady Mary Dean
                (Thom) Janklow
             Children: Russell, Pamela (Derheim), and
                Shonna (Haugen)

2003-2011   Governor M. Michael and First Lady Jean (Vedvei) Rounds
             Children: Christopher, Brian, Carrie (Larson), and John

History of the South Dakota Governors Residence

In the 1904 election, voters decided to make Pierre the permanent seat of government and plans for a new Capitol were approved. With the new Capitol under construction, permanent housing for the First Family did not exist. South Dakota governors, year-round residents of the capital city, had to find their own living quarters.

From 1889 to 1925, governors found housing where they could on a monthly housing allowance of $75. These residences are documented in historical pictures and city directories of the time.

Legislative steps to provide for a Governors Residence began in 1913. After failed bills, legislative studies, and property searches by the State Capitol Commission, the commission purchased a large tract east of Capitol Lake in 1920, which included the Hodoval home on Court Place. The house was not used as a Governors Residence until 1925. Governors Carl Gunderson, William Bulow, Warren Green, and Tom Berry made this residence their home.

Governor Tom Berry (1933-1937) thought better quarters were needed. He lacked legislative support to build a residence with state funds and turned to the federal government for aid. The project was approved. In early 1936, Works Progress Administration (WPA) workers began construction on a new Governors Residence. The original yellow cottage was sold for $1,270 and was moved to another location in Pierre. By late 1936, the WPA completed the structure with $1,800 provided by the state and $25,861 provided by the federal government.

Before the new Governors Residence was completed, there had been a change in political power. Republican Governor Leslie Jensen had defeated Democrat Governor Tom Berry. Democratic legislators had supported the construction of the residence, but they now opposed the

furnishings. One Democratic legislator commented, "My party found means to build the house without cost to the state and if your party can find means to furnish it without cost to the state, I am...with you." By mid-February, a compromise appropriation of $9,000 was approved. Governor Jensen promised South Dakotans to spend "only enough of this appropriation now to make habitable the rooms we absolutely need" and he would buy furniture "appropriate to the governor of a great state" only "after we get rains and a crop."

Governor Jensen and his wife moved into the residence in 1937, but it was not until 1939 that the house was totally furnished. First Lady Vera Bushfield, along with an interior decorator, furnished the residence. The design was keeping with a practical look. The official state reception room had linoleum floors, no curtains, and was furnished with rugged bamboo furniture.

Since 1939, the Governors Residence has had several face-lifts. This building served as the Governors Residence for sixteen first families from 1937 to 2003.

Because of severe infrastructure problems and outdated facilities, the Bureau of Administration and the Capitol Beautification Commission recommended the Governors Residence be replaced with a new facility, which would better serve the needs of the governor, the first family, and the citizens of South Dakota.

The former residence was officially closed on November 3, 2003, and Governor Rounds and his family returned to their private residence in Pierre. The residence was relocated to a lot in east Pierre in December 2003. The building was sold and was moved to the Rapid City area.

Construction on the 14,000-square-foot residence began in the spring of 2004, and the new residence was completed in June 2005. Thousands of South Dakotans and numerous corporations and companies from across the state contributed substantial amounts of money, products, and services. The estimated total cost was $2.87 million. It has private living quarters for the governors' families and room for public receptions. A time capsule was placed in the double fireplace located in the public area.

Table of Contents

APPETIZERS & BEVERAGES

(Photo courtesy of the South Dakota State Historical Society Archives)

WELLS HOUSE

Governor Arthur C. Mellette and his family frequently stayed at the Wells House. Governor Charles H. Sheldon and family leased the same rooms as Mellette until 1895.

William S. Wells built the Wells House in 1883 for $25,000. It was a three-story structure 60x60 feet. On the first floor was a large dining hall, which could seat 100, a very large parlor with a billiard table, and a well-equipped kitchen.

With 80 rooms, The Wells House was the best hotel in Dakota Territory. It was finished inside with imitation black walnut and French veneer. Even though Pierre had no water or sewer system when the hotel was built, the hotel provided a water system from an outside cistern with a 700-barrel capacity. The cistern was a force pump with enough power to force water to any part of the hotel. The washrooms contained marble basins, each supplied with hot and cold water pipes and elegant faucets. The very spacious parlor and bedrooms were all elegantly and tastefully furnished.

One famous guest of the Wells House was U.S. Senator Benjamin Harrison in July 1885. Competition from the new Locke Hotel forced the Wells House to close in 1892. Bishop Thomas O'Gorman bought the Wells House intending to use it as a hospital. The Wells House instead was torn down and used by the Pierre Catholic Church for the building of S.S. Peter and Paul Academy.

TIDBITS

Margaret Wylie Mellette married Arthur Mellette in 1866 and, in 1879, moved to Springfield, Dakota Territory to find a desirable climate for her delicate health. She died at the age of 95. She was a china painter and portrait painter and was the hostess at the South Dakota building at the 1893 Columbia Exhibition in Chicago.

———⇒◇⇐———

Martha Frizzell Sheldon came with her husband Charles H. Sheldon in 1881 to Groton, Dakota Territory. They took up a Government Claim near Pierpont, SD.

———⇒◇⇐———

Annie Chappelle Lee's husband, Andrew E. Lee, was the third Governor of South Dakota and her nephew, Carl Gunderson, was the 11th Governor of South Dakota.

———⇒◇⇐———

Eunice Slye Herreid was affectionately called "Nettie".

———⇒◇⇐———

Annie Chappelle Lee was active in the Women's Christian Temperance Union and wore the little hatchet pin of the WCTU on her inaugural gown.

APPETIZERS & BEVERAGES

ARTICHOKE - PROSCIUTTO GRATIN

First Lady Linda Mickelson Graham

2 (14-oz.) cans artichoke hearts,
  drained and quartered
6 oz. thinly sliced prosciutto
1 cup whipping cream
1-½ cups crumbled Gorgonzola
  cheese

½ cup pine nuts, toasted
¼ cup grated Parmesan cheese
1 tsp. chopped fresh sage

Pat quartered artichoke hearts dry with paper towels. Cut each prosciutto slice crosswise in half. Wrap each artichoke quarter in halved prosciutto slice. Place wrapped artichoke hearts in single layer in 9 x 13 inch glass baking dish. Pour cream on top. Sprinkle with Gorgonzola, pine nuts, Parmesan, and sage. Bake until gratin is bubbling - about 25 minutes. Serve warm with crusty bread. This is a good "heavy hors d'oeuvre!!"

ARTICHOKE DIP

Kris Carmody Reaves

2 (13.75-oz.) cans artichoke
  hearts
1 cup parsley
1 cup scallions (green top
  onion)
1 (6-oz.) pkg. goat cheese
  crumbles

4 oz. Gorgonzola cheese
  crumbles
1 (6-oz.) pkg. pine nuts
2-¼ cups fresh Parmesan
  cheese
1 pint heavy whipping cream

Chop artichokes, parsley, and onion and toss evenly into a large mixing bowl. Add goat cheese crumbles, Gorgonzola crumbles, 1-½ cups of Parmesan cheese and whipping cream. Combine all ingredients thoroughly. Spread mixture into a 9 x 13 glass pan. Sprinkle top with pine nuts and ¾ cup of Parmesan cheese. Preheat oven at 350° bake for 30 minutes or until mixture is bubbly and top is golden brown. Serve with bread or crackers.

Granddaughter of Governor George T. Mickelson and niece of Governor George S. Mickelson

ARTICHOKE RANCH DIP

Rob Skjonsberg
Governor's Staff

1 cup mayonnaise
1 cup sour cream
1 (1-oz.) pkg. Hidden Valley The
Original Ranch dressing &
seasoning mix
1 tbls. lemon juice (more if
desired)
2 (15-oz.) cans artichoke
quarters in water, drained &
chopped

$\frac{1}{2}$ cup chopped roasted red bell
peppers
1-$\frac{1}{2}$ cups shredded Swiss
cheese
1-$\frac{1}{2}$ cups French fried onions,
divided
tortilla chips

Preheat oven to 350°F. Spray a 1 quart baking dish with olive oil cooking spray; set aside. In medium mixing bowl, whisk together mayonnaise, sour cream, seasoning mix and lemon juice until smooth. Stir in artichokes, peppers, cheese and $\frac{1}{2}$ cup French fried onions. Transfer to baking dish and top with remaining French fried onions. Bake 40-45 minutes, until set and top is golden brown. Serve warm with tortilla chips.

BACON CRESCENT BITES

Cindy Louder
Former Governor's Staff

1 (3-oz.) pkg. Philadelphia
Cream Cheese, softened
6 slices bacon, crispy cooked,
crumbled

1 green onion, thinly sliced
$\frac{1}{2}$ tsp. Worcestershire sauce
1 pkg. refrigerated crescent
dinner rolls

Mix cream cheese, bacon, onion and Worcestershire sauce. Separate crescent rolls into 8 triangles. Cut each triangle in half lengthwise. Spread one generous tsp. cream cheese mixture on each triangle. Roll up, starting at shortest side of triangle and rolling to opposite point. Place on ungreased cookie sheet. Bake at 375° 12 to 15 minutes or until golden brown. Serve warm.

85104-07

BACON WRAPPED GOOSE HORS D'OEUVRES

Jeff Vonk
Governor's Cabinet

2 cleaned, boned goose breasts
  (4 pieces)
1 qt. buttermilk

1 lb. maple cured bacon
1 onion, sliced
3-4 jalapeño peppers, sliced

Cut cleaned goose breasts into 1-½" cubes. Punch hole through each cube. Marinate goose cubes in buttermilk for 12-24 hours (keep refrigerated). Take each goose cube, place a piece of onion and jalapeño pepper inside hole in cube. Wrap each "stuffed" goose cube with a piece of bacon just long enough to encircle goose cube. Hold in place with toothpick. Grill on medium heat; turn frequently to avoid burning bacon (10-15 minutes or until cooked). Serve as appetizer.

BACON-CRAB DIP

Susanne Ruhnke
Residence Staff

1 (8-oz.) pkg. cream cheese,
  softened
½ cup sour cream
2 tsp. prepared horseradish
⅛ tsp. pepper
4 imitation crabmeat sticks,
  chopped (1 cup)
4 slices bacon, crisply cooked,
  crumbled

2 medium green onions, sliced
  (2 tbls.)
toasted bagels, cut into fourths
  or whole-wheat crackers, if
  desired
green onion flower, if desired

In medium bowl, using electric mixer, beat cream cheese and sour cream on medium speed until smooth and fluffy. By hand, stir in remaining ingredients except bagels and onion flower. Cover, refrigerate at least 1 hour to blend flavors. Place dip in serving bowl. Serve with bagels. Garnish with onion flower. Cover and refrigerate any remaining dip.

Note: Per Serving (2 tbls.): Calories 110; Total Fat 10g; Sodium 220mg; Dietary Fiber 0g.

BAKED GARLIC WITH ROQUEFORT AND ROSEMARY

Jackie Rounds

6 whole heads of garlic
3 tbls. butter (cut into 6 slices)
¼ cup olive oil
1 (14-½-oz.) can chicken broth
 (extra broth may be needed)
¼ cup dry white wine

2 tsp. chopped fresh rosemary
8 oz. Roquefort cheese,
 crumbled
fresh rosemary sprigs
crusty French bread
½ tsp. ground black pepper

Preheat oven to 375°. Cut ½ inch off top end of each garlic head (exposing top of garlic cloves). Remove any loose papery outer skin. Place garlic side up in non aluminum baking dish. Top with butter slices. Pour oil over garlic heads and butter. Add 1 can broth and the white wine to the dish. Sprinkle chopped rosemary over garlic. Place 2 rosemary sprigs in dish. Season with pepper. Bake uncovered until garlic is tender (about 1 hour, 15 minutes), baste every 15 minutes with pan juices (add more broth if necessary to maintain some sauce in dish). Add cheese to the dish and continue baking until cheese is almost melted (about 10 minutes). Discard cooked rosemary sprigs. Garnish with fresh rosemary sprigs. Dip crusty French bread into cooking juices, then spread it with the garlic and melted cheese.

Sister-in-Law of Governor M. Michael Rounds

85104-07

BERTSCH BASH GRILLED DEER CHISLIC

Dale Bertsch
Governor's Staff

4 lbs. deer meat trimmed and cut into 1 inch cubes (can use beef)

1 large onion cut into pieces large enough to skewer

1- 2 large bell pepper(s) cut into pieces large enough to skewer

Marinade:

4 cups vegetable oil
2 cups white vinegar
½ cup plain yellow mustard

2 tbls. garlic salt
9" wooden bamboo skewers

Trim and cube meat. Deer meat is easier to cut if not completely thawed. Cut onions and peppers into large pieces. Stick the meat, onions, and peppers on skewers alternating meat with vegetables. Place skewered kabobs in a plastic tub. Stir vegetable oil, vinegar, mustard, and garlic salt until blended. Pour over kabobs. If not completely covered, make more marinade or rotate kabobs once or twice a day. Refrigerate for at least 2 days and up to 4 days. Place kabobs on well heated grill and cook for 5-8 minutes, turning as needed. Vegetable oil will cause grill to flame up and smoke at first. Use a spray bottle of water to keep flames down. Remove from grill and season with more garlic to taste.

Comments from friends: "This doesn't even taste like deer meat."

Note: The longer the kabobs are marinated, the more tender the meat will be. If more marinade is needed to cover the kabobs, mix two parts oil to one part vinegar. Add mustard and garlic salt to taste.

BREAD BOWL DIP

Catherine Sulzle
Former Governor's Staff

1-½ cups sour cream
1-⅓ cups mayonnaise
2 tsp. Accent
2 tsp. dill weed
2 tbls. parsley, chopped
3 green onions, chopped

2 pkgs. Buddig Beef or Pastrami (can also use small jar of dried beef)

1 round loaf sour dough bread or sheepherder's bread, unsliced

Mix all ingredients (except bread) well. Chill. Cut top off round loaf of bread (like you cut a pumpkin lid). Pull out bread in small chunks for dipping. Just before serving, fill bread with dip. You can also have bagel bits, chips, etc. handy for dipping.

CARIBBEAN SHRIMP COCKTAIL

Michele Rounds Brich

½ cup catsup
½ cup lime juice
2 tsp. Tabasco or other hot
  sauce
1 lb. fresh or frozen shrimp,
  peeled, deveined & cooked

1 large tomato, chopped
½ cup chopped onion
¼ cup fresh cilantro, snipped
2 avocados, peeled and
  chopped

Mix catsup, lime juice, and Tabasco in a large bowl. Add shrimp, tomato, onion and cilantro. Cover and chill. Just before serving, add avocados and toss. Serve with crackers or tortilla chips.

Sister of Governor M. Michael Rounds

CHEESE SNACKS

Susan Bushfield Beckman

½ cup butter
1 cup flour
½ tsp. salt
dash cayenne pepper

1 cup extra sharp cheddar,
  grated
36 stuffed green olives, if
  desired

Cream butter, then mix in flour, salt, cayenne pepper, and cheddar cheese. Knead lightly until smooth. Roll into a 2" roll then slice into about 1" thick rounds. They can be baked at this point or wrapped around olives and baked. Bake at 350° until brown, about 10 minutes.

Granddaughter of Governor Harlan Bushfield

CHEX CEREAL STUFFED MUSHROOMS

Dale Bertsch
Governor's Staff

1 8 oz. pkg. button mushrooms
¼ cup butter
⅓ cup onion, finely diced
½ tsp. salt
¼ tsp. garlic salt
⅛ tsp. nutmeg

½ tsp. pepper
1 cup Corn Chex crushed to ¼
  cup
3 tbls. shredded Parmesan
  cheese
paprika

Remove stems from mushrooms and dice finely. Melt butter in microwave on high for 40 seconds. Add diced mushroom stems and diced onions to butter. Microwave for 4-5 minutes until onions are tender. Add the salt, garlic salt, nutmeg, pepper, crushed Corn Chex, and Parmesan cheese to melted butter, onions, and stems and mix. Fill mushroom caps and place in glass baking dish lined with paper towel. Microwave on high for 2-3 minutes. Sprinkle with paprika.

85104-07

CHICKEN EGG ROLLS

Michael Gorman
Governor's Cabinet

6 cups cabbage (shredded)
6 cups celery (thinly sliced)
water
oil (2 tbls. plus oil to fry)
1 lb. skinless, boneless chicken
  breast (cut into ½" bits)

1 cup green onions (chopped)
2 tbls. soy sauce
¼ tsp. black pepper
salt to taste
12 egg roll skins
1 egg white (slightly beaten)

Place cabbage and celery in a sauce pan. Add enough water to cover and simmer until tender (about 5 minutes). Drain, pat mixture with paper towel to remove most of the water, and set aside to cool. Heat 2 tbls. oil in wok, add chicken cubes and stir-fry until chicken is done. Add onion and stir-fry another minute. Combine soy sauce and pepper. Put cabbage mixture, chicken mixture, and soy sauce mixture into a large bowl and stir. Add salt to your taste. Spread mixture on a baking pan to cool. Then assemble the egg rolls sealing with the beaten egg white. Keep covered with a damp towel until fried. Deep fat fry a few at a time at 375° until golden brown, turning as needed. Drain on paper towel, but do not stack because they will loose their crispness. Serve with your favorite sauce or mustard. Serves 6 (two egg rolls each).

CHICKEN/JALAPEÑO NACHO DIP

Dar Baum
Former Governor's Cabinet

2 8 oz. pkg. cream cheese
2 cups Louis Rich chicken,
  chopped
1 (4-oz.) can diced jalapeños
  and 2 tbls. jalapeño juice

1 (16-oz.) tub sour cream
½ cup Parmesan cheese
½ tsp. white pepper

Place all in crock pot and heat. Serve with nacho chips.

CHIP DIP

Aaron Miller
Governor's Staff

1-½ lbs. hamburger
1-½ lbs. Jimmy Dean Hot
  Sausage (3 round tubes)
onion, chopped

2 tomatoes
1 can chopped green chilies
1 2 lb. box Velveeta Cheese

Brown hamburger and sausage with chopped onion. Drain grease. Add tomatoes, chilies and cheese. Warm until cheese is melted. Keep dip in crock pot - serve warm.

CLASSIC GUACAMOLE

*Recipe Box at the
Governors Residence*

2 ripe avocados
1 clove garlic, minced
1 tsp. coarse salt
2 plum tomatoes, seeded and
  diced

2 jalapeño chiles, minced
1 small red onion, minced
1/2 cup fresh cilantro
3-4 tbls. fresh lime juice

Pit, dice, and peel the avocados; gently mash in medium bowl with garlic and salt. Mix in tomatoes, jalapeño chiles, red onion cilantro, and lime juice. Serve immediately, or press plastic wrap directly onto surface of guacamole (to prevent discoloration), and store in refrigerator up to 1 day.

COLA-GLAZED CHICKEN WINGS

First Lady Nancy Kneip Paprocki

2 lbs. chicken wings
1 can (12 oz.) cola

1 cup ketchup
1 tbls. Worcestershire sauce

Preheat oven to 375°. Place wings in a large shallow baking dish. Combine cola, ketchup, and Worcestershire sauce, pour over wings. Bake about 1 hour turning occasionally. Makes 4 appetizer servings. (Diet soda may lack the proper sugar content to form the glaze).

CORN DIP

*Jerus Campbell
Former Governor's Staff*

1 (8-oz.) pkg. cream cheese,
  softened
8 oz. mayo
8 oz. shredded cheddar, finely
  shredded

2 can mexi-corn, drained
1 can Ro-tel tomatoes, drained
4 green onions, chopped
salt and pepper to taste

Mix together and let set for several hours or overnight (refrigerate). Serve with Fritos Scoops.

85104-07

CRAB SALAD

*Recipe Box at the
Governors Residence*

1 pkg. imitation crab, shredded
½ cup mayonnaise
½ cup black olives, chopped
½ cup celery, chopped

½ cup green onion, chopped
½ cup shredded cheese
½ tsp. onion salt
ground black pepper

Combine all ingredients; serve on assorted crackers.

CUCUMBER DIP

*Connie Tveidt
Governor's Staff*

1 8 oz. pkg. cream cheese
¼ cup mayonnaise
¼ cup sour cream
1 or 2 cucumbers

optional seasonings: salt,
pepper, garlic salt, lemon
pepper

Beat cream cheese until smooth. Add mayonnaise and sour cream and blend well. Peel cucumbers, cut into long slices to remove seeds and chop into small pieces. Stir cucumbers into cream cheese mixture and season to taste. Chill. Serve with crackers.

CUCUMBER SANDWICHES

*Tanna Zabel
Governor's Staff*

2 (8-oz.) pkgs. cream cheese
½ cup sour cream
several cucumbers - peeled and
 sliced
¼ cup chopped green onion

½ cup chopped green pepper
3 shakes each of salt, pepper,
 garlic salt, celery salt and
 onion powder
2 dozen silver dollar buns

Combine cream cheese, sour cream, green onion, green pepper, salt, pepper, garlic salt, celery salt and onion powder. Chill 1 hour. Add sandwich spread and 1 slice of cucumber to each bun. Serve and enjoy!

DEVIL DIP

George Mark Mickelson

1 2 lb. box Velveeta, cubed
1 1 lb. pkg. Jimmy Dean spicy
  sausage

2 (10-oz.) cans Ro-tel tomatoes
tortilla chips

In a skillet, sauté the ground beef and sausage into crumbles until thoroughly cooked. In a large saucepan, melt the Velveeta over low heat, stirring constantly. Add the Ro-tel and beef/sausage mixture. Serve warm with your favorite tortilla chips.

Son of Governor George S. Mickelson and grandson of Governor George T. Mickelson

DEVILED EGGS

Recipe Box at the
Governors Residence

18 eggs
1 cup mayonnaise
1 tbls. mustard

1/2 cup sweet relish plus 1/4 tsp.
1/2 tsp. sugar
celery salt to taste

Hard-boil the eggs. When cooled, cut each egg in half and remove yolks. Mash yolks and then combine with remaining ingredients. Scoop yolk mixture into each half of egg.

DOWN SOUTH (DAKOTA) SALSA

Patricia Van Gerpen
Former Governor's Staff

1 large tomato, chopped
1 small onion chopped
cilantro, half a bunch, chopped

juice from 1/2 squeezed lime, to
  taste
1/4 tsp. kosher salt

Combine the chopped ingredients in a mixing bowl. Add the lime juice and kosher salt, to taste. Refrigerate for 1 hour before serving with nacho chips. This is best served the day it is prepared.

DRIED BEEF DIP

Tanna Zabel
Governor's Staff

2 8 oz. pkg. cream cheese
4.5 oz. jar dried beef
1/2 cup chopped onion

1/2 cup green pepper
1 1/2 tbls. Worcestershire Sauce
1 1/2 tsp. Nature' s Seasoning

Combine cream cheese, dried beef, onion, green pepper, Worcestershire sauce and Nature's seasoning. Chill for 1 hour and serve with crackers.

85104-07

FLAKY PIZZA SNACKS

Susanne Ruhnke
Residence Staff

1 (8-oz.) can Pillsbury refrigerated crescent dinner rolls
1/3 cup pizza sauce
1/4 cup grated Parmesan cheese

1 cup finely chopped tomato
1/3 cup shredded mozzarella cheese
chopped fresh basil leaves, if desired

Heat oven to 375°. Spray cookie sheet with cooking spray. Unroll dough into 1 large rectangle; press perforations to seal. Spread pizza sauce evenly over rectangle to within 1 inch of edges. Sprinkle with Parmesan cheese. Starting at short side, roll up rectangle, jelly-roll fashion. With a sharp knife, cut into 16 slices. Place cut side down on cookie sheet. Top each slice with 1 tbls. tomato and about 1 tsp. mozzarella cheese. Bake 9-11 minutes or until edges are golden brown and cheese is melted. (Bottoms will be very deep golden brown). Top with basil.

Note: Per snack: Calories 70; Total Fat 4g; Sodium 170mg; Dietary Fiber 0mg.

FRENCH QUARTER MUFFULETTA SANDWICH

Lavon Mickelson Meyers

Olive Salad:

2/3 cup pitted, chopped green olives
2/3 cup pitted, chopped black olives
1/2 cup chopped pimento
3 cloves garlic, minced

1 anchovy fillet, mashed
1 tbls. capers
1 tsp. oregano
1/3 cup chopped fresh parsley
1/4 tsp. black pepper
1/2 cup good olive oil

Mix together thoroughly. Cover and refrigerate at least 12 hours. Enough for one large sandwich. Constructing the sandwich: 1 large loaf Italian bread, preferably round. 1/3 lb. each; hard salami, ham, provolone cheese. Slice bread horizontally and scoop out about half of the soft bread from top and bottom. Brush bottom of loaf with olive oil or juice from the olive salad marinade. Next, layer cold cuts and cheese. Top with as much olive salad as will fit without spilling out. Replace top of the loaf; wrap tightly in foil or plastic wrap for a couple of hours before slicing.

Daughter of Governor George T. Mickelson and sister of George S. Mickelson

FRUIT & ORANGE FLUFF

Lynnette M. Hauschild Eckert
Governor's Staff

1 (3-¾-oz.) pkg. instant vanilla
pudding mix
2 cups cold milk

1 cup dairy sour cream
¼ cup orange juice
cut-up fruit

To prepare slowly beat pudding mix and milk in mixing bowl with rotary beater until well blended, about 1-2 minutes. Gently beat in sour cream. Fold in orange juice. Chill. Prepare your fruit and serve.

FRUIT DIP

Tanna Zabel
Governor's Staff

1-½ cups buttermilk
1 pkg. fat-free/sugar-free vanilla
pudding

1 carton fat-free Cool Whip
cut-up fruit

Combine buttermilk, pudding mix, Cool Whip, and whip. Chill 1 hour. Serve with cut-up fruit.

FRUIT DIP

Kelly (Donahue) Wheeler
Former Governor's Staff

1 (3-oz.) pkg. French vanilla
instant pudding
1 cup milk

1 (12-oz.) container sour cream
1 tsp. vanilla or almond extract
cut-up fruit

Combine all ingredients and refrigerate. Serve with cut up bananas, apples, oranges, pineapple, strawberries, etc.

GARLIC CHEESE SPREAD

Susanne Ruhnke
Residence Staff

1 (8-oz.) pkg. cream cheese
1 (8-oz.) jar Cheez Whiz
¾ tsp. garlic powder, or to taste

⅛ tsp. seasoned salt
⅛ tsp. pepper

Combine all ingredients and beat with hand mixer for 2 minutes or until smooth. Serve with freshly toasted French bread.

85104-07

GENERAL KILLEY HORS D' OEUVRES

MG (ret.) Phil G. Killey
Former Governor's Cabinet

2 tbls. olive oil
4 to 6 garlic cloves, chopped
4 to 6 Portobella mushrooms,
  chunky chopped
1/4 cup red onion, chopped

sour dough baguette bread
Brie cheese
1/4 cup green olives, chopped
1 tsp. balsamic vinegar
fresh ground pepper

Sauté chopped garlic, red onion, and portobella mushrooms in olive oil until tender. Add green olives, balsamic vinegar, and pepper. Set aside. Slice baguette into 1/4 inch slices; spread with Brie cheese and melt on bread. Add sautéed ingredients to baguette. Serve warm and enjoy!

GINGER BEEF MARINADE

Dottie Howe
Former Governor's Cabinet

1 lean 3 lb. beef roast

Bake until done. Cut into small, thin, bite-size pieces. Combine marinade ingredients and pour over beef, refrigerate. Can be done a day ahead of serving.

Marinade:

12 oz. soy sauce
1 cup white vinegar
1/4 cup oil
1 (4-oz.) piece of fresh ginger
  root, grated

2 tbls. sugar
pepper to taste

Before serving, add raw carrot slices and small broccoli florets. Provide tongs for serving.

GOUDA CHEESE BALL

Recipe Box at the
Governors Residence

1 (8-oz.) tub cream cheese
spread
2 cups shredded Gouda or
Colby cheese
1/4 cup chopped fresh chives
1/4 cup sliced drained oil packed
sun-dried tomatoes

1/4 tsp. garlic powder
1/4 cup finely chopped fresh
parsley
assorted crackers

In medium bowl, mix cream cheese spread and Gouda cheese until blended. Stir in chives, tomatoes, and garlic powder. Shape mixture into one large or two small balls or logs. Roll in parsley. Wrap in plastic wrap. Refrigerate at least 2 hours until firm. Serve with crackers.

GRAND OLD FLAG CHEESE SPREAD

Julie M. Johnson
Former Governor's Cabinet

1 (8-oz.) pkg. Philadelphia
Cream Cheese, softened
1/4 cup Kraft Mexican Style
Shredded Cheddar Jack
Cheese

2 tbls. sliced pitted ripe olives
1/4 cup Taco Bell Home
Originals Thick 'N Chunky
Salsa
Ritz Crackers

Place cream cheese between two sheets of wax paper. Roll out to 6 x 4-inch rectangle with rolling pin. Remove top sheet of wax paper; coat top and sides of cream cheese with shredded cheese. Invert onto serving plate. Remove wax paper. Arrange three rows of olives in top left corner of cream cheese rectangle for the "stars" of the "flag." Make four (1/4-inch deep) rows, using rounded end of 1/4 tsp. measuring spoon for the "flag's stripes," leaving a 1/4-inch-wide space between the rows. Fill rows with salsa. Serve immediately or cover and refrigerate until ready to serve. Serve as a spread with crackers.

HOT ARTICHOKE DIP

Recipe Box at the
Governors Residence

2 (6.5-oz.) cans artichoke hearts
1 (10-oz.) pkg. frozen chopped
spinach

1/2 cup sour cream
1/2 cup mayonnaise
3 oz. Parmesan cheese (3/4 cup)

Combine ingredients and bake at 375° for 20-25 minutes.

85104-07

HOT BEAN DIP

Bonnie Untereiner Bjork
Former Governor's Staff

6 green onions
1 dash Tabasco
½ lb. cheddar cheese

1 can Hormel Hot Chili
1 can green chilies

Combine and bake at 300° for 1 hour. Serve with taco chips.

HOT MAMMAS

Alice Wright
Former Governor's Staff

1 gallon apple cider
1 bottle Cinnamon Schnapps

cinnamon sticks

Heat apple cider with cinnamon sticks. When hot, pour into cup adding a half shot of Cinnamon Schnapps. Great drink at holiday time.

JANE NIELSEN'S CHEESEBALL

Betty Oldenkamp
Former Governor's Cabinet

1 8 oz. pkg. cream cheese
1-¼ cups Velveeta cheese (⅔ of 1 lb. box), cubed
4 oz. shredded cheddar cheese

½ stick margarine
½ cup black olives, chopped
½ onion, finely chopped
chopped walnuts or pecans

Have all ingredients at room temperature. Mix everything except the nuts until well blended. Separate the mixture in half for two cheese balls. Place large piece of plastic wrap on counter, put chopped nuts on plastic wrap. Shape cheese mixture into a ball with hands and roll in chopped nuts. Wrap ball in plastic wrap and refrigerate overnight. Repeat with remaining cheese mixture. Serve with any type crackers or celery sticks.

JEAN'S CHEESE BALLS

R. Van Johnson
Former Governor's Cabinet

1 (5-oz.) jar Old English cheese
¼ cup butter
½ cup flour

½ tsp. salt
olives

Cream cheese and butter. Add dry ingredients. Mix well. Form into balls. Make depression with thumb. Fold over and around a stuffed olive. Freeze on cookie sheets. When frozen, can be placed in plastic bag. Do not thaw before baking. Bake @ 400° for 15 - 20 minutes. Makes about 30-35 depending on size of olives.

JIMMY DEAN'S SNACK SANDWICHES

Brian Burma

1 lb. ground beef, cooked and
drained
1 pkg. Jimmy Dean's hot
sausage, cooked and drained

1 jar Cheez Whiz

Mix together and spread on pumpernickel bread. Brown under broiler for 5 minutes, cut each sandwich into 4 diagonal pieces and serve.

Great-grandson of Governor Walter Dale Miller

KALAMATA OLIVE PESTO

Dale Bertsch
Governor's Staff

1 (10-oz.) jar pitted Kalamata
olives
1 tsp. dry oregano
1 tsp. dry basil
1-1/2 tsp. balsamic vinegar

1/2 tsp. sugar
2 tsp. olive oil
2-6 cloves fresh garlic,
depending on taste
crackers or cocktail breads

Add all ingredients to food processor. Process until well blended. Refrigerate overnight for flavors to intensify. Serve with crackers or breads.

KRAB SALAD

Josh Albers

1 pkg. krab meat (imitation crab)
1 (2.25-oz.) can sliced black
olives
3 - 5 green onions, finely
chopped

1 cup cheddar cheese, shredded
3/4 cup real mayonnaise
3/4 cup sour cream

In a large bowl, shred krab meat. Add drained black olives, chopped green onions and shredded cheddar cheese. Stir carefully. In a separate bowl, combine mayo and sour cream. Add to krab meat mixture and stir until thoroughly incorporated. Chill well. Serve with Club or Ritz Crackers.

Grandson of Governor Walter Dale Miller

85104-07

MARY'S BEAN DIP

Susan Edwards Johnson
Former Governor's Cabinet

1-½ lbs. lean hamburger
1 (15-oz.) can refried beans
2 tbls. chopped onion
4 oz. sliced black olives
4 oz. green olives
(10-oz.) can Ro-tel tomatoes

8 oz. cheese or Velveeta
8 oz. green salsa sauce
8 oz. red salsa sauce
1 pkg. taco seasoning
4 oz. jalapeños or green chilies

Brown onion. Add hamburger and brown. Add taco seasoning mix. Place mixture in crock pot. Add olives, cheese, refried beans, salsa, chilies and Ro-tel tomatoes. Cook on medium heat for 3 hours. Serve hot with chips.

MOUNTAIN MAN POPPERS

Steve Pirner
Governor's Cabinet

frozen deer hearts
soy sauce
cream cheese

jar of sliced jalapeño peppers
bacon

Trim fat from partly thawed deer hearts. Slice trimmed heart lengthwise into thin slices or strips. Soak overnight in salt water, changing water a couple times. Marinate for 8 hours in soy sauce and drain. Spread cream cheese on each strip of meat, top with a jalapeño pepper slice, roll up, and wrap with bacon. Fasten with toothpicks that have been soaked in water to prevent burning. Cook on a gas grill under low heat until done. To serve, keep warm in a crock pot set on low.

MUSHROOM CRESCENT SNACK

Susanne Ruhnke
Residence Staff

3 cups chopped fresh
  mushrooms
2 tbls. margarine
½ tsp. garlic salt
2 tbls. chopped onions
1 tsp. lemon juice

1 tsp. Worcestershire sauce
1 (8-oz.) can Pillsbury Quick
  Crescent Dinner Rolls
1 (8-oz.) pkg. cream cheese
¼ cup Parmesan cheese

Brown mushrooms in margarine. Stir in salt, onion, lemon juice, Worcestershire sauce, and cook until liquid evaporates. Spread (separate) crescent roll dough into two rectangles, place on an ungreased 13 x 9 pan. Press over bottom to form crust. Spread cream cheese over dough. Top with mushroom mixture, top with Parmesan cheese. Bake at 350° for 20-25 minutes.

PARTY BREAD STICKS

Jason Burma

2 pkgs. large breadsticks (cut
  into 1-inch lengths)
1 cup vegetable oil
2 tbls. Worcestershire sauce
2 tsp. Lawry Seasoned Salt

1 tsp. dill weed
½ tsp. celery salt
2 tsp. onion powder
1 tsp. garlic powder

Place breadsticks in cake pan and pour above ingredients over them.
Bake at 250° for 2 hours, stirring every 15 minutes. Place on paper
towel to cool. Can be made in advance and kept for several weeks.
Best if kept in old coffee can with sealed cover.

Great-grandson of Governor Walter Dale Miller

PEPPERONI PIZZA SPREAD

Linda Dykstra
Governor's Staff

2 cups shredded mozzarella
  cheese
2 cups shredded cheddar
  cheese
1 cup mayonnaise
1 cup chopped turkey pepperoni
1 (4-oz.) can drained and
  chopped mushrooms (optional)

½ cup diced onion
½ cup chopped green pepper
1 (6-oz.) can sliced ripe olives
1 cup sliced pimento stuffed
  green olives

Combine all ingredients into 11 x 7 inch or 12 inch round baking dish
and bake uncovered at 350° for 25-30 minutes. Serve with crackers
(Triscuits are good).

85104-07

PEPPERONI SWIRLS

Susanne Ruhnke
Residence Staff

1 sheet frozen puff pastry (from
  17.3 oz. pkg.), thawed
3 tbls. country-style Dijon
  mustard

4 oz. pepperoni, chopped
1 cup shredded mozzarella
  cheese (4 oz.)
2 tsp. dried oregano leaves

On lightly floured surface, roll puff pastry into 16 x 14 inch rectangle.
Spread mustard over pastry. Sprinkle pepperoni evenly over mustard.
Sprinkle cheese and oregano over pepperoni. Starting at 16-inch side,
tightly roll up pastry; gently pinch edge into roll to seal. Wrap in plastic
wrap and refrigerate 2-3 hours. Heat oven to 425°. Line cookie sheets
with foil; lightly spray foil with cooking spray. Cut pastry into 1/2-inch
slices. Place on cookie sheets. Bake 15-20 minutes or until golden
brown and slightly puffed. Serve warm. Makes 32 appetizers.

Note: 1 Appetizer: Calories 65 (Calories from fat 45); Fat 5g (Saturated
2g); Cholesterol 10mg; Sodium 140mg; Carbohydrate 3g (Dietary Fiber
0g); Protein 2g

PROSCIUTTO-WRAPPED ASPARAGUS SPEARS

Recipe Box at the
Governors Residence

2 cups cream cheese or herb
  cream cheese
zest of 1 lemon
1/2 bunch chives, finely chopped

24 slices Prosciutto
24 stalks asparagus (do not use
  pencil asparagus, it should be
  approximately 1/2-inch thick)

Spread the cheese on top of the Prosciutto and top with lemon zest
and chopped chives. Place the asparagus in the middle and roll on
an angle.

PUNCH WITH JELL-O

Rosemary Rounds

2 (3-oz.) pkgs. Jell-O (cherry,
  raspberry, strawberry) for red
  punch
3-1/2 cups boiling water

1-1/4 cups sugar
2 (12-oz.) cans frozen lemonade
1 (46-oz.) can pineapple juice
6 cups cold or ice water

Dissolve Jello in boiling water. Add sugar, frozen lemonade, pineapple
juice, and cold water. Stir together. Divide into two ice cream pails.
Freeze. Thaw for at least 2 hours before serving. Add about 1 quart
7-Up or ginger ale to each pail of punch.

Stepmother of Governor M. Michael Rounds

RACHEL'S BAGEL DIP

Deb Bowman
Governor's Cabinet

1-1/3 cups sour cream (can use
  light)
1-1/3 cups mayonnaise
2 tsp. Accent seasoning
2 tsp. dill weed
2 tsp. onion salt

3 pkg. corned/dried beef,
  chopped
parsley flakes for garnish
  (optional)
6 bagels

Mix all ingredients together, refrigerate for at least 3 hours prior to serving. Cut bagels into bite size pieces for dipping.

RO-TEL SAUSAGE DIP

Kimberly Orr

1 (6-oz.) pkg. Jimmy Dean hot
  sausage
1 can Ro-tel diced tomato with
  green chilies

1 (8-oz.) pkg. Philadelphia
  Cream Cheese - cubed

Brown sausage. Add can of tomatoes (do not drain). Add cream cheese stirring until melted. Serve with tortilla chips or corn chips.

Granddaughter of Governor Joe Foss

ROLLED TORTILLA WITH SPINACH APPETIZER

Darrell Butterwick
Former Governor's Cabinet

1 pkg. 10-inch soft flour tortillas
  (lightly buttered)
1 pkg. cleaned spinach leaves
2 shredded carrots
1 bunch small green onions -
  chopped

2 (8-oz.) pkg. cream cheese
1/4 tsp. garlic powder
1/2 cup chopped walnuts
  (optional)
1 small can chopped ripe
  olives - drained

If washing fresh spinach leaves, be sure to completely dry. In small bowl, mix together softened cream cheese, garlic powder, shredded carrots, walnuts (optional), and olives. Lay out tortilla, layer with spinach leaves, then spread cream cheese in thin layer on top of spinach. Roll tortilla jelly roll style. Wrap each in saran wrap and refrigerate before slicing into bite size pieces. Serve cold.

85104-07

SAUSAGE-STUFFED MUSHROOM

Mary Farrar Turner

2 Italian sweet sausages, about
  1/3 lb.
1/4 tsp. fennel seeds
pinch red pepper flakes
  (optional)
1/4 cup finely minced yellow
  onion
1 clove garlic, peeled and
  minced
olive oil, as necessary

1/4 cup chopped parsley
1/4 cup chopped black olives,
  preferably imported
1/3 cup thick Béchamel Sauce
salt and freshly ground black
  pepper to taste
12 large white mushrooms
imported Parmesan cheese to
  taste

Remove sausage meat from casings and crumble into a small skillet. Sauté gently, stirring often, until meat is thoroughly done. Season with fennel and, if desired, red pepper flakes. With a slotted spoon, remove sausage to a bowl, leaving the rendered fat in the skillet. Sauté onion and garlic in the rendered fat, adding a little olive oil if necessary, until tender and golden, about 25 minutes. Stir in chopped parsley and add to reserved sausage meat. Stir olives and Béchamel sauce into the sausage mixture; combine thoroughly. Taste the mixture, and season with salt and pepper if necessary. Pull the stems off the mushrooms and save for another use. Wipe mushroom caps with a damp cloth and season lightly with salt and pepper. Fill each cap generously with the stuffing. Arrange caps in a lightly oiled baking dish. Sprinkle the tops of the stuffing with Parmesan cheese to taste. Bake at 450° for about 15 minutes, or until bubbling and well browned. Let settle for 5 minutes before serving. Makes 3-4 portions.

Béchamel Sauce

4 tbls. sweet butter
6 tbls. unbleached all-purpose
  flour
2 cups milk

salt, freshly ground black
  pepper, and freshly grated
  nutmeg, to taste

Melt butter in a heavy saucepan. Sprinkle in the flour and cook gently, stirring almost constantly, for 5 minutes. Do not let the flour and butter brown at all. Meanwhile, bring the milk to a boil. When milk reaches a boil, remove butter and flour mixture from heat and pour in the boiling milk all at once. As the mixture boils and bubbles, beat it vigorously with a wire whisk. When the bubbling stops, return the pan to medium heat and bring the Béchamel to a boil, stirring constantly for 5 minutes. Season to taste with salt, pepper and nutmeg. Use at once, or scrape into a bowl, cover and refrigerate until use. Makes 2 cups thick sauce.

Note: For 2 cups medium sauce, use 3 tbls. butter and 4 tbls. all-purpose flour with the same amount of milk.

Daughter of Governor Frank Farrar

SCRATCH BLOODY MARY MIX

Jerry Hofer
Governor's Cabinet

1 qt. tomato juice
1/4 tsp. black pepper
1/2 tsp. celery salt
1 tsp. Worcestershire sauce

1/2 tsp. Tabasco sauce
3 tsp. pickle juice
3 tsp. green olive juice
3 tsp. lemon juice

Combine all ingredients and refrigerate overnight. Serve with vodka on ice, garnishing with pickle spear, green olives and celery stick.

SHISH KABOBS

Tim Reisch
Governor's Cabinet

1-1/2 cup salad oil
1/4 cup Worcestershire sauce
2 1/4 tsp. salt
1/2 cup vinegar
1/3 cup fresh lemon juice

3/4 cup soy sauce
2 tbls. dry mustard
1 tbls. pepper
1-1/2 tsp. dried parsley flakes

Combine all ingredients and mix well. Store in refrigerator in tightly covered jar until ready to use. Sauce can be put back in fridge and reused. Cut 2-3 lbs. of round steak in 1-1/2 inch cubes. Marinate meat for several hours. Put meat, salad tomatoes, thick celery, green peppers, mushrooms, onions, and whatever on skewers.

SIZZLING SHRIMP DIP

Alice Wright
Former Governor's Staff

1 lb. Velveeta cheese
2 cans cream of shrimp soup

3 cans broken shrimp pieces

In a crock pot set on low, place cheese slices and melt. Once cheese is creamy, add cream of shrimp soup and drained shrimp pieces. Stir together and serve hot. Flavored breads, scoop chips, and crackers are wonderful with this treat!

85104-07

SPINACH ARTICHOKE DIP

Deonne Bloomberg
Former Governor's Staff

1 (12-oz.) jar or can artichoke hearts
1 cup mayonnaise
1 cup grated Parmesan cheese

¼ cup chopped onion or more
½ tsp. pepper or more
1 or 2 cloves garlic - chopped
½ pkg. frozen spinach

Drain artichoke hearts and mix mayonnaise, cheese, onion, pepper, garlic and spinach. Bake 350° uncovered in casserole dish for 30 - 35 minutes. Serve with crackers.

STRAWBERRY & BRIE BRUSCHETTA

Sarah Adam Axtman

12 slices French bread, cut ½ inch thick
⅓ cup butter, softened
⅓ cup packed brown sugar
2 tsp. ground cinnamon
12 slices Brie cheese (about 12 oz.)

1-½ lb. (about 4 to 5 cups) sliced, stemmed strawberries
½ tsp. vanilla extract
1 cup sliced almonds, toasted

Heat oven to 375°. Spread one side of each bread slice with butter; arrange, butter side up, on large baking sheet. In small bowl, combine sugar and cinnamon; sprinkle 1 tsp. over each slice of bread. Reserve remaining sugar mixture. Toast bread in oven for 5 minutes. Remove from oven. Top each toast slice with one slice of cheese; return to oven. Bake an additional 4 to 6 minutes or until cheese is melted. Meanwhile, in large bowl, combine strawberries, vanilla, and remaining sugar mixture; toss lightly. Place two bruschetta on each serving plate. Spoon ⅓ cup strawberry mixture over each; sprinkle with almonds. Serve immediately. This is a wonderful dish to serve with brunch or at a wedding or baby shower. Pour a mimosa and enjoy!

Granddaughter of Governor George T. Mickelson and niece of Governor George S. Mickelson

STUFFED MUSHROOMS

Recipe Box at the
Governors Residence

18 large mushrooms, cleaned,
 with stems removed and
 chopped fine
2 tbls. melted butter
1 tsp. garlic salt

2 tbls. minced onion
1 tsp. Worcestershire sauce
4 oz. jumbo lump crab
1 tbls. mayonnaise
3 oz. Brie, cut into 18 pieces

Place mushroom caps on a cookie sheet. Brush caps with some butter
and sprinkle with garlic salt. In a skillet, sauté mushroom stems with
onion, Worcestershire sauce and remaining butter. In a bowl, combine
crab and mayonnaise. Fill caps with mushroom and onion mixture; top
with crab mixture and one piece of cheese. Bake at 350° for 10-15
minutes or until mushrooms are tender and cheese is melted.

SUSANNE'S & SARAH'S ARTICHOKE SPREAD

Tanna Zabel
Governor's Staff

2 cups mayonnaise
1 can artichoke hearts (non-
 marinated)
2 tbls. dill weed (start with 1
 tbls., taste and add if
 necessary)

1 cup cheddar/mozzarella
 cheese (thinly shredded)
1 shake garlic salt
2 shakes pepper
1 loaf cocktail rye bread

Combine mayonnaise, artichoke hearts, dill weed, cheese, garlic salt
and pepper. Spread on cocktail rye bread and bake at 350° for 5
minutes. Serve and enjoy!

SWEET CHICKEN BACON WRAPS

Recipe Box at the
Governors Residence

1-¼ lbs. boneless, skinless
 chicken breasts (about 4)
1 1 lb. pkg. sliced bacon

⅔ packed cup brown sugar
2 tbls. chili powder

Preheat oven to 350°. Cut chicken breasts into 1 inch cubes. Cut each
bacon slice into thirds. Wrap each chicken cube with bacon and secure
with a wooden pick. Stir together brown sugar and chili powder. Dredge
wrapped chicken in mixture. Coat a rack and broiler pan with nonstick
cooking spray. Place chicken wrap on rack in broiler pan. Bake at 350°
for 30-35 minutes or until bacon is crisp.

85104-07

TACO DIP

Nancy Jahnke

1 lb. ground beef, cooked and
  drained
1 pkg. taco seasoning mix
1 (8-oz.) can tomato sauce
1 (4-oz.) can chopped green
  chilies

1 tsp. Worcestershire sauce
1 (16-oz.) box Velveeta Cheese
  or 8 oz. Velveeta and 8 oz.
  Velveeta Mexican
dash garlic salt

Cut cheese into chunks and mix all together and warm until cheese is melted. Serve warm with taco chips.

Daughter of Governor Walter Dale Miller

TEXAS CAVIAR

Pam Janklow Derheim

1 can black-eyed peas (with
  jalapeño), drained
1 can pinto beans (with
  jalapeño), drained
1 small jar pimento, finely
  chopped

1 small onion, finely chopped
1 cup celery, finely chopped
1 cup green pepper, finely
  chopped
1 cup white shoepeg corn,
  drained

Dressing:

1 tsp. salt
¾ cup cider vinegar
½ tsp. pepper

½ cup oil
1 tbls. water
1 cup sugar

Place all ingredients in bowl with a lid. Cover with the dressing and marinate for at least 24 to 48 hours before serving. When ready to serve, drain well. Best when served with Frito Scoops. For the dressing, combine all ingredients in saucepan. Bring to a boil, stirring constantly until the sugar is dissolved. Remove from heat and cool completely. Pour over bean mixture to marinate.

Daughter of Governor William J. Janklow

TEXAS CAVIAR

Monica Harding
Former Governor's Staff

2 large tomatoes, chopped
3 large avocados, chopped
1/2 bunch of cilantro leaves, chopped
4 green onions, finely chopped
1 (15-oz.) can black beans, rinsed and drained

1 (11-oz.) can corn, drained
1 - 2 tsp. garlic salt
1 tsp. Tabasco sauce
3 tbls. red wine vinegar
2 tbls. olive oil
1 lime

Combine all the ingredients except the lime. Mix together. Cut the lime in half and squeeze the juice over the mixture. Chill for 2 hours before serving. Serve with tortilla chip scoops.

TOMATO BRUSCHETTA

Recipe Box at the
Governors Residence

3 ripe medium tomatoes, seeded and chopped
1 small onion, chopped
2 tbls. fresh basil leaves, snipped, or 2 tsp. dried basil leaves
1 clove garlic, pressed

1/4 tsp. salt
1/4 tsp. coarsely ground black pepper
24 slices French bread, cut 1/4 inch thick
2 tbls. olive oil

Preheat oven to 375°. Cut tomatoes in half crosswise; squeeze out seeds. Chop tomatoes and onion. Snip basil; add to tomato mixture. Add garlic to salt and pepper; mix gently. Place bread slices on greased baking sheet. Lightly brush bread with olive oil. Bake 10-12 minutes or until lightly browned and crisp. Remove bread from oven; scoop tomato mixture onto toast slices. Serve immediately.

VEGETABLE PIZZA

Jim Hagen
Former Governor's Cabinet

2 pkgs. crescent rolls
2 (8-oz.) pkgs. cream cheese, soft
1/2 cup Miracle Whip
1 envelope Hidden Valley Ranch Dressing Mix

cheddar cheese
vegetables, cut up (broccoli, carrots, green peppers, onions, black olives, etc.)

Spread crescent rolls on 11 x 17 inch baking sheet. Bake as directed and cool. Beat cream cheese, Miracle Whip, and dressing mix. Spread over cooled crust. Top with cheese and vegetables. Cover and refrigerate at least an hour.

85104-07

VEGGIE TORTILLA ROLL-UPS

Recipe Box at the
Governors Residence

1 (3-oz.) pkg. cream cheese
½ cup sour cream
½ cup finely shredded cheddar
cheese
¼ cup finely chopped red bell
pepper

2 tbls. sliced ripe olives,
chopped
1 tbls. chopped fresh parsley
3 flavored or plain flour tortillas
(8-10 inch)

In medium bowl, mix all ingredients except tortillas. Spread about ½ cup of the cheese mixture over one side of each tortilla. Tightly roll tortilla up. Repeat with the remaining tortillas and cheese mixture. Wrap each tortilla roll individually in plastic wrap. Refrigerate at least 3 hours but no longer than 24 hours. To serve, cut each tortilla roll into 1 inch slices. About 30 servings.

WILD PURPLE SMOOTHIE

Luz Naasz
Residence Staff

½ cup frozen blueberries
1 frozen banana
2 tbls. soy protein powder
1 cup water

1 cup vanilla soy milk
cinnamon and vanilla extract to
taste
carob powder (optional)

Combine in blender.

Recipe Favorites

Recipe Favorites

85104-07

(Photo courtesy of the South Dakota State Historical Society Archives)

COE-CRAWFORD-DAVEY-PETTYJOHN HOUSE

Coe Crawford built this Queen Anne house in 1885. He lived here while he was Attorney General from 1892 to 1896. He later served as governor from 1907 to 1909. Robert S. Vessey succeeded Crawford as governor and lived in the house built by Crawford during his 1909 to 1913 term of office.

Cut stones are used in the house's foundation. The basement of the house contains a large uncut boulder that has resisted attempts to break it up or move it. In essence, the house is built on a rock.

The house's Queen Anne appearance came about from a 1908 rebuilding project. The house's front facades has an open porch that wraps around the right side and is supported by Doric columns. Directly above the porch is a second-story balcony. A tower dormer with segments appears on the combination hip-gable roof.

The interior of the house has oak trim on the first level and fir on the second. The floors were of sugar maple or black walnut and have some of the most ornate parquet floors in the state.

The house is listed on the National Register of Historic Places. Today it is a private residence and is located at 129 South Washington.

TIDBITS

Elizabeth Ward Jensen worked many years in her family's business, the People's Telephone and Telegraph Company, in Hot Springs, SD.

Karen Jensen was the first child of a South Dakota governor born during his term in office. Her parents were Governor Leslie and First Lady Elizabeth Jensen.

Vera Cahalan Bushfield entertained the legislator's wives at tea every Tuesday.

Vera Cahalan Bushfield was appointed to the U.S. Senate to complete her husband's term after his death in 1948.

Vera Cahalan Bushfield was the Kappa Alpha Theta house mother at Purdue University.

Lorna Sharpe, daughter of Governor Merrill Q. and Emily Auld Sharpe, was married while Governor Sharpe was in office. The wedding breakfast was held at the Governors Residence. Lorna married Lieutenant Dan Leedy of Rapid City.

Governor Harlan and First Lady Verna Bushfield christened the SS South Dakota during World War II.

Governor Joe and First Lady June Foss christened the SS Sioux Falls Victory ship in 1944.

The newly built 1936 Governors Residence had to be remodeled in 1939 because the dining room was too narrow. First Lady Vera Bushfield enlarged the small dining room by combining it with the butler's pantry.

Governor Harlan Bushfield planted cottonwood trees along the shore of Capitol Lake.

SOUPS & SALADS

Soups

5 CAN SOUP

Bonnie Untereiner Bjork
Former Governor's Cabinet

1 can mixed veggies
1 can diced tomatoes
1 can corn

1 can black beans
1 can Progresso Light
 Minestrone

Combine ingredients and heat. (This one is 1 Weight Watcher point for the whole pot).

BOE FAMILY POTATO SOUP

Mrs. Sissel Boe

4 medium red potatoes, cooked
 in skins
5 tbls. butter
4 tbls. flour
1 small onion, minced

1 cup minced celery or 1 tsp.
 celery salt
salt and pepper
3 cups milk (add more if soup is
 too thick)

Melt 1 tbls. of butter and slowly cook minced onion and celery until slightly done. Stir constantly and don't let them burn. Cool cooked potatoes and remove skins. Dice and set aside. In a Dutch oven or heavy kettle melt the remaining 4 tbls. of butter. Whisk in flour. Stir and cook 2 minutes over medium heat. Add milk and make a thin white sauce. Cook 2 minutes. Add cooked onion, potatoes and celery. (If you use celery salt instead of celery, add it now). Salt and pepper to taste. Cook slowly over low heat for 20 minutes. Mash slightly with potato masher and cook 10 more minutes. (Do not let the mixture burn or scorch - stir often). Will keep in refrigerator several days. Leftovers may be frozen.

Mother of Governor Nils Boe

Note: Recipe submitted by Carol Mashek, Minnehaha County Historical Society

BROCCOLI CHEESE SOUP

Don Rounds

1 large onion, chopped
½ stick margarine (4 tbls.)
3 heaping tbls. chicken bouillon
3 cups milk (1 can evaporated)
3 cups water

2 cups dry noodles
1 (16-oz.) pkg. frozen broccoli or
 1 head fresh broccoli
¾ lb. Velveeta Cheese
⅓ tsp. garlic powder

Sauté onion in margarine. Add water and bouillon. Bring to boil. Then add broccoli and noodles and simmer until tender (about 11 minutes). Add milk and cheese and stir until cheese is melted. Add garlic powder and stir well. DO NOT BOIL.

Father of Governor M. Michael Rounds

CHEESE SOUP

Doreen Kayser
Former Governor's Staff

⅔ cup grated carrots
1 cup green onions, thinly
 sliced

2 cups water
1 medium white onion, chopped
1 cup flour

In a 5 quart pot, parboil the carrots, green onions, and water for 5 minutes. Add the flour to the white onion and mix together. Combine this with the ingredients in the 5-quart pot to make rue.

1 stick butter
4 cups milk
4 cups chicken broth
1 (15-oz.) jar Cheez Whiz

¼-½ tsp. cayenne (red) pepper
1 tbls. wet mustard
1 lb. bacon, fried crisp and
 crumbled

Add these ingredients to the rue. Cook until heated through.

Note: This is great with homemade bread.

85104-07

CHICKEN AND SALSA SOUP

Lori Shangreaux
Governor's Staff

1-³/₄ cups water
1 (14-¹/₂-oz.) can chicken broth
¹/₂ lb. skinless, boneless
  chicken, cut into bite-size
  pieces
1 - 2 tbls. chili powder
1 (11-oz.) can whole kernel corn
  with sweet peppers, drained

1 cup chunky garden-style salsa
3 cups broken baked or fried
  corn tortilla chips
2 oz. Monterey Jack cheese with
  jalapeño peppers, shredded

In a 3-quart saucepan combine water, chicken broth, chicken, and chili powder. Bring to boiling; reduce heat. Cover and simmer for 8 minutes. Add corn. Simmer, uncovered, for 5 minutes more. Stir in salsa; heat through. Serve with chips and cheese on top.

CHICKEN TORTILLA SOUP

Michael Gorman
Former Governor's Cabinet

2 cups onion, chopped
3 stalks celery, chopped
2 carrots, chopped
2 tbls. olive oil
1 lb. fajita chicken, cubed (see
  below)
1¹/₂ tbls. fresh parsley, chopped
1¹/₂ tbls. fresh cilantro, chopped
1 (10-oz.) can Ro-Tel diced
  tomatoes with green chilies

2 (14-¹/₂-oz.) can Hunt's diced
  tomatoes
1 (49-¹/₂-oz.) can chicken broth
1 tsp. sesame oil
1 cup Uncle Ben's converted
  rice, uncooked
shredded cheddar cheese
tortilla chips

In deep pan, sauté onion, celery, and carrots in olive oil until onion is transparent. Remove mixture with slotted spoon and set aside. Brown chicken in same pan until crispy brown - add no more oil. Add cooked onion, celery, carrot, parsley, cilantro, 3 cans of tomatoes, chicken broth, and sesame oil. Stir and bring to a boil, then add uncooked rice. Bring back to a boil and reduce heat to simmer. Simmer the mixture, covered, for 20 minutes. To serve, top the bowl of soup with cheese and tortilla chips.

Fajita Chicken - cut chicken into ³/₄ inch cubes. Shake some Cajun seasoning on chicken to taste (experiment a little first by crisping up a little chicken chislic.) Add a small amount of olive oil...mix well...put in zip lock bag to marinate for a couple hours in the refrigerator. I like to use boneless, skinless thighs, but breasts are good, too, depending on your personal preference.

CHILI IN NO TIME

Bonnie Untereiner Bjork
Former Governor's Cabinet

1-½ lbs. ground beef
1 medium onion
1 (28-oz.) can crushed tomatoes
1 (30-oz.) jar spaghetti sauce

2 (16-oz.) cans kidney beans,
  drained
2 - 4 tbls. chili powder

In a large kettle or Dutch oven, brown beef and onion. Drain. Add remaining ingredients. Simmer for at least 15 minutes. Stirring occasionally. Yield: 10 servings (2-½ qts.)

CREAM OF POTATO SOUP

Mardell Davis
Governor's Staff

6 cups potatoes, sliced
½ cup carrots, sliced
1 cup onion, chopped
1 cup celery, sliced
1-½ tsp. salt

¼ tsp. pepper
2 cups milk
2 cups light cream
2 tbls. cheddar cheese, finely
  shredded

Cook potatoes and carrots in boiling water until done; drain. Sauté bacon until crisp; drain and crumble. Sauté onion and celery in 2 tablespoons bacon fat. Combine cooked vegetables, bacon, salt, pepper, milk and cream. Simmer for 30 minutes. Do not boil. Garnish with shredded cheese. Makes 2 quarts.

EASY CHICKEN CORN CHOWDER

DeeAnn Rounds

2 cans chicken broth
1 can water
2 potatoes, peeled and diced
2 stalks celery, diced

1 onion, diced or minced
celery salt, regular salt, pepper
  (add to own liking)

In large pot over medium heat, place potatoes, celery and onion in the chicken broth and water. Bring to a boil and boil until potatoes are tender (about 10 minutes). Reduce heat.

1 cup Velveeta Cheese, diced
1 large canned chicken,
  undrained

2 cans creamed corn
1 can whole corn, undrained
1 can evaporated milk

Over low heat, add to broth mixture. Simmer 20 minutes.

Sister-in-law of Governor M. Michael Rounds

85104-07

FIVE CAN SOUP

Bonnie Untereiner Bjork
Former Governor's Cabinet

1 can beef or chicken broth
1 can carrots
1 can zucchini with tomato
 sauce

1 can sliced potatoes
1 can diced tomatoes with basil,
 garlic and oregano

Combine and heat. (This is 3 Weight Watcher points for the whole pot.)

GROUND BEEF/VEGETABLE STEW

Dean Anderson
Former Governor's Cabinet

2 lbs. ground beef
½ cup chopped onion
1 clove garlic, minced
2 tsp. salt
1 tbls. dried parsley flakes
1 tsp. dried basil leaves
½ tsp. pepper

1 (28-oz.) can tomatoes, cut up
 (or 2 quarts)
6 medium potatoes, pared and
 cut in ¾" cubes (4 cups)
1 (16-oz.) can pork and beans in
 tomato sauce
1 (10-oz.) pkg. frozen peas

Brown ground beef in 4 quart Dutch oven. When meat begins to change color, add onion, garlic, salt, parsley, basil and pepper. Sauté until well browned. Add tomatoes. Simmer, covered, 50 minutes. Stir occasionally. Add potatoes and pork and beans; cook 20 minutes. Add peas, cook 10 minutes longer. Serves 8.

HUNGARIAN MUSHROOM SOUP

Former Lt. Gov. Carole Hillard

1 lb. fresh mushrooms, chopped
1 clove garlic, crushed
2 tbls. chopped parsley
1 small onion, chopped
3 tbls. butter

1 tsp. salt
1 tsp. paprika
3 tbls. flour
4 cups chicken broth
½ pt. sour cream

Brown mushrooms, garlic, parsley and onion in butter. Stir in salt, paprika, and flour. Add half of chicken broth. Cook over low heat until thick and smooth. Blend in remaining stock and heat to boiling. Just before serving, add sour cream. Stir slightly.

ITALIAN PASTA SOUP

Susan L. Walker
Former Governor's Cabinet

8 oz. mild Italian sausage
1 cup sliced celery
1 thinly sliced carrot
$1/2$ cup chopped onions
5 cloves garlic, minced
1 (49-$1/2$-oz.) can chicken broth
 (about $6 1/4$ cups)
2 tsp. dried Italian Seasonings,
 crushed
$1/4$ tsp. crushed red pepper
 (optional)

1 cup small dried pasta (such as
 bow ties, shells or elbow
 macaroni)
$1/4$ cup snipped fresh parsley
1 (28-oz.) can diced tomatoes
 (undrained)
shredded Parmesan cheese
toppers, sliced green or black
 olives; canned artichoke
 hearts, rinsed, drained and cut
 into wedges

Remove casings from sausage, if present. In a 4-quart heavy cooking pot cook and stir sausage over medium heat about 10 minutes or until done. Remove sausage from cooking pot with a slotted spoon, reserving drippings in pan. Cook celery, onion, carrot and garlic in drippings about 5 minutes or until tender. Drain off fat. Add chicken broth to pan along with herbs and crushed red pepper (if using). Bring to boiling. Simmer for 10 minutes. Add pasta; return to boiling. Boil gently for 8-10 minutes or until pasta reaches desired tenderness, stirring occasionally. Add cooked sausage and undrained tomatoes and heat through. Stir in parsley. Season to taste with salt and black pepper. Ladle into serving bowls and top with shredded Parmesan cheese and add desired toppers. Serve with garlic toast or garlic-Parmesan cheese toast. Makes 5 or 6 servings. This soup tastes like it has been cooking all day with the very first serving!

85104-07

KNEPFLA SOUP

Rachel Hansen Kippley
Former Governor's Staff

6 cans chicken broth
1 lb. cooked ham
1 can cream of mushroom soup
1 can cream of celery soup

1 can evaporated milk
diced vegetables - your choice
  (carrots, celery, potatoes,
  onion, etc.)

Simmer chicken broth, ham, cream of mushroom soup, cream of celery soup, evaporated milk, and veggies in a slow cooker for 3 hours. When veggies are cooked, proceed to make the knepfla.

Knepfla:

¾ cup milk
1 egg
1-½ cups flour

for added flavor, save a small
amount of finely chopped
onion and ham to add

Increase temperature of soup until gently boiling. Drop dime-sized knepfla into boiling pot until mixture is gone. Turn down heat again to simmer for ½ hour.

LOW CAL CHILI

Recipe Box at the
Governors Residence

1 lb. lean ground beef
½ cup onion, chopped
2 cups celery, sliced
½ cup green pepper, chopped
½ tsp. garlic salt (optional)
1-¾ cups undrained kidney
  beans (15 oz. can)

4 cups undrained tomatoes
  (3-lb. cans)
salt to taste
½-1 tbls. chili powder (to taste)
1 bay leaf

Brown meat and onion in large fry pan. Thoroughly drain all excess fat. Place 2 cans undrained tomatoes in blender and liquify. Cut up tomatoes from remaining can. Add this and all other ingredients except kidney beans to drained meat mixture. Simmer, covered 1 - 2 hours. Add kidney beans, remove bay leaf. Serve hot, topped with shredded cheddar cheese and crackers.

MIKE'S POTATO CHEESE/SAUSAGE SOUP

Michael Gorman
Former Governor's Cabinet

4 cups chicken broth
4 cups potatoes, cubed
1-¹/₂ cup onion, chopped
³/₄ cup celery, chopped
¹/₂ cup carrots, shredded

1¹/₂ cup Velveeta Cheese, cubed
1 cup fully cooked smoked
  sausage ring, cubed
salt and pepper, to taste

Bring chicken broth, potatoes, onion, celery, and carrots to a boil and
then reduce heat. Simmer until potatoes are very tender. DO NOT
DRAIN. Add cheese and heat on low until cheese melts. Add sausage
and continue to heat for 5 minutes, stirring frequently. Serves 4.

MY SISTER'S GRILLED CHICKEN & BLACK BEAN CHILI

Susan Edwards Johnson
Former Governor's Cabinet

2 cans black beans
4 chicken breasts, grilled and
  cubed
2 cups half and half (use low fat
  if you'd prefer)
1 cup Velveeta Cheese, cubed
1 (10-oz.) can Ro-tel tomatoes
1 cup Monterey Jack pepper
  cheese, cube

¹/₄ cup diced pimentos
1 cup diced tomatoes
¹/₂ cup diced onion
1 tsp. cumin
1 tbls. chili powder
1 tsp. cilantro
¹/₄ tsp. cayenne pepper
pinch salt

Grill chicken, cool, cut into cubes. Place half and half in a large pot and
bring to a simmer. Add Velveeta and lower heat stirring constantly until
cheese melts. Add pepper cheese and stir until melted. Add Ro-tel
tomatoes, black beans, chicken, diced tomatoes, pimentos, onion,
and spices.

36

OYSTER STEW

First Lady Madge Turner Mickelson

1 pt. oysters, in their juice
1/4 cup butter
1 pt. milk

1/2 cup cream
1 tsp. salt
1/8 tsp. pepper

Pick over the oysters, discarding any pieces of shell. Melt butter in saucepan, add oysters and cook gently until edges curl. Scald milk and cream and add to oysters. Season with salt and pepper. Let stand for an hour to let flavors combine. Reheat gently to serving temperature. Makes 4 servings.

My Mother, Madge Turner Mickelson, died this past December at age 103. She was a wonderful cook and gave my sisters and me an appreciation for the basic task of preparing good food for family and friends. I have one of her recipe boxes, and have selected this recipe and another for your cookbook.

PHEASANT WILD RICE SOUP

Bonnie Unteriner Bjork
Former Governor's Cabinet

1/2 cup butter plus 2 tbls.
1 cup flour
2 tbls. butter
1 cup finely chopped celery
1 cup diagonally sliced carrot
1 cup finely chopped onion
1/3 cup finely chopped green bell
  pepper
1/3 cup finely chopped red bell
  pepper
2 cups white shoe peg corn or
  corn niblets
2 cups sliced mushrooms

1 medium jalapeño
1 gal. chicken broth
1 tbls. finely chopped parsley
1 tsp. salt
1/4 tsp. black pepper
1/4 tsp. white pepper
1/4 tsp. ground nutmeg
1/4 tsp. cayenne
1-1/2 lbs. pheasant, cooked,
  chopped
3 cups cooked wild rice
1 cup heavy whipping cream

Heat the butter in a skillet until hot. Stir in the flour. Cook over low heat for 2 minutes or until the consistency of a roux, stirring constantly; do not brown. Heat 2 tablespoons butter in a large saucepan until hot. Add the celery, carrot, onion, green pepper, and red pepper. Sauté until the onion is tender. Stir in corn, mushrooms, and jalapeño. Cook until the mushrooms begin to turn golden brown, stirring frequently. Remove from heat. Bring broth to a boil in a 2-gallon stockpot. Stir in roux. Simmer until thickened, stirring frequently. Stir in vegetable mixture, parsley, salt, black pepper, white pepper, nutmeg, and cayenne. Bring to a simmer, stirring occasionally. Add pheasant, wild rice, and whipping cream and mix gently. Cook until heated through, stirring occasionally. Ladle into soup bowls.

This is a little work, but definitely worth the effort.

REUBEN SOUP

Recipe Box at the
Governors Residence

1 gal. milk
8 oz. corned beef
8 oz. Swiss cheese

1 lb. sauerkraut
rye bread croutons (optional)

Combine all ingredients except croutons and heat to boiling point. Cook until cheese is melted using care to as not to burn. May garnish with croutons.

Note: This soup was a favorite at the Pierre Elks Club. Serves 14-16.

85104-07

SISSEL'S CREAM OF TOMATO BISQUE SOUP

Mrs. Sissel Boe

2 cups cooked, peeled and
  strained tomatoes
4 tbls. butter

4 tbls. flour
2 - 3 cups milk
salt and pepper

If using fresh tomatoes, blanch and remove skins. Quarter tomatoes and cook slowly in their own juice until done. Strain, keeping 2 cups. Set aside. Melt butter over medium heat. Add flour and mix until there are no lumps and the mixture thickens. Add the milk, a bit at a time, making a thin white sauce. Add tomatoes. Turn heat down before mixture begins to bubble. Simmer at least 20 minutes or until soup is smooth. Salt and pepper to taste. Serve immediately. (May be frozen).

Mother of Governor Nils Boe

Note: Recipe submitted by Carol Mashek, Minnehaha County Historical Society

TACO SOUP

Bonnie Untereiner Bjork
Former Governor's Cabinet

2 lbs. ground beef
1 onion
1 (4-oz.) can green chilies,
  chopped
1 tsp. salt
$\frac{1}{2}$ tsp. pepper
1 pkg. taco seasoning
1 pkg. Hidden Valley dressing
  mix

1 can hominy, undrained
1 can kidney beans, undrained
1 can pinto beans, undrained
2 cans stewed tomatoes
1 can Ro-tel tomatoes
1-$\frac{1}{2}$ cups tomato juice (can use
  water)

Brown beef and onion - add everything else. Bring to boil and simmer 30 minutes. Serve with grated cheese on top and Fritos in bottom of bowl.

VENISON SOUP

Jeff Vonk
Governor's Cabinet

olive oil
1-½ lbs. ground venison
1 (46-oz.) can tomato juice
1 large can tomatoes
1 (8-oz.) can minced clams, drained
1 cup diced carrots
1 tbls. Worcestershire sauce
1 can yellow string beans (with juice)
1 can green string beans (with juice)
1 tbls. garlic powder
2 cups chopped celery
3 tbls. chopped onion
2 tsp. basil
½ head finely chopped cabbage (optional)
salt and pepper to taste

Brown ground meat in olive oil in large soup kettle. Add all the ingredients. Simmer everything 2 hours. Sprinkle grated cheese over top when ready to serve.

WEST TEXAS SOUTHWESTERN BEEF SOUP

Dr. James Hansen
Former Governor's Cabinet

2 lbs. stew meat

Brown stew meat in oil.

¾ cup chopped onion
2 cloves minced garlic
2 cans stewed tomatoes (12 - 14 oz.) (typically use Mexican-style stewed tomatoes)
1 can fiesta tomato or regular tomato soup
1 can beef broth
1 can chicken broth
¼ cup water
1 tsp. cumin
1 tsp. chili powder
1 tsp. salt
½ tsp. lemon pepper
2 tsp. Worcestershire sauce
½ cup picante sauce

Mix ingredients. Add in cooked stew meat. Cook for 10 hours minimum. Serve with cut-up flour tortilla shells, shredded cheddar cheese and sour cream.

85104-07

WHITE CHILI

Kellie Kneip

1 lb. boneless skinless chicken breasts, cut into 1/2 inch cubes
1 tsp. garlic powder
1 small onion
1 tbls. vegetable oil
2 (15-oz.) cans great northern beans, rinsed and drained
1 (14-1/2-oz.) can chicken broth
2 (4-oz.) cans chopped green chilies
1 tsp. salt
1 tsp. ground cumin
1/2 tsp. pepper
1/4 tsp. cayenne pepper
1 cup sour cream
1/2 cup whipping cream

In a large pot, sauté chicken, onion, and garlic powder in oil until chicken is no longer pink. Add beans, broth, chilies, and seasonings. Bring to a boil. Reduce heat, simmer, uncovered for 30 minutes. Remove from heat, stir in sour cream and whipping cream.

Daughter-in-law of Governor Richard F. Kneip

WILD RICE PHEASANT SOUP

Jerry Hofer
Governor's Cabinet

2 tbls. butter
1/3 cup onion, finely chopped
1 clove garlic, minced
1/4 cup all-purpose flour
1/2 tsp. salt
1/4 tsp. pepper
4 cups chicken broth, divided
2-1/2 cups cooked wild rice
2 cups cut-up cooked pheasant
1 cup thinly sliced carrots
1 cup half & half
2 tbls. dry sherry

In 6 qt. Dutch oven or stockpot, melt butter over medium heat. Add onion and garlic. Cook 2-3 minutes or until onion is tender, stirring frequently. In separate bowl, combine flour, salt and pepper. Blend in 2 cups broth and all other remaining ingredients except the half & half and the sherry. Bring to boil over medium heat. Reduce heat to low and simmer for 30-35 minutes, or until carrots are tender. Stir in half & half and sherry, then simmer for 15-20 minutes or until flavors are blended.

WILD RICE SOUP

Kevin Forsch
Governor's Staff

6 tbls. butter
1 tbls. minced onion
½ cup flour
3 cups chicken broth
2 cups cooked wild rice
⅓ cup minced ham
½ cup finely grated carrots

3 tbls. chopped silvered
  almonds
½ tsp. salt
1 cup half and half
1 cup dry Sherry
minced parsley or chives

Melt butter in saucepan; sauté onion until tender. Blend in flour; gradually add broth. Cook, stirring constantly, until mixture comes to a boil; boil 1 minute. Stir in rice, ham, carrots, almonds, and salt; simmer about 5 minutes. Blend in half and half and Sherry; heat to serving temperature. Garnish with minced parsley or chives.

ZUPPA TUSCANO

Rebecca Caldwell Bauer

1 lb. Jimmy Dean hot sausage
  (roll)
2 large russet baking potatoes,
  sliced into ¼" slices (do not
  peel)
1 large Vidalia onion
6 slices bacon

2 cloves garlic, minced
2 cups kale or Swiss chard,
  chopped
2 cans chicken broth
1 qt. water
1 cup heavy cream

Cook sausage, drain. Cook bacon, drain. Place onion, potatoes, chicken broth, water and garlic in pot, and cook on medium heat until potatoes are done. Add sausage, bacon, salt and pepper to taste - simmer for another 10 minutes. Turn to low heat, add kale and cream. Heat through and serve with baguette or bread sticks (don't be afraid to dunk).

Daughter of Governor Walter Dale Miller

42

Salads

ALL AMERICAN FLAG MOLD

Julie Johnson
Former Governor's Cabinet

1 qt. boiling water, divided
2 pkgs. Jell-O Brand Berry Blue
Flavor Gelatin
2 pkgs. Jell-O Brand Gelatin,
any red flavor

3 cups ice cold water, divided
1 pkg. Jell-O Brand Lemon
Flavor Gelatin
1 (8-oz.) tub Cool Whip Whipped
Topping, thawed

Add 1-½ cups boiling water to dry berry blue gelatin mix in medium bowl; stir at least 2 minutes until gelatin is dissolved. Dissolve dry red gelatin mix in 1-½ cups boiling water in separate bowl. Stir 1-½ cups ice cold water into dissolved gelatin in each bowl. Spray 10 cup flag mold (or sprayed rectangular cake pan); place on baking sheet. Pour red gelatin into mold. Refrigerate 45 minutes until set but not firm (gelatin should stick to finger when touched and should mound). Meanwhile, refrigerate berry blue gelatin in bowl for 45 minutes. Meanwhile, stir remaining 1 cup boiling water into dry lemon gelatin mix in bowl at least 2 minutes until dissolved. Refrigerate 25 minutes or until slightly thickened (consistency of unbeaten egg whites), stirring occasionally. Stir in whipped topping with wire whisk. Gently spread over red gelatin in mold. Refrigerate 10 minutes or until set but not firm. Gently spoon thickened berry blue gelatin over lemon gelatin mixture in mold. Refrigerate 4 hours or overnight until firm. Unmold.

BAKED POTATO SALAD

Michele Rounds Brich

12 Russet potatoes, baked and
diced (unpeeled)
4 eggs, hard-boiled and
chopped
2 stalks celery, diced

3 pieces bacon, cooked, cooled
and crumbled
1 green bell pepper, diced
1 red pepper, diced

In a large bowl, combine potatoes, eggs, celery, bacon, green pepper, and red pepper.

Dressing:

6 tbls. dill
2 cups mayonnaise
1 cup yellow prepared mustard

6 tbls. sweet relish
½ cup apple cider vinegar

Combine all ingredients and mix well. Toss with potato mixture and refrigerate at least 2 hours.

Sister of Governor M. Michael Rounds

BLEU CHEESE DRESSING

*Recipe Box at the
Governors Residence*

1 pkg. Hidden Valley Ranch
  dressing
1 cup mayonnaise

1 cup milk
bleu cheese, crumbled

Combine in blender. Add crumbled bleu cheese and mix by hand. Refrigerate.

BLUEBERRY SALAD

Ida Covey

First Layer:

1 (3-oz.) pkg. Raspberry Jell-O

2 cups hot water

Stir well and pour into 9 x 13 pan. Chill until firm.

Second Layer:

1 envelope Knox Gelatin
$\frac{1}{2}$ cup cold water
1 cup half and half cream
1 cup sugar

1 tsp. vanilla
1 (8-oz.) pkg. cream cheese
  (room temp)
$\frac{1}{2}$ cup chopped nuts

Dissolve Knox gelatin in cold water. Heat sugar and cream to boiling point, do not boil. Mix gelatin mixture into hot mixture. Add vanilla and cream cheese and beat until smooth. Add nuts. When cool pour over first layer. Chill until firm.

Third Layer:

1 (3-oz.) pkg. Raspberry Jell-O
1 cup hot water

1 #2 can blueberries (do not
  drain)

Dissolve Jello in hot water and cool. Add blueberries. Blend carefully and spoon over second layer. Allow to chill. Cut in squares to serve.

Granddaughter-in-law of Lieutenant Governor Hyatt Covey

85104-07

BONNIE'S CORN SALAD

Deb Bowman
Governor's Cabinet

4 ears sweet corn (may
  substitute 2 cans of niblets
  corn, drained)
1 small purple onion
1 small green pepper
4 ripe Roma tomatoes

2 large cucumbers
$\frac{1}{2}$ cup mayonnaise or salad
  dressing
$\frac{1}{4}$ cup sour cream
$\frac{1}{2}$ tsp. cracked black pepper
Beau Monde seasoning to taste

Cook sweet corn and slice from cob, or use drained canned corn. Quarter the tomatoes and remove seeds and pulp, cut into chunks. Quarter the cucumbers and scoop out the seeds, cut into chunks. Dice the onion and green pepper. Mix all together and then add the salad dressing or mayonnaise, sour cream and seasonings. Adjust seasonings to your taste preference. Best served after refrigerating for 2 hours or more.

BROCCOLI CAULIFLOWER SALAD

Pam Janklow Derheim

Salad:

2 bunches of broccoli cut into
  bite size pieces
1 bunch of cauliflower cut into
  bite size pieces
$\frac{1}{2}$ lb. bacon, cooked and cut
  into pieces

$\frac{1}{4}$ cup chopped green onions
1 (8-oz.) pkg. mozzarella cheese
  (shredded)
$\frac{1}{3}$ cup Parmesan cheese
  (shredded)

Dressing:

2 cups Light Miracle Whip
2 tbls. red wine vinegar

$\frac{1}{2}$ cup sugar

Combine broccoli, cauliflower, bacon, and green onions. Just before serving add the mozzarella and Parmesan cheese and toss with dressing. For the dressing, combine all ingredients in small bowl. Pour over salad mixture just before serving.

Daughter of Governor William J. Janklow

CABBAGE SALAD

First Lady Florence Vessey

1 small cabbage, chopped
1 egg
1/2 cup sugar
1/2 cup vinegar

1 tsp. mustard
1 tsp. salt
1 large spoonful butter

Combine all ingredients but the egg and cabbage and boil. Pour over beaten egg and boil again. Pour over cabbage which must be chopped very fine. Add 1/2 cup of sweet thick cream.

Note: This recipe submitted by Arlein Fransen, Dunham Historical Society, Wessington Springs, SD.

CAULIFLOWER SALAD

First Lady Linda Mickelson Graham

1 tsp. Accent
1/2 tsp. dry mustard
1/2 tsp. salt
1/3 cup tarragon vinegar
2/3 cup salad oil
1 clove garlic, halved

2 cups cauliflowerets
1 red onion, diced and
  separated
1 cup pitted ripe olives
6 cups salad greens
3 tbls. chopped parsley

Beat first five ingredients until well mixed. Add garlic and parsley. Pour over cauliflowerets, onions, and olives in large jar. Cover and refrigerate for one day, shaking occasionally. To serve, drain dressing and reserve. Discard garlic. Add vegetables to greens in salad bowl, sprinkle with Accent and toss with enough dressing to moisten greens. If desired, top with croutons, blue cheese, or hard cooked egg. Serves 8.

CHERRY SALAD

Kevin Forsch
Governor's Staff

2 cans cherry pie filling
(8-oz.) container Cool Whip
1 can sweetened condensed
  milk

walnuts

Mix together all ingredients and chill before serving.

85104-07

CHICKEN AND PINEAPPLE SALAD

Sandra Zinter
Governor's Cabinet

3-1/2 lb. chicken breasts -
 poached and skinned
2 cups diced celery
2 cups diced (1/2-inch) fresh
 pineapple
1/2 cup heavy whipping cream,
 whipped

1 cup Hellmann's Mayonnaise
salt and freshly ground pepper,
 to taste
lettuce leaves

Cut chicken into 1-inch chunks. Combine the chicken, celery, and pineapple in a bowl. Whisk the whipped cream and mayonnaise together until blended, and pour over chicken. Toss and coat thoroughly. Season to taste with salt and freshly ground pepper. Line six salad plates with lettuce leaves. Mound the salad on the leaves and serve immediately.

CHICKEN SALAD

Recipe Box at the
Governors Residence

3 cups chicken, cooked and
 cubed
1/2 cup green pepper, diced
3 tbls. minced onion
1/2 cup black olives

1 cup crushed pineapple,
 drained
1-1/4 cups mayonnaise
1 can mandarin oranges
salt and pepper to taste

Toss everything together, then gently fold in the mandarin oranges.

CHICKEN SALAD

Diane Wollman

4 cups diced cooked chicken
1 (15-oz.) can pineapple chunks,
 drained
1 cup chopped celery
1 (11-oz.) can mandarin
 oranges, drained

1/2 cup sliced ripe pitted olives
1/2 cup chopped green pepper
2 tbls. grated onion
1 cup mayonnaise
1 tbls. mustard

Blend mayonnaise and mustard and toss over chicken, fruit, and vegetables. Cover and chill several hours. Serve in lettuce-lined bowl. Serves 8.

Sister-in-law of Governor Harvey Wollman

COLESLAW

*Recipe Box at the
Governors Residence*

1 qt. cabbage, shredded
2 tsp. salt

1 cup onion, chopped
1 cup green pepper, chopped

Dressing:

1 cup sugar
$\frac{1}{2}$ cup water
$\frac{1}{2}$ cup white vinegar

1 tsp. mustard seed
1 tsp. celery seed

Boil dressing ingredients for 1 minute. Cool, and pour over cabbage.
Store in covered bowl in refrigerator. Make this salad at least 2 days
in advance - slaw keeps indefinitely, and will taste better.

CRANBERRY-RASPBERRY MOLD

Pam Janklow Derheim

6 cups boiling water
2 (6-oz.) pkgs. Raspberry Jell-O
4 cups sour cream

2 1 lb. cans whole cranberry
 sauce
crushed walnuts

In a large bowl, pour boiling water over Jell-O; stir until dissolved. Place
in the refrigerator and chill until very thick but set. With rotary beater,
beat in sour cream and cranberry sauce along with walnuts. Divide
between two 9x13 inch pans or use a decorative Jell-O mold. Chill until
firm. The recipe can be halved and placed in 8 x 8 inch pans instead.

Daughter of Governor William J. Janklow

CRUNCH SALAD

*Doug Loen
Former Governor's Staff*

1 cup chopped broccoli (bite-
 size)
1 cup green grapes
1 cup red grapes

1 cup chopped celery
$\frac{1}{4}$ cup sliced green onion
4 oz. slivered almonds

Mix all together, then add dressing and let sit overnight.

Dressing:

1 cup Miracle Whip
1-$\frac{1}{4}$ cups sugar

1 tbls. vinegar

CRUNCHY CAULIFLOWER SALAD

Mandy Burma

1 pkg. frozen baby peas, thawed
1 cup diced celery
1 cup chopped cauliflower
1/4 cup chopped onions

1 cup cashews
1/2 cup Kefir
1 cup mayonnaise

Mix together and serve.

Great-granddaughter of Governor Walter Dale Miller

CRUNCHY CHICKEN SALAD

Harla Jessop
Former Governor's Staff

1 bag shredded cabbage
1/2 cup olive oil
2 tbls. soy sauce

2 tbls. balsamic vinegar
2 tbls. white vinegar
2 bags chicken ramen noodles

Dissolve seasonings in liquids. Mix in cabbage. Right before serving, mix in ramen noodles. Sprinkle with sunflower seeds.

CUCUMBER TOMATO SUMMER SALAD

Dale Bertsch
Governor's Staff

2 large cucumbers, seeded and
  diced in large pieces
4 - 6 large garden ripened
  tomatoes, seeded and diced in
  large pieces
4 oz. fresh mozzarella cheese
  diced

1 pkg. Good Seasons Italian
  Dressing
1/4 cup aged balsamic vinegar
3 tbls. water
1/2 cup olive oil
4 - 6 fresh sweet basil leaves
  torn into small pieces

Place seeded and diced cucumbers and tomatoes in large service bowl. Add fresh mozzarella and stir. Mix Good Seasons Italian Dressing according to package directions. Pour 1/2 - 2/3 of dressing over vegetables and cheese. Mix in torn basil leaves reserving a few for garnish. Refrigerate, turning often for at least 1 hour. Serve within a few hours. Best when fresh. Unused dressing keeps for several weeks in refrigerator.

ESTELLE'S CRANBERRY SALAD

Dr. Howell W. Todd
Former Governor's Cabinet

2 small boxes Raspberry Jell-O
1 cup hot water
2 cans Ocean Spray Whole
  Berry Cranberry Sauce
1 small can crushed pineapple,
  including juice

1 apple grated
1 orange, diced
grated rind of one orange
1 cup chopped pecans

Heat Jell-O and water until fully dissolved and then cool. Add remaining ingredients and chill overnight in appropriate bowl/container.

FARFALLE AND BROCCOLI SALAD

First Lady Linda Mickelson Graham

1 lb. broccoli, tops cut into
  florets and stems into rounds
1 lb. farfalle (bow-tie pasta)
¾ cup mayonnaise
½ cup sour cream
3 tbls. white wine vinegar

2 cups Gorgonzola cheese,
  crumbled
6 green onions, chopped
3 celery stalks, thinly sliced
3 tbls. fresh parsley chopped

Cook broccoli stems in large pot of boiling salted water 2 minutes. Add florets and cook 2 minutes longer. Transfer broccoli to strainer and refresh with cold water. Drain. Whisk mayonnaise, sour cream and vinegar in large bowl. Add half of Gorgonzola cheese and mash until almost smooth. Stir in remaining cheese. Add pasta, green onions, celery, parsley, and broccoli; toss to coat. Season with salt and pepper. Cover and refrigerate until cold.

FRENCH DRESSING

Recipe Box at the
Governors Residence

1-½ cups oil
½ cup onion
½ cup sugar
½ cup chili sauce

¼ cup lemon juice
¼ cup vinegar
1 tsp. salt
1 tsp. paprika

Combine all ingredients in bowl; stir until well blended. Refrigerate.

85104-07

FROZEN FRUIT SALAD

Luz Naasz
Residence Staff

1 (3-oz.) pkg. cream cheese
1/2 cup salad dressing
1/2 pt. cream, whipped
1 cup pineapple, diced
1 cup seeded grapes or fruit
  cocktail

1/2 cup maraschino cherries
1/4 cup pecans or walnuts
10 marshmallows, cut up

Blend cream cheese and salad dressing. Add whipped cream. Fold in the rest of the ingredients. Put in a 9 x 9 inch Pyrex baking dish. Freeze. Serve in slices.

FRUIT SALAD

Deb Hall
Former Governor's Staff

1 can fruit cocktail, drained
1 can mandarin oranges,
  drained
1 can pineapple chunks
2 - 3 bananas

1 (4-oz.) pkg. vanilla instant
  pudding (regular or sugar-free)
1 (8-oz.) container Cool Whip
1 cup marshmallows (optional)
nuts (optional)

Cut bananas in bowl, add pineapple chunks with juice (pineapple juice will keep bananas from getting brown), add other cans of fruit, instant pudding, and Cool Whip. Stir until everything is coated. Add marshmallows and nuts. Chill at least 2 hours.

GINGER-TOMATO SALAD

Robin Albers

2 tbls. rice vinegar
1 tbls. fresh ginger, finely
  minced
1 tbls. honey

1/8 tsp. salt
2 cups cherry or grape
  tomatoes (cut in half)

Whisk together the rice vinegar, ginger, honey, and salt. Toss gently with the tomatoes. Chill 1- 4 hours. Serves 4.

Granddaughter-in-Law of Governor Walter Dale Miller

GLAZED GRAPES

Tom Dravland
Governor's Cabinet

1 cup slivered almonds
8 - 10 cups red and/or green
  seedless grapes (larger grapes
  work better)

1 cup sour cream
3/4 cup brown sugar
1 (4-oz.) container Cool Whip

Brown almonds in 350° oven for 10 minutes turning frequently. Combine sour cream, brown sugar, and Cool Whip. Mix all with grapes.

HERBED TOMATO SALAD

Robin Albers

1/2 cup Light Miracle Whip
1 cucumber, peeled, seeded,
  chopped
1/3 cup sweet onion, finely
  chopped

1/3 cup fresh basil, finely
  chopped
1/4 tsp. salt
3 tomatoes, sliced

Mix all ingredients, except tomatoes, until well blended; refrigerate. Spoon over tomatoes. Serves 6.

Granddaughter-in-Law of Governor Walter Dale Miller

JACKSON SALAD

Mary Joe Foss Finke

1/4 small onion, chopped
3 tbls. cider vinegar
2 tsp. spicy brown mustard
1/2 tsp. salt
1/4 tsp. ground pepper
1 cup vegetable oil
1/2 lb. bacon

2 bunches romaine or red leaf
  lettuce-bit size pieces
1 (8-1/2-oz.) can can artichoke
  hearts - drained and quartered
4 oz. bleu cheese - crumbled
1 cup walnuts or pecans

Purée onion with vinegar in blender. Transfer to medium bowl. Using electric mixer, blend in mustard, sugar, salt and pepper. Gradually add oil in steady stream and continue beating until thick. Cook bacon until crisp. Cool and crumble bacon. Combine lettuce, artichoke hearts, bleu cheese, bacon, and walnuts or pecans. Toss with dressing to taste and serve.

Daughter of Governor Joe Foss

85104-07

JEANNINE'S CRANBERRY SALAD

Mitch Krebs
Governor's Staff

2 bags fresh cranberries
3 cups miniature marshmallows
1-1.2 cups sugar
2 - 3 red apples
1 small pkg. English walnuts,
  chopped

½ cup pineapple chunks
2 pints heavy whipping cream
1 tsp. salt
½ tsp. vanilla

Cranberry preparation: Fill blender halfway with cranberries, add enough water to cover and blend until cranberries are chopped into small pieces (don't purée!). Pour the cranberries into a colander and repeat until both bags are done. Squeeze water out of the chopped cranberries in the colander. Combine 2 heaping cups of cranberries with 3 cups of the miniature marshmallows and one cup sugar in a large mixing bowl and refrigerate overnight.

Next day:

Dice 2 or 3 red apples and add to cranberry/marshmallow mixture. Stir in the chopped walnuts and pineapple chunks. After that is well mixed, stir in 1 tsp. salt and set mix aside. Shortly before serving, fold in whipped cream (I use heavy cream, whipped to stiff peaks by gradually adding sugar and vanilla to taste, and save the leftover for pie. You can substitute regular or low fat non-dairy whipped cream, but it may not taste as good) to desired consistency and color (light pink, shouldn't be too white or too red). Serves 10.

Note: My Mom would make this every Thanksgiving and Christmas.

JELL-O & JUICE FLAG MOLD

Julie Johnson
Former Governor's Cabinet

3 cups boiling water
2 pkgs. Jell-O Brand Strawberry
  Flavor Gelatin (8 serving size
  each)

3 cups cold orange juice or
  other fruit juice
2 cups Cool Whip Whipped
  Topping, thawed

Spray 10 cup flag mold with cooking spray (or well-sprayed cake pan, preferable glass cake pan); place on baking sheet. Add boiling water to dry gelatin mix in large bowl; stir at least 2 minutes until gelatin is completely dissolved. Stir in juice. Pour into prepared mold. Refrigerate 6 hours or overnight until firm. Unmold onto serving tray or platter. Decorate with whipped topping just before serving.

JOAN'S SPINACH RICE SALAD

*Recipe Box at the
Governors Residence*

1 cup raw rice
½ cup Zesty Italian salad
  dressing
1 tbls. soy sauce
½ tbls. sugar

2 cups fresh spinach, cut into
  thin strips
½ cup chopped celery
½ cup chopped green onions
⅓ cup chopped crisp bacon

Cook rice per package directions. When done, transfer to a bowl and cool slightly. In a separate bowl, combine Italian dressing, soy sauce, and sugar. Pour over warm rice. Cover and chill. After cutting up vegetables, place in separate bowl and chill. When ready to serve, mix together prepared rice, vegetables and bacon.

LARGE VEGETABLE SALAD

Stacie Olson

1 head cauliflower, cut up
1 bunch broccoli, cut up
3 tomatoes
2 cups diced celery
1 cup sliced radish
1 cup sliced carrots

1 can black olives sliced
1 onion
1 (16-oz.) bottle Kraft Zesty Lite
  or Free Italian dressing
1 tsp. garlic powder
½ tsp. pepper

Mix the bottle of Kraft Zesty Lite or Free Italian dressing with garlic powder and pepper. Pour over vegetables. Marinate 1 hour or overnight. I don't measure vegetables - can always stir every so often so all the vegetables get in the dressing.

Niece of Governor M. Michael Rounds

85104-07

LAYERED GARDEN PASTA SALAD

*Recipe Box at the
Governors Residence*

1 (7-oz.) pkg. macaroni shells,
 cooked, drained and cooled
1/2 cup green onions, sliced
1/2 cup imitation bacon or
 cooked, crumbled bacon
2 cups mayonnaise or salad
 dressing
1/4 cup lemon juice concentrate
5 tbls. grated Parmesan cheese

1 tbls. sugar
1/2 tsp. garlic powder
4 cups mixed salad greens
1 med. zucchini, sliced
1 cup fresh cauliflower florets,
 sliced
1 cup fresh broccoli florets
2 med. tomatoes, cut into
 wedges or cherry tomatoes

In a medium bowl, combine macaroni, onions, and half of bacon bits. In small bowl, combine mayonnaise, lemon juice, cheese, sugar, and garlic powder, and mix well. Set aside. In large salad bowl, layer greens, macaroni mixture, zucchini, cauliflower, broccoli florets, and tomatoes. Pour dressing evenly over top; cover. Chill several hours. Just before serving, toss with remaining bacon bits.

MACARONI SALAD

*Linda Dykstra
Governor's Staff*

2 cups dry elbow macaroni
2-3 shredded carrots

1 cup diced celery
1 small chopped red onion

Boil macaroni according to directions on box and rinse in cold water. Drain and add vegetables.

Dressing:

1 cup mayonnaise
1/4 cup cider vinegar
1/2 cup sugar
1/2 tsp. salt

1/4 tsp. pepper
1/2 can sweetened condensed
 milk

Combine all ingredients and pour over macaroni and vegetable mixture. Chill and occasionally rotate upside down to thoroughly coat macaroni/vegetable mixture with dressing.

MARINATE IT SALAD

Recipe Box at the
Governors Residence

1 head broccoli florets
1 can sliced water chestnuts
1 pt. cherry tomatoes
1 red onion, sliced and ringed

$1/2$ lb. mushrooms, sliced
1 (12-oz.) jar Italian dressing
1 can black olives
cauliflower florets

Prepare vegetables in large bowl. Pour Italian dressing over to marinate. Add cherry tomatoes when ready to serve.

MAVIS' GREEN SALAD

Randy Miller

1 pkg. lime Jell-O
1 cup hot water
1 cup 7-Up
1 (8-oz.) pkg. cream cheese, softened

1-$1/2$ cups Cool Whip
1 can crushed pineapple, drained
1 cup pecans

Combine Jell-O, hot water and 7-Up; let set until jiggly. Beat cream cheese and Cool Whip together. Combine Jell-O, cream cheese mixture, pineapple and pecans. Refrigerate until ready to serve.

Son of Governor Walter Dale Miller

ORANGE - LEMON SALAD

Melanie Vedvei

2 (3-oz.) pkg. Orange Jell-O
1 (3-oz.) pkg. Lemon Jell-O
1 can lemon pie filling
1 can mandarin oranges, drained

1 can crushed pineapple, drained
whipped cream

Add 2 cups hot water to the Jell-O, dissolve. Then add 3 cups cold water, mix and cool. When Jell-O is syrupy add pie filling, oranges and pineapple. Put in a 9 x 13 inch pan or bowl and chill until set. May top with whipped cream.

Niece of Governor M. Michael Rounds

85104-07

ORIENTAL SALAD

First Lady Mary Dean Janklow

Salad:

1 head leaf lettuce
1/4 head romaine lettuce
1 can mandarin oranges, drained
1 small red onion, sliced very thin

1/3 lb. bacon, fried crisp and crumbled
1/2 pkg. sliced almonds, toasted

Dressing:

1/3 cup sugar
2-1/2 tbls. red wine vinegar
1/2 tbls. lemon juice
2-1/2 tbls. honey

1/2 tsp. paprika
1/2 tsp. celery seed
1/8 tsp. salt
1/4 cup oil

In a large bowl, combine greens, oranges and bacon. Just before serving, add onion rings and toasted almonds. Toss with dressing. To prepare dressing, combine sugar, red wine vinegar, lemon juice, honey, paprika, celery seed, and salt in saucepan. Heat until sugar is dissolved. Cool completely and add oil. Mix well.

PASTA CRAB SALAD

Janie Beeman
Former Governor's Staff

1 small pkg. linguine
1 small bottle Italian dressing
some sliced green onions

2 cans shredded crab met, drained
1 box frozen peas

Cook linguine according to package. Empty peas into strainer. When linguine is cooked, pour into strainer with peas. Rinse with cold water. In large Tupperware bowl, combine all the ingredients. Stir. Then refrigerate for a couple of hours until cold. You might want to stir the mixture every once in awhile so that the dressing is mixed in well. Also, sometimes the dressing really absorbs into the pasta and you might need to add a little more.

PEACH TAPIOCA SALAD

Recipe Box at the
Governors Residence

2 pkgs. vanilla tapioca pudding
1 large can sliced peaches (reserve juice)

1 (3-oz.) pkg. Peach Jell-O
1 (9-oz.) container Cool Whip

Cook pudding and peach Jell-O with peach juice and enough water to make 3 cups. Cool, then add peaches and Cool Whip. Chill.

POTATO SALAD

Clara D. Williamson
Wife of Wm. Williamson

4 medium cold, boiled potatoes
2 boiled eggs
³/₄ cup stuffed olives

³/₄ cup sweet pickles
³/₄ cup mayonnaise

Mix mayonnaise with sweet cream. Then combine with rest of ingredients. Stir all together. Amounts may be varied according to taste. Leave in refrigerator several hours before using.

RASPBERRY SALAD

Deonne Bloomberg
Former Governor's Staff

2 pkgs. raspberry gelatin
2 cups boiling water
1 (24-oz.) bag frozen raspberries

1-¹/₂ cups cold milk
1 pkg. instant vanilla pudding
1 (8-oz.) pkg. cream cheese

Mix gelatin, water, and raspberries; refrigerate 1 hour.

Crust:

2 cups graham cracker crumbs
¹/₄ cup brown sugar

¹/₂ cup melted butter

Mix graham cracker crumbs, brown sugar, and butter. Press into 9 x 13 greased pan. Beat milk, pudding and cream cheese until smooth. Pour over graham cracker crust. Pour raspberry mixture over pudding mixture and refrigerate until set.

REPUBLICAN WOMEN'S LUNCHEON PASTA SALAD

Dar Baum
Former Governor's Cabinet

2 boxes rotini pasta
1 pkg. sliced pepperoni
2 large cans black olives, sliced
2 cups fresh Parmesan cheese, grated
1 pkg. dry Good Seasons Italian dressing
³/₄ lb. Provolone cheese, cubed

3 cans artichokes, drained and chopped
2 cartons grape tomatoes, halved
3 (4-oz.) jars button mushrooms, halved
1 bottle Zesty Italian salad dressing

Cook rotini according to package directions. Drain and set aside. In a large mixing bowl, combine Provolone, pepperoni, artichoke pieces, black olives, tomatoes, Parmesan, and mushrooms. Sprinkle with Good Seasons, add Zesty Italian and toss until evenly coated. Refrigerate until ready to serve.

85104-07

RHUBARB SALAD SUPREME

Dottie Howe
Former Governor's Cabinet

2 cups rhubarb - cut fine   **½ cup sugar**

Mix and let set for 30 minutes, then bring to boiling point, simmer 10 minutes. Remove from stove and add:

(3-oz.) pkg. cream cheese, cut   **1 (3-oz.) pkg. Strawberry Jell-O**
  up

Stir until Jell-O is dissolved and cheese is melted. Cool, then add the following:

1 (8-oz.) container Cool Whip   **⅔ cup chopped pecans**
⅔ cup celery, cut fine

Mix well and refrigerate. Serve on lettuce leaf.

SALAD DRESSING

First Lady Mary E. Elrod

4 tbls. butter   **1 tsp. mustard**
1 tbls. flour   **1 tbls. sugar**
3 eggs   **½ cup vinegar**
1-½ tsp. salt

Beat flour in the butter; add 1 cup milk and put on stove to boil. Beat eggs, salt, mustard, sugar and vinegar together and add to boiling milk.

Note: Submitted by Ailene Luckhurst - Clark County Historical Society.

SALAD THE WRIGHT WAY

Alice Wright
Former Governor's Staff

apples   **almonds**
celery   **grilled chicken pieces**
raisins   **green grapes**
green leaf lettuce   **red grapes**

Slice apples in bite size pieces, cut celery in bite size pieces. Add apples and celery along with 2 cups of raisins and green leaf lettuce to a large serving bowl. Add one to two cups almonds, add chicken pieces (3 cups) and toss. Cover with green and red grapes - 2 cups total should do the trick. Serve with low fat honey mustard dressing.

SEATTLE SALAD

First Lady Linda Mickelson Graham

2 heads romaine lettuce
2 peeled tomatoes
2 tbls. olive oil
salt
1 clove garlic

¼ cup chopped green onion
½ cup grated Romano cheese
1 lb. bacon, cooked and finely
   chopped
¼ cup croutons, homemade

Slice romaine into 1" strips. Cut tomatoes into eighths. Pour olive oil into a large wooden bowl, sprinkle with salt, and rub firmly with the garlic. Remove the garlic. In the bowl place the tomatoes and then the romaine. Add the green onion, grated cheese, and bacon.

Dressing:

juice of 1-½ lemons
1 tsp. chopped mint
½ tsp. ground black pepper

¼ tsp. dried oregano
1 coddled egg
½ cup olive oil

Into a small bowl combine the lemon juice and seasonings. Add the coddled egg and whip vigorously. Add olive oil slowly, whipping constantly. When ready to serve pour dressing over salad. Toss and add croutons.

Note: This salad is worth the effort!

SEVEN LAYER SALAD

Joshua Albers

1 head lettuce, torn
1 cup celery, chopped
1 cup green peppers, chopped
1 cup onion, chopped
1 cup frozen peas

1 cup sour cream
1 cup Miracle Whip
2 tbls. sugar
bacon bits
shredded cheddar cheese

Layer lettuce, celery, green peppers, onion, then frozen peas in large glass serving dish. Mix together sour cream, Miracle Whip, and sugar; put on top of vegetables. Sprinkle with bacon bits and cheddar cheese. Refrigerate until ready to serve.

Grandson of Governor Walter Dale Miller

85104-07

SHRIMP CHEESE CHOWDER

Dick Beringson
Former Governor's Cabinet

2 cup onions, thinly sliced
2 tbls. margarine
2 tbls. flour
1 tbls. dried garlic chips
1 cup chicken stock
1-1/2 cup water
2 cups potatoes, diced
1 cup celery, sliced
1-1/2 tsp. salt
1/4 tsp. pepper
1 tsp. seasoned salt

leafy tops from celery stalks
2 tbls. chives, chopped
1-1/2 cup milk
2 (4-1/2-oz.) cans whole tiny
  shrimp, rinsed & drained
2-1/2 cups sharp cheddar
  cheese, shredded
1 shot (1-1/2 oz.) sherry
paprika
imitation bacon bits

Sauté onions and garlic in margarine until tender, blend in flour. Stir in stock, water, potatoes, celery and seasonings. Cover and simmer 20 minutes or until potatoes are tender. Add remaining ingredients and stir until cheese melts. Ladle into bowls. Top with a sprinkle of paprika and bacon bits.

SNICKER BAR SALAD

Robert Houck

2 pkgs. instant vanilla pudding
  (dry)
2 cups milk
1 (8-oz.) tub Cool Whip

4 diced apples (peeled & cored)
2 large Snicker bars (chopped
  fine)

Combine pudding and milk. Beat until thick. Add Cool Whip, apples, and Snicker bars. Stir these ingredients together until well-mixed. Serve and enjoy.

Nephew of Lieutenant Governor L. R. "Roy" Houck

SOUR CREAM JELLO

Recipe Box at the
Governors Residence

2 small pkgs. Strawberry Jell-O
1 cup boiling water
2 (10-oz.) pkgs. frozen
  strawberries (take off 1/2 cup
  liquid)

3 bananas, mashed
1 (20-oz.) can crushed
  pineapple, drained
1 cup chopped walnuts
1 pt. sour cream

Mix together strawberry Jell-O, boiling water, then add strawberries, bananas, crushed pineapple and walnuts. Pour half in a flat dish, let set. Add the sour cream, then spread rest of Jell-O mixture on top.

SOUTHWEST SALAD

Michele Rounds Brich

1 lg. head romaine lettuce
3 green onions, sliced
3 tomatoes, chopped
2 cups jicama, cut in strips
1 avocado, chopped

1 can black beans, drained
1 can white corn, drained
1 cup Monterey jack or
   mozzarella cheese, shredded

(Can add cooked chicken to make this a main course meal). Combine all above ingredients in a large bowl. For dressing: Add 2 tablespoons of BBQ sauce to 1 cup of ready-made ranch dressing. Serve on the side.

Sister of Governor M. Michael Rounds

STRAWBERRY LETTUCE SALAD

Rick Melmer
Governor's Cabinet

1 bag romaine lettuce
1 cup strawberries, cut up
1 small can mandarin oranges

1 cup grapes, cut in half
$\frac{1}{2}$ cup slivered almonds (I use
   Almond Accents)

Dressing:

3 tbls. red onion
$\frac{1}{2}$ cup vinegar
$\frac{1}{2}$ cup sugar

$\frac{1}{2}$ cup oil
1 tbls. poppy seed

Put dressing ingredients in a blender for 30 seconds to 1 minute. Mix lettuce, strawberries, oranges, grapes, and almonds together in serving bowl. Add dressing before serving.

STRAWBERRY PRETZEL SALAD

Recipe Box at the
Governors Residence

1 (8-oz.) pkg. cream cheese
1 large pkg. Strawberry Jell-O
1 pkg. pretzels

1 (8-oz.) tub Cool Whip
1 (12-oz.) pkg. frozen or fresh
   sliced strawberries

First layer: 2 cups lightly rolled pretzels, $\frac{3}{4}$ cup butter, and 3 tbls. sugar mixed well and spread in bottom of 9x13 inch pan. Bake 10 minutes at 400°. Second layer: Cream package of cream cheese and 1 cup sugar; add Cool Whip and mix well. Spread over cooled crust. Third layer: Mix Strawberry Jell-O in 2 cups of boiling water. Add strawberries and refrigerate until mixture begins to gel. Keep refrigerated until ready to serve.

85104-07

SUMMER STRAWBERRY SALAD

Monica Harding
Former Governor's Staff

1 head romaine lettuce
½ red onion
1 pt. strawberries
½ cup sugar

¾ cup mayo
¼ cups milk
1 - 2 tbls. poppy seeds
4 tbls. red wine vinegar

Mix together 1 head romaine lettuce, washed and torn into pieces, ½ red onion, sliced thin and 1 pint strawberries, sliced. Dressing: Mix sugar, mayo, milk, poppy seeds, and red wine vinegar. Pour on salad and toss just before serving.

SUMMERTIME NEW POTATO SALAD

Patricia Mickelson Adam

4 cups new potatoes
½ each red, green, and yellow
  peppers
¼ cup chopped celery

¼ cup chopped red onion
¼ cup fresh chives
2 tbls. chopped fresh parsley

In large bowl combine potatoes, chopped peppers, celery, red onions, chives, and parsley. Toss gently.

Dressing:

¼ cup oil
2 tbls. red wine vinegar

1 tbls. chopped fresh thyme
salt and pepper to taste

In small bowl, combine oil, vinegar, thyme, salt, and pepper. Pour dressing over potato mixture and toss gently to combine. This makes appropriately six servings. Serve at room temperature.

Daughter of Governor George T. Mickelson and Sister of Governor George S. Mickelson

THOUSAND ISLAND DRESSING

Recipe Box at the
Governors Residence

2 tbls. chopped pickle
2 tbls. finely chopped green
  pepper
2 tbls. chopped red pepper or
  pimento
2 tbls. finely chopped onion

1 cup mayonnaise or cooked
  salad dressing
2 tbls. chili sauce
2 tbls. milk
1 egg, hard-boiled

Combine all ingredients in small bowl; stir until well blended. Refrigerate, covered at least 2 hours before serving. Makes 1-¾ cups.

TOKYO SALAD

Governor Richard F. Kneip

1 (16-oz.) can drained bean sprouts
1 can tuna, shrimp or chicken
1 cup frozen peas (just defrosted)
2 cups cooked spaghetti (2 oz. uncooked, break into 2-inch pieces)

1 cup diced celery
1 can water chestnuts, diced
1 (4-oz.) can mushrooms, sliced
onions, if desired
Chinese noodles

Dressing:

¾ cup mayonnaise
2 tbls. soy sauce
1 tsp. prepared mustard

¼ tsp. garlic powder
1 dash pepper

Mix dressing and salad and chill until cold. Add Chinese noodles before serving. May add less noodles if desired. Serves 15.

TOP HAT SALAD

Governor Frank L. Farrar

1 1 lb. can whole cranberry sauce
¼ cup lemon juice
1 cup cream, whipped

¼ cup confectioners sugar
¼ cup salad dressing
½ cup walnuts, chopped

Combine cranberry sauce and lemon juice. Pour into 1 quart mold. Freeze. Fold confectioners sugar into whipped cream with salad dressing and chopped nuts. Pour over cranberry mixture and freeze until firm. Serve on endive or similar greens.

85104-07

TROPICAL CHICKEN SALAD

*Recipe Box at the
Governors Residence*

4 boneless chicken breasts
¼ cup olive oil
3 tbls. red wine vinegar
1 tsp. Dijon mustard
¼ tsp. dried rubbed sage
6 cups mixed greens
1 papaya, peeled, seeded,
chopped

1 mango, peeled, pitted,
chopped
1 (6-oz.) basket raspberries or
strawberries
1 tbls. minced fresh mint
½ cup chopped toasted pecans

Preheat over to 425°. Place chicken in baking pan. Season generously with salt and pepper. Bake until cooked through, about 20 minutes. Cool completely; cut chicken into bite-size pieces. Whisk olive oil, vinegar, mustard and age to blend in small bowl. Combine chicken, salad greens, papaya, mango, berries and mint in large bowl. Add dressing and toss well. Divide mixture among 4 plates. Sprinkle with walnuts and serve. Serves 4.

VEGETABLE SALAD

*Luz Naasz
Residence Staff*

1 large head cauliflower,
chopped
1 bunch broccoli, chopped
½ cup onions, sliced
1 large tomato or several small,
sliced

1 cup olives, chopped
2 (4-oz.) cans mushrooms (or
fresh)
1 large green pepper, chopped
1 pkg. dry Italian dressing mix

Sprinkle dry Italian dressing mix over vegetables and refrigerate overnight.

Dressing:

1 cup mayonnaise
3-4 tbls. chili sauce

1 tsp. dill weed
1 tsp. salt

Put dressing on vegetables 2 hours before serving (after they have been refrigerated overnight).

WHEAT BERRY SALAD

Robert Houck

1-½ - 2 cups wheat
2 pkg. instant vanilla pudding
 (dry)
1 (8-oz.) pkg. cream cheese
1 (20-oz.) can crushed
 pineapple, undrained

3 tbls. lemon juice
½ cup nuts, chopped
1 (8-oz.) tub Cool Whip

Clean and wash wheat. Soak overnight. Simmer an hour or until cooked to the desired crunchiness. Drain well and set aside. Mix together pudding, cream cheese, pineapple, lemon juice, and nuts. Fold in Cool Whip and cooked wheat. Refrigerate at least 2 hours; overnight is better.

Nephew of Lieutenant Governor L. R. "Roy" Houck

Recipe Favorites

VEGGIES & SIDE DISHES

(Photo courtesy of the South Dakota State Historical Society Archives)

ST. CHARLES HOTEL

"South Dakota's Most Prestigious Address" is how one owner of the St. Charles Hotel described the building. The building, listed on the National Register of Historic Places, was a favorite of lawmakers, lobbyists and state officials. The hotel, located at 207 W. Capitol Ave., was home to William McMaster while he served as governor from 1921 to 1925.

The St. Charles Hotel is linked with Pierre's most energetic promoter, Charles L. Hyde. Hyde moved to Pierre in 1887 and immediately set out to promote Pierre as a major metropolitan city. Hyde built the hotel that bears his first name in 1910. The rectangular block structure soared five stories into the sky and was built of yellow brick and trimmed with glazed terra cotta tile on the first and fifth stories. Composed of seven bays on the axial, front facade and five bays along the north facade. The building is capped with a projecting cornice, which feature acanthus leaf motif antefix and block modillions. A glazed terra cotta belt course marks the division between the fourth and fifth floors. A one-story portico shelters the main entrance.

Gov. Robert S. Vessey signed in as the first guest. Today, the building houses apartments, office space, and a restaurant.

TIDBITS

Gertrude Bertelesen Gunderson graduated
from the University of South Dakota in 1892.

———•———

Gertrude Bertelesen Gunderson was a poet
of renown and served as co-editor and president
of a magazine of poems, *Pasque Petals*.

———•———

Sarah Johnson Farrand Bulow operated a millinery
and ready to wear store in Beresford.

———•———

Sarah Johnson Farrand Bulow was the first
governor's wife to have bobbed hair.

———•———

Elizabeth Jane Parliament Green lived to be
99 years old. At age 83, she was still rising at 5 a.m.
to begin an active day of gardening, bargain hunting,
canning, entertaining, and keeping up to date
on the latest political issues.

———•———

Lorena McLain Berry had a love for music and
published several pieces of music she composed.

———•———

Lorena McLain Berry christened the balloon Explorer
II, which was launched from the Strata Bowl in the
Black Hills. This event ushered in the Space Age and
was man's first ascent into the stratosphere.

———•———

A legislative study in 1915 showed that twenty-three
states provided a governors mansion; three states rented a mansion; and the remainder had no mansion.

———•———

A bill to appropriate funding for a "home for the
governor and his family" died in the 1915 legislature
because they could not agree whether to call it a
mansion or a residence.

VEGETABLES & SIDE DISHES

ALVANIA'S CARROTS

*Recipe Box at the
Governors Residence*

1-½ cups sugar
4 lbs. carrots
1 cup concentrated orange juice (diluted)

nutmeg to taste
½ stick butter or oleo
raisins (optional)

Boil carrots until tender. Drain well. Put in casserole, pour syrup on and bake 15 minutes at 350°.

Note: We always get raves on this, even from people who do not like carrots!

APPLESAUCE

*Dottie Howe
Former Governor's Cabinet*

2 qts. apples, chopped
2 tbls. tapioca
⅔ cup water
1 tsp. cinnamon

1 tsp. apple pie spice
1-½ cups white sugar
red food coloring

Mash apples. Add 1 tablespoon butter and 1-½ teaspoon vanilla when removed from the stove.

BAKED BEAN CASSEROLE

Pam Janklow Derheim

½ lb. hamburger
½ lb. bacon, cooked and diced
1 onion, minced
1 can red kidney beans, drained
1 can butter beans, drained
2 cups pork and beans, drained
⅓ cup brown sugar
¼ cup white sugar

¼ cup ketchup
½ cup barbecue sauce
2 tbls. mustard
2 tbls. molasses
½ tsp. chili powder
1 tsp. salt
½ tsp. pepper

In a large skillet, brown and drain the hamburger and onion. In a large bowl, combine the hamburger mixture with the bacon and beans; set aside. In a small bowl, combine the sugars, ketchup, barbecue sauce, mustard, molasses and spices. Pour over the hamburger and beans; mix well. Place in an oven safe 2 qt. casserole dish and refrigerate overnight. Bake at 350° for 1 hour.

Daughter of Governor William J. Janklow

BAKED BEANS

Patti de Hueck Clodfelter
Former Governor's Cabinet

2 (28-oz.) cans B & M beans
1 lb. bacon, cut up
2 medium onions
2 green peppers, chopped

2 tbls. Worcestershire sauce
1 med. size size bottle ketchup
2 cups brown sugar

Mix all ingredients in large pot or crock. Bake at 300° for 3 hours.

BEEF CONSOMME RICE

Ron Zylstra
Former Governor's Staff

1 cup white rice
1 stick butter, melted
2 cans beef consomme soup

1 scant can water (use soup
can, don't completely fill)

Dump all ingredients into casserole dish. You can add mushrooms or almonds. Place in preheated oven and cook covered for 45 minutes. Cook uncovered until liquid is soaked up by rice.

CALICO BEANS

Sandra Zinter
Governor's Cabinet

1 can butter beans, drained
1 can kidney beans, drained
1 can Bush's pork & beans
1 cup onion, finely chopped
1/2 lb. hamburger
1/2 lb. bacon

1/2 cup ketchup
2 tbls. vinegar
1 tsp. dry mustard
1 tsp. salt
1/2 cup brown sugar

Brown together hamburger, bacon, and onions. Crumble the bacon. Pour off fat and add all the remaining ingredients. Pour into casserole dish. Bake 1 hour and 30 minutes at 375°.

85104-07

CHEESE GRITS SOUFFLÉ

First Lady Mary Dean Janklow

1-½ cups quick grits
2 tsp. salt
6 cups boiling water
1 lb. grated cheddar cheese
3 eggs, beaten

1 dash Tabasco
1-½ sticks margarine, melted
1 tbls. seasoned salt
⅛ tsp. paprika
1 tsp. Worcestershire sauce

Cook grits and salt in water for 5 minutes. If regular grits, cook 20 minutes. Mix all ingredients and pour into well-greased 3 quart casserole (or use two pans and freeze one for future use). Bake at 350° for 1 hour; or 275° for 2-½ hours.

CHEESE POTATOES

Monica Harding
Former Governor's Staff

2 (16-oz.) bags hash browns
2 cans cream of potato soup

8 oz. shredded cheddar cheese
1 (16-oz.) tub sour cream

Mix together and put into a greased 9 x 13 inch pan. Pour a little melted butter on top and bake at 350° for at least 1-½ hours.

CHEESE POTATOES

First Lady Jean Rounds

1 pkg. frozen hash browns
1 pt. half & half or whipping
  cream
⅔ lb. Velveeta Cheese

1 (8-oz.) pkg. grated cheddar
  cheese
½ cup margarine

Spread potatoes in baking dish. Heat cream, margarine and cheeses over low heat until melted. Pour over potatoes. Bake 1 hour at 350°.

DIRTY RICE

Ron Zylstra
Former Governor's Staff

1 stick butter, melted
1 cup rice
1 cup chicken broth

1 can French onion soup
1 small can mushrooms
1 cup shredded cheddar cheese

Dump all ingredients into casserole dish. Season with garlic salt and pepper. Cook 1-½ hours at 350°. You can put several chicken breasts in with this mixture and cook at same time.

DRESSING

Deb Vedvei

1 cup butter or margarine	1 tsp. poultry seasoning
2 cups chopped onion	1-$\frac{1}{2}$ tsp. salt
2 cups chopped celery	1-$\frac{1}{2}$ tsp. sage
2 (8-oz.) cans mushrooms, drained	1 tsp. dried thyme
	$\frac{1}{2}$ tsp. pepper
12 - 13 cups slightly dry bread cubes	3-$\frac{1}{2}$ - 4-$\frac{1}{2}$ cups chicken broth
	2 eggs, well beaten

Melt butter in skillet and sauté onion, celery, and mushrooms. Pour over bread cubes in a very large mixing bowl. Add all seasonings and toss together well. Pour in enough broth to moisten; add beaten eggs and mix together well. Pack lightly into crock pot. Cover and set to high for 45 minutes; then reduce to low to cook for 4 to 8 hours.

Sister-in-Law of Governor M. Michael Rounds

ESCALLOPED HASH BROWNS

Kevin Forsch
Governor's Staff

2 lbs. frozen hash browns	1 tsp. salt
$\frac{1}{2}$ cup melted butter	$\frac{1}{4}$ tsp. pepper
$\frac{1}{2}$ cup onion	1 pint sour cream
1 can cream of mushroom soup	2 cups crushed corn flakes
2 cups grated cheese	$\frac{1}{4}$ cup melted butter

Lay hash browns in a 9 x 13" pan. Mix $\frac{1}{2}$ cup butter, onion, soup, cheese, salt, pepper, and sour cream and pour over potatoes. Melt $\frac{1}{4}$ cup butter. Coat corn flakes with butter and pour over potato mixture. Bake at 450° for 45 minutes.

GARLIC MASHED POTATOES

Tim Reisch
Governor's Cabinet

4-5 lbs. russet potatoes	salt and pepper to taste
9 oz. cream cheese	garlic to taste (I use jar garlic)
1 cup sour cream	

Boil potatoes with skins on. Mash. Add other ingredients. Can make the day before and warm up in crockpot.

85104-07

GOURMET POTATOES

Rosemary Rounds

6 med. potatoes
2 cups shredded cheddar
  cheese
1/4 cup butter or margarine
1-1/2 cups dairy sour cream

1/4 cup finely chopped onion
1/4 tsp. black pepper
1 tsp. salt
2 tbls. butter
paprika

Cook potatoes in skins, cool. Peel and shred coarsely. In saucepan over low heat, combine cheese and 1/4 cup butter; stir until almost melted. Don't be concerned if the cheese and butter separate. Remove from heat and blend in sour cream, onion, pepper, and salt. Fold in potatoes and turn into a greased 2 qt. casserole. Dot with 2 tablespoons butter and sprinkle with paprika. Bake uncovered at 350° for 45 minutes. Yield: 8 servings

Stepmother of Governor M. Michael Rounds

GOVERNMENT POTATOES

Bonnie Untereiner Bjork
Former Governor's Cabinet

1 pkg. hash browns
2 cups shredded cheddar
  cheese
1/4 cup butter
1-1/2 cups sour cream

4 tsp. onion, finely chopped
1 tsp. salt
1/4 tsp. pepper
paprika

In saucepan over low heat, combine cheese and 1/4 cup butter. Stir until almost melted. Remove from heat and blend in sour cream, onion, salt, and pepper. Fold in has browns and put in 2 quart casserole. Dot with 2 tsp. butter and sprinkle with paprika. Bake uncovered for 35 minutes at 350° or until heated through.

GRATIN POTATOES

LaVonne Johnson
Former Governor's Staff

3 tbls. melted butter
4-5 cups Country Style frozen
  hash browns, slightly thawed
1 clove garlic, minced very
  small

1 cup shredded Gruyere cheese
1/2 tsp. salt
1/8 tsp. freshly ground black
  pepper
1 cup 2% milk, heated

Preheat oven to 425°. Butter 8 x 8" cake pan well. Arrange potatoes, garlic, melted butter, salt, pepper, and most of the Gruyere cheese. Pour warmed milk over all and then add the rest of the cheese. Bake for 40 minutes or until potatoes are tender, milk is absorbed, and top is browned. Serves 4. (Very easy and good).

GREEN BEANS AND SAUSAGE

MG(ret.) Phil Killey
Former Governor's Cabinet

1-½ pounds green string beans

Clean. Cut off stem end. Blanch for about 5 minutes.

Sauce:

1 lb. Hot Italian Sausage, bulk
preferred

If you have to use links, take the sausage out of the casing. Brown sausage with 3 cloves of garlic and ½ of a large onion in small amount of olive or canola oil. Add 1 large can of tomatoes - you can choose from tomato sauce, tomato in heavy purée, or a combination of tomato sauce and chopped tomatoes. Now, I know you want definite, but a little more tomato is not a problem. I am very inconsistent with this part. Depends how runny you want the mixture, how many beans, etc. Add 1 tsp. of dried basil or 4-6 leaves of fresh basil. If you like Italian oregano, you can put in a small amount of that, too. I'm not real fond of the oregano purchased in the store, as it is too strong. I would likely eliminate this initially. Salt and pepper to taste. Simmer for 15-20 minutes. Add a touch of baking soda and a touch of sugar to decrease acidity. Add beans and cook as long as you like, at least 30 minutes. Each day this sits, it gets more flavorful. Freezing works too; however, the beans get kind of wimpy for my taste.

GREEN BEANS WITH PINE NUTS

Paula Adam-Burchill

3 lbs. green beans, trimmed
4 tbls. olive oil
½ cup pine nuts (about 3 oz.)

4 garlic cloves, minced
30 large fresh basil leaves,
chopped

Cook beans in large pot of boiling water, salted until crisp/tender about 6 - 7 minutes. Drain. Place beans in bowl of ice water to cool. Dry, drain, and pat dry. (can make 1 day ahead, wrap in paper towels and refrigerate). Heat oil in heavy large skillet over med-low heat. Add pine nuts and sauté until light-brown about 7 - 8 minutes. Add garlic; stir 2 minutes. Add green beans to skillet, sauté, heat through 6 - 7 minutes. Stir in basil. Season to taste; transfer to bowl and serve.

Granddaughter of Governor George T. Mickelson and Niece of Governor George S. Mickelson

85104-07

HOBO POTATOES

*Mardell Davis
Governor's Staff*

2 cups peeled, cubed potatoes	½ tsp. salt
1 cup onions, chopped	⅛ tsp. pepper
1 cup thinly sliced carrots	8 slices bacon, cut into 2-inch
½ cup sliced celery	pieces, crisply cooked
2 tbls. water	2 tbls. butter

Microwave to grill. In 3-quart microwave-safe casserole, combine potatoes, onions, carrots, celery, and water. Cover with microwave-safe plastic wrap. Microwave on High for 5-6 minutes or until vegetables are hot and just begin to cook, stirring once during cooking. Drain, stir in salt and pepper. Place potato mixture on 18 x 18 inch square of heavy-duty foil. Top with bacon and dot with butter. Wrap securely with double fold seal. Place on grill and cook 25-30 minutes or until vegetables are tender. 8 servings

HOT FRUIT COMPOTE

*Darrell D. Butterwick
Former Governor's Cabinet*

1 (29-oz.) can pear halves	1 (29-oz.) can peach halves or
1 (20-oz.) can chunk pineapple	slices

Drain fruit well. Discard juice and lay fruit in buttered 9 x 13 inch casserole. On stove top mix and boil paste of:

½ cup brown sugar	1 tbls. cornstarch
¼ cup butter	1 tsp. curry powder

Allow brown sugar and butter to melt together, then add cornstarch and curry powder. Stir and blend ingredients together and spoon warm mixture over fruit. Bake 1 hour at 350°. Add drained maraschino cherries for color before baking.

85104-07

73

MACARONI CORN CASSEROLE

Shelly Rounds

1 can creamed corn
1 can corn, drained
½ cup dry macaroni
½ cup butter or margarine,
  melted

2 tsp. minced onion
1 cube Velveeta Cheese, cubed

Combine ingredients and bake 1 hour at 350° uncovered. Stir after ½ hour.

Sister-in-Law of Governor M. Michael Rounds

Note: Double for potlucks. Triple for Rounds' Family get togethers.

MAKE AHEAD PARTY POTATOES

Harla Jessop
Former Governor's Staff

5 lbs. potatoes
1 (8-oz.) pkg. cream cheese
1 cup sour cream
2 tsp. garlic salt

¼ tsp. pepper
1 tsp. salt
2 tbls. butter or margarine

Peel potatoes and cut into medium sized pieces. Boil until soft. Drain and mash potatoes. Add remaining ingredients and beat well. Dot top with butter. Cover and refrigerate or freeze. Bake at 350° for 30-45 minutes to warm up.

85104-07

MARVELICIOUS MAC & CHEESE

*Recipe Box at the
Governors Residence*

2-1/2 cups fat-free milk
2 cups uncooked elbow
  macaroni
1 tbls. butter
3 tbls. all-purpose flour
3/4 tsp. salt

1/2 tsp. dry mustard
2 cups shredded reduced fat
  sharp cheddar cheese
1/2 cup shredded reduced fat
  sharp cheddar cheese
  (optional)

Preheat oven to 375°. Cook macaroni according to package directions. Meanwhile, heat milk and butter in a medium saucepan over medium heat. Gradually whisk in flour, salt, and dry mustard and simmer for 1 minute, whisking occasionally. Remove from heat; stir in 2 cups of the cheddar cheese until melted. Add drained macaroni to saucepan and toss with cheese sauce. Transfer mixture to an 8 inch or 9 inch square baking dish. Sprinkle 1/2 cup cheddar cheese on top (optional). Bake uncovered until hot and bubbly, about 20 minutes. Let stand 5 minutes before serving.

Nutrition facts per serving: 285 calories; 8 g fat; 5 g saturated fat; 20 mg cholesterol; 635 mg sodium; 33 g carbohydrates; 20 g protein; 40% Daily Value Calcium; 15% Daily Value Vitamin A; 10% Daily Value Vitamin D; 8% Daily Value Iron.

MASHED POTATOES FOR COMPANY

*Linda Dykstra
Governor's Staff*

9 large potatoes
2 (3-oz.) pkg. cream cheese
1 cup dairy sour cream

2 tsp. onion salt
1/4 tsp. pepper
4 tbls. butter (divided)

Boil potatoes and mash until smooth. Add remaining ingredients and beat until light and fluffy. Cool, cover and refrigerate. This will keep up to two (2) weeks in refrigerator. To use: put in baking dish and dot with additional butter (2 tbls.). Bake in preheated oven at 350° for 30 minutes. Yields 8-12 servings.

MOM'S BAKED BEANS

Pam Roberts
Governor's Cabinet

1 lb. ground beef
1 small onion
$\frac{1}{2}$ green pepper, chopped
2 (14-oz.) cans baked beans

$\frac{1}{2}$ cup ketchup
$\frac{1}{4}$ cup molasses
$\frac{1}{2}$ cup brown sugar
2 tsp. mustard

In a frying pan, fry ground beef, onions and green pepper together until browned. Pour into a large baking bowl. Mix with beans and add the rest of the ingredients. Stir, and bake for 1 hour at 350°.

MOM'S ESCALLOPED CORN AND OYSTER CASSEROLE

Gretchen Lord Anderson
Former Governor's Staff

1 pint oysters, coarsely cut, with juice
2 (12-16-oz.) cans niblets corn, drained
$\frac{1}{4}$ cup half & half

1 dash Tabasco sauce
2 cups crackers, coarsely broken
$\frac{1}{2}$ cup melted butter
$\frac{1}{4}$ tsp. salt

Mix together in a bowl: broken crackers, melted butter or margarine, and salt. In a separate bowl, mix oysters, corn half & half and Tabasco sauce. Using a buttered casserole, alternate 3 layers of crackers and 2 layers of corn and oysters. Bake uncovered at 375° for 40 minutes.

PATRICIAN POTATOES

Susan L. Walker
Former Governor's Cabinet

4 cups instant mashed potatoes (prepared)
2 tsp. minced onion
1 lb. carton cottage cheese
$\frac{3}{4}$ cup sour cream
1 tsp. fresh minced garlic
$\frac{1}{2}$ tsp. dried dill (optional)

$\frac{1}{2}$ tsp. dried or 1 tsp. fresh chives (optional)
salt and pepper to taste (recommend to use white pepper)
2 tbls. butter

Cook instant potatoes according to instructions for 4 cups. Add the minced onion to the water when cooking the instant potatoes. Mix the instant potatoes, cottage cheese, sour cream, garlic, dill, and chives in large bowl until combined. Salt and pepper to taste. Place in a greased 9 x 13 inch baking dish. Dot with butter. Sprinkle with dill (optional). Bake at 350° for $\frac{1}{2}$ hour or until lightly browned and bubbly. Important to let stand 20 minutes before serving. Serves 8-10.

Note: This is a recipe I've used often over the years to rave reviews. It also heats up great for leftovers!

85104-07

POTATO BRUNCH CASSEROLE

Catherine Sulzle
Former Governor's Staff

½ cup butter or margarine
1 can chopped green chilies
1 tsp. salt
½ cup bacon, fried crisp and
  crumbled
2 cups grated cheddar cheese

1 can cream of potato soup
1 2 lb. pkg. frozen hash brown
  potatoes
1 tbls. minced onion
2 cups sour cream

Thaw hash browns. Melt butter. Combine all ingredients. Bake in 9 x 13 inch pan at 350° for 45-60 minutes.

POTATOES (FANTASTIC)

Recipe Box at the
Governors Residence

2 lb. frozen hash browns
  (thawed)
1 tsp. salt
½ cup chopped onion
1 cup sour cream

1 cup grated processed cheese
½ cup butter
¼ tsp. pepper
1 can cream of chicken soup
1 cup milk

Mix all ingredients together. Put in greased 9 x 13 inch pan or 3 quart casserole.

Topping:

2 cups corn flakes or potato
  chips, crushed

¼ cup butter, melted (only ⅛
  cup or 2 tbls. is needed)

Mix together and put on top of hash brown mixture in pan. Bake at 350° for 45 minutes to 1 hour. This may be prepared and refrigerated or frozen until ready to bake.

RICE PILAF

Darrell Butterwick
Former Governor's Cabinet

6 tbls. melted butter
1 small chopped onion
1 cup Uncle Ben's long grain
  rice (not instant)

1 can beef consomme soup
1 can water

On stove top simmer onion in melted butter until opaque. Add Uncle Ben's Rice and coat in melted butter mixture. Mix can of consomme that has been heated separately with water. Add consomme mixture to rice. Pour into 1-½ quart casserole. Bake 30 minutes at 350° - covered.

SCALLOPED CORN

Michele Rounds Brich

½ cup butter or margarine - melted
2 eggs - beaten
1 cup sour cream (low fat is OK)
1 (8-½-oz.) pkg. cornbread muffin mix
1 (15-oz.) can creamed corn
1 can whole kernel corn (don't drain)

Preheat oven to 375°. Combine all ingredients. Pour into greased casserole dish. Bake for 40 minutes or until center is set (no longer jiggles when dish is shaken).

Sister of Governor M. Michael Rounds

SCALLOPED CORN

Aaron Johansen

1 can creamed corn
2 eggs, beaten
¼ cup sugar
½ cup saltine cracker crumbs
2 tbls. melted butter
½ cup milk
½ cup cream

Mix all ingredients together and pour into casserole dish. Bake at 325° about 45 minutes or until knife comes out clean.

Son-in-Law of Governor Walter Dale Miller

SEA MONSTER

Deonne Bloomberg
Former Governor's Staff

1 box frozen chopped broccoli
1 box frozen cauliflower
1 can sliced mushrooms, drained
1 can French cut green beans, drained
2 cups shredded Velveeta cheese
¼ cup slivered almonds
1 tbls. dehydrated onion
1 can cream of mushroom soup
crushed Ritz crackers
butter

Cook broccoli and cauliflower. Add onion and drain. Combine this mixture with mushrooms, green beans, cheese, almonds and soup in oven proof dish. Crush Ritz crackers on top and dot with butter. Bake 350° until bubbly - about 30 minutes.

85104-07

STUFFED ZUCCHINI

Mary Bisson
Former Governor's Staff

1 lb. ground pork
2 medium zucchini, scooped out
1 medium onion, chopped
1 can tomato paste
1 (12-oz.) container cottage cheese

1 can mushrooms (can also use fresh)
1 - 2 cloves garlic, crushed
oregano, to taste
Parmesan cheese

Brown ground pork. Chop pulp and sauté zucchini with onion. Combine pork with browned pulp, tomato paste, cottage cheese, mushrooms, garlic, and seasonings. Stuff zucchini and sprinkle with Parmesan cheese. Cover with foil and bake at 350° for 30 minutes. Remove foil after 30 minutes and check. Continue cooking 15 minutes to brown.

SWEET POTATO CASSEROLE

Kellie Kneip

1-1/2 lb. sweet potatoes
1/2 cup granulated sugar
1/2 cup milk
1 beaten egg
3 tbls. butter, cubed

1-1/2 tsp. vanilla
1/2 cup packed brown sugar
1/3 cup all-purpose flour
2 tbls. butter

Peel and cut potatoes into cubes. Cook, covered, in a small amount of water for 25 or 35 minutes or till tender. Drain. Combine hot sweet potatoes, granulated sugar, milk, egg, the 3 tbls. butter, and vanilla. Stir to break up potatoes. Put mixture into a greased 2-quart square baking dish. Combine brown sugar and flour, cut in the 2 tbls. butter until mixture resembles coarse crumbs. Sprinkle crumb mixture on top of potatoes. Bake uncovered in a 350° oven about 25 minutes or till set.

Daughter-in-Law of Governor Richard F. Kneip

SWEET POTATOES WITH APPLES

Robin Albers

8 lbs. sweet potatoes
 (approximately 12)
1 cup orange juice
1 cup heavy cream
1 stick melted butter

½ cup brown sugar
2 tsp. ground nutmeg
1 tsp. cinnamon
4 tsp. salt
2 tsp. pepper

Preheat oven to 375°. Bake the sweet potatoes, cool and scoop out the inside. Combine the orange juice, cream, butter, brown sugar, cinnamon, salt, and pepper. Place ½ of the potatoes into a bowl and add ½ of the mixture; beat with mixer and pour into a large baking dish. Repeat with the remaining potatoes and juice mixture and add to the baking dish.

Topping:

6 tbls. butter
6 McIntosh apples, peeled and
 cut into eighths

6 tbls. brown sugar

Melt the butter and add apple wedges and brown sugar, cook about 10 minutes until soft and lightly browned. Place on top of sweet potatoes and bake 30 minutes or until heated through. You can prepare and refrigerate before baking. Serves 20.

Granddaughter-in-Law of Governor Walter Dale Miller

ULTIMATE TWICE BAKED POTATOES

*Recipe Box at the
Governors Residence*

4 large baking potatoes
8 slices bacon
1 cup sour cream
½ cup milk
4 tbls. butter

½ tsp. salt
½ tsp. pepper
1 cup shredded cheddar cheese,
 divided
8 green onions, sliced, divided

Preheat oven to 350°. Bake potatoes in preheated oven for 1 hour. Meanwhile, place bacon in a large, deep skillet. Cook over medium high heat until evenly brown. Drain, crumble and set aside. When potatoes are done, allow them to cool for 10 minutes. Slice potatoes in half lengthwise and scoop the flesh into a large bowl; save skins. To the potato flesh add sour cream, milk, butter, salt, pepper, ½ cup cheese, and ½ the green onions. Mix with a hand mixer until well blended and creamy. Spoon the mixture into the potato skins. Top each with remaining cheese, green onions, and bacon. Bake for another 15 minutes.

85104-07

WILD RICE CASSEROLE

Kevin Forsch
Governor's Staff

1 cup butter
2 cups wild rice
1 cup water chestnuts
6 oz. mushrooms

$^1/_3$ cup slivered almonds
$^1/_4$ cup onions
3 cups broth

Melt butter in saucepan; sauté wild rice, water chestnuts, mushrooms, slivered almonds, and onions for 15 minutes. Pour into casserole dish and add chicken broth. Cover and bake at 325° for 2 hours.

WILD RICE CASSEROLE

Steve Wegman
Former Governor's Staff

4 cups water
1 cup uncooked wild rice
1 can cream of mushroom soup
1 can cream of chicken soup
2 small cans mushrooms, drained
2 beef bouillon cubes in 1 cup water
1 tsp. salt (optional)
1 bay leaf

$^1/_2$ cup slivered almonds (optional)
$^1/_4$ tsp. celery salt
$^1/_4$ tsp. garlic powder
$^1/_4$ tsp. pepper
$^1/_4$ tsp. onion powder
$^1/_4$ tsp. paprika
$^3/_4$ cup chopped celery
6 tbls. chopped onion
1-$^1/_2$ lbs. lean ground beef

Cook rice in water until rice is tender, drain. Place rice in large casserole; add soups, mushrooms, water, and seasonings. Mix gently. Sauté onions and celery in butter until transparent. Add to casserole. Brown meat and add. Sprinkle with almonds and refrigerate overnight. Bake at 350° for 1 to 1-$^1/_2$ hours or until heated.

Recipe Favorites

MAIN DISHES

(Photo courtesy of the South Dakota State Historical Society Archives)

1936 GOVERNORS RESIDENCE

This 5,474-square-foot, two-story home was built as a Works Progress Administration project. It was built from native brick manufactured at Belle Fourche, lumber prepared by men in CCC camps, and cement from the state cement plant. The cost to construct in 1937 was $27,661.

The original description of the interior homes mentioned affording living accommodations for the family. The ground floor consisted of a governor's study, a reception hall, living room, family dining room, kitchen, and a long dining room for large dinners. There are two sets of French doors. At the far end of the reception hall was a fireplace made of petrified wood. A mantel, with teakwood panel from the famed Battleship X, was later added.

There were three additional fireplaces, one in the reception area, one in the living room, and one in the master bedroom. Upstairs there were six bedrooms and four bathrooms, two included shower baths. The recreation room was a feature of the basement. A bomb fallout shelter was built in the basement during the 1950s.

The exterior had wide siding painted white with the foundation trimmed in red, ironclad brick. A two-car garage complemented the 1936 home.

This Governors Residence, which served 16 First Families, went through many remodels and upgrades over its 67-year history. It currently is located east of Rapid City.

TIDBITS

Governor and Mrs. William J. Janklow converted the two-car garage into a family room.

Governor and Mrs. George S. Mickelson had a berm built south of the residence to create more privacy for an outdoor patio area. The outdoor patio area was composed of bricks from each of the railroad depots in South Dakota.

The 30-year-old heating and water pipes gave out in the late 1960s and caused extensive damage to the walls. While the walls were repaired, insulation was added for the first time.

First Lady Pat Farrar received 16 place settings of Mikasa China in the Mount Holyoke pattern from Smith Jewelry in Sioux Falls.

The Capitol Club, with proceeds from the Centennial Cookbook, provided funding for many of the furnishings in the Governors Residence, including state seal china and dining room furniture.

Mary Dean Thom Janklow participated in the lighting of the National Christmas Tree in 1998 in Washington, D.C. The tree came from the Black Hills of South Dakota.

Jean Vedvei Rounds has initiated "Go Red for Women" day in South Dakota. This day, held in February each year, promotes women's cardiovascular health awareness.

Governor M. Michael and First Lady Jean Rounds hosted wedding receptions for two of their children at the Governors Residence. Brian Rounds married Kerry Ingram on June 17, 2006 and Carrie Rounds married Justin Larson on July 6, 2007.

Governor William and First Lady Mary Dean Thom Janklow had an audience with Pope John Paul II.

MAIN DISHES

(EASY) CREAMY BAKED CHICKEN BREASTS

Susan Stoneback
Former Governor's Staff

6 chicken breasts (boneless,
  skinless)
6 pieces Swiss cheese
1 can cream of chicken soup
½ cup milk

2 cups Pepperidge Farms
  herbed stuffing mix (blue bag,
  not cubed)
⅓ cup melted butter

Place the chicken breasts in a baking dish sprayed lightly with Pam. Place on slice of Swiss cheese on each piece of chicken. Mix the soup with the milk and spoon over the chicken. Sprinkle the stuffing mix over the top and drizzle the melted butter over all. Bake uncovered at 325° for 1 hour. Goes well with asparagus.

MEAT LOAF

Jeanette Crawford Lusk

1 lb. ground round
¼ lb. pork sausage
2 tbls. chopped onion
5-6 soda crackers, broken

pinch sage
dash salt
1 cup tomato juice

Combine ground round, pork sausage, chopped onion, soda crackers, sage and salt. Form loaf and place in greased loaf pan. Cover with tomato juice. Bake for 1 hour at 350°.

Daughter of Governor Coe I. Crawford

Note: Recipe submitted by Vicki Coe Lusk, Jeanette's daughter.

ASPARAGUS AND EGG CASSEROLE

Dick Beringson
Former Governor's Cabinet

Arrange cooked asparagus spears in a butter baking dish. Place deviled eggs over the asparagus. Mix a can of Campbell's cream of asparagus or cream of celery soup (undiluted) with a cup of Best Food Mayonnaise, add a few slivered almonds, and put over the deviled eggs. Sprinkle 1 cup of shredded sharp cheddar cheese over the top. Heat in 350° oven for about 30 to 40 minutes. I plan one per person.

AUNT MILLIE'S LASAGNE

Connie Tveidt
Governor's Staff

Meat Sauce:

1 lb. sausage
1 lb. hamburger
1 clove garlic, minced or ½ tsp.
 garlic salt

1 tbls. basil leaves
1 large can crushed tomatoes
2 (6-oz.) cans tomato paste
14 lasagne noodles, cooked

Brown sausage and hamburger together and drain grease. Add garlic, basil, tomatoes and tomato paste. Simmer uncovered about 30 minutes, stirring occasionally.

Cheese Filling:

1 large container cottage cheese
½ cup grated Parmesan cheese
2 tbls. parsley
2 eggs

2 tsp. salt
½ tsp. pepper
1 lb. grated mozzarella cheese

Beat eggs lightly with a fork in large bowl. Add all remaining ingredients and stir well.

Place 7 lasagne noodles to cover bottom of 9 x 13 inch pan. Cover with ½ the cheese filling and ½ the meat sauce. Repeat these layers. Bake at 350° for 45 minutes. It may take longer if you refrigerate and cook later. Let stand for 10 minutes before cutting to serve.

BAKED OR GRILLED WALLEYE

Bonnie Untereiner Bjork
Former Governor's Cabinet

Layer onions in an aluminum pan. Sprinkle with butter and lemon juice. Place walleye in pan. Spread mayonnaise over fish. Cover with Parmesan cheese. Bake or grill for 15-20 minutes.

BAKED PORK CHOPS

Nancy Jahnke

6 center cut pork chops,
 browned
1 onion

dry mustard
1 can chicken gumbo soup

Place pork chops in a flat baking dish. Put a slice of onion on each chop. Sprinkle each with dry mustard. Spoon soup on each chop so each has rice and pimento on top. Pour rest of juice in baking dish beside chops. Cover and bake at 325° for 1-½ hours.

Daughter of Governor Walter Dale Miller

85104-07

BAR-B-QUE BEEF BRISKET

Mary Joe Foss Finke

8 lb. beef brisket
1/4 cup liquid smoke
2 tsp. meat tenderizer
2 tsp. onion salt
1 tsp. ground nutmeg

1 tsp. black pepper
2 tsp. garlic salt
2 tsp. paprika
1 cup brown sugar
your favorite barbeque sauce

Pierce brisket with fork and pour liquid smoke over meat. Sprinkle with tenderizer. Combine onion salt, nutmeg, pepper, garlic salt, and paprika - sprinkle over top of meat. Coat entire top of brisket with brown sugar. Cover roasting pan with aluminum foil. Roast 325° for 25 - 30 minutes per pound. Remove from oven and let stand 20 minutes. Slice thin across grain. Let juice cool and skim off fat. Combine juice with equal amount of barbeque sauce. Pour over meat, heat and serve.

Daughter of Governor Joe Foss

BARBEQUES

Doug Loen
Former Governor's Staff

2 lbs. hamburger
1 onion, chopped
1 cup water

1 cup ketchup
2 - 3 tsp. chili powder
2 tsp. dry mustard

Simmer water, ketchup, onion, chili powder, and mustard for 10 minutes. Then add raw hamburger. Simmer 2 hours. Drain any grease.

BEEF AND ASPARAGUS NEGIMAKI

*Recipe Box at the
Governors Residence*

salt for water
24 thick stalks asparagus, or 12
  thick stalks sliced in half
  lengthwise
1/2 cup soy sauce

1/4 cup sugar
1 bunch scallions, greens only
1-1/2 lbs. beef tenderloin
freshly ground black pepper to
  taste

Preheat a grill or grill pan until hot, or prepare oven broiler. Bring medium saucepan of salted water to a boil. Cut off asparagus stalks 1/2 inch from tips; reserve bottoms for another use. Place in water; cook until bright green but still crunchy, about 1 minute. Prepare ice-water bath. Drain asparagus; transfer to an ice-water bath to stop cooking. Drain asparagus again in a colander, and set aside. Whisk together soy sauce and sugar until dissolved; set aside. Cut scallions into 3-1/2 inch lengths, julienned lengthwise; set aside. Slice tenderloin into 1/4 inch thick pieces. Place one slice between two pieces of plastic; pound lightly to an even thickness. Remove plastic. Meat should be a 2 x 5 inch rectangle. Repeat with remaining beef. Dip a piece of beef in soy sauce mixture, and place on a cooking sheet. Season with pepper. Place 1 piece of scallion and 2 asparagus stalks at end of beef piece so vegetables extend over edges; roll. Set aside. Repeat with remaining beef and vegetables. Grill or broil negimaki, brushing with sauce and turning occasionally until charred and medium-rare, about 2 minutes. Serve.

BEEF BOURGUIGNONNE (BEEF BURGUNDY)
(A French Stew)

Governor Ralph Herseth

3 tbls. salad oil
2 lbs. lean beef chuck, cubed
2 tbls. flour
1 tsp. salt
1/4 tsp. pepper

1/4 tsp. thyme
1 cup undiluted beef broth
1 cup burgundy
1 (3-oz.) can mushrooms
1 small can white onions

The night before, heat salad oil, brown meat on all sides. Heat oven to 325°. When meat is browned, stir in flour, salt, pepper, and thyme. Mix well with meat, scraping bottom of pan. Put everything into a 3-quart casserole. Mix beef broth and wine. Pour over meat. Put covered casserole in oven. Bake 2-1/2 hours. Cool slightly, refrigerate. Before serving: heat oven to 325°. If liquid has evaporated, add wine and broth in equal parts. Add drained mushrooms and onions. Stir, cover and bake 35-40 minutes. Serve with rice. Serves 4 to 5 generously. Recipe can be doubled if needed.

85104-07

BEEF BRUSCHETTA SKILLET

Corrie Holt

1 lb. sirloin cut into cubes
2 tsp. vegetable oil
4 cloves garlic
2 cups chopped tomatoes
1 can beef broth

1 tsp. dried basil leaves
1½ cups Minute Rice (white),
 uncooked
½ cup Velveeta cheese, cubed

Brown meat in oil. Remove from skillet. Add garlic, tomatoes, broth, and basil to skillet. Bring to a boil. Stir in rice. Return to boil. Reduce heat to medium. Stir in meat and Velveeta cheese. Cover and simmer 8 - 10 minutes, or until heated throughout. Stir until cheese is completely melted and mixture is well blended. Serve.

Niece of First Lady Jean Rounds

BEEF BUNDLES

Aaron Miller
Governor's Staff

1 lb. ground beef
1 medium onion
½ medium cabbage, chopped
salt, pepper, and garlic powder
 to your own taste

Rhoades frozen bread dough,
 thawed

Brown meat and onion. Season with salt, pepper, and garlic powder. Drain grease. Add cabbage and cook for 10 - 15 minutes. Roll dough out to about ½ thick - cut in 4-5 inch squares. Put filling (meat) in center and shape into a bun. Seal dough well and put sealed side down on baking sheet. Bake at 400° for 15 minutes, until bread crust is golden outside. Serve right away.

BEEF NOODLE CASSEROLE

Rosemary Rounds

1-1-½ lb. ground beef
2 tbls. chopped onion
2 tbls. chopped green pepper
1 (10.5-oz.) can tomato soup
¾ cup water

¾ tsp. sugar
¾ tsp. salt
¼ lb. dry noodles, cooked
½ lb. Velveeta cheese, grated

Brown meat with pepper and onion. Add soup, water, sugar, and salt. Simmer 30 minutes. Alternate layers of meat, noodles, cheese, meat, noodles, cheese. Bake 30 minutes at 350° degrees. Yield: 6 - 8 servings

Stepmother of Governor M. Michael Rounds

BEEF STROGANOFF

Shirley Jenssen
Former Governor's Staff

1 lb. beef tips
2 cans cream of mushroom
  soup

1 envelope Lipton's dry onion
  soup mix
1/2 cup water

Place all ingredients in a crock pot. Cover and cook on medium all day. Serve on cooked rice, cooked noodles or use as gravy on bread or mashed potatoes.

BEEF STROGANOFF

Steve Wegman
Former Governor's Staff

1-1/2 cups cubed beef
1/4 cup flour
1/4 cup margarine
1/2 cup chopped onion
1 small clove garlic, minced
1 (4-oz.) can mushrooms,
  drained

1 (10.5-oz.) can condensed beef
  broth
1 cup sour cream
salt and pepper

Dust meat with flour and brown in margarine. Add mushrooms, garlic and onion. Stir in soup and add 1 can of water. Cover and simmer for 1 hour. Add sour cream and serve over hot noodles.

85104-07

BEEF TENDERLOIN WITH COGNAC MUSTARD CREAM SAUCE

Paula Adam-Burchill

2 lbs. tenderloin in one piece
1 tbls. olive oil
1 tbls. salt
¼ tsp. fresh ground pepper
2 tbls. butter
1 large shallot, minced

½ lb. fresh mushrooms, minced
⅓ cup cognac or brandy
1 cup whipping cream
1 tbls. Dijon mustard
1 tsp. minced fresh thyme
leaves

425° oven. Heat oil over high heat - season beef with salt and pepper - brown quickly on all sides. Place in foil-lined roasting pan; cook to medium - rare, about 25 minutes, or to 130°. Remove from pan, let rest loosely tented with foil. Melt butter in original skillet, add shallots - cook, stirring occasionally until slightly softened about 1 minute. Add mushrooms, cook for 4 minutes. Pour in cognac, raise heat to high - boil, scraping bottom of pan until reduced to half - about 2 minutes. Stir in cream, mustard, and thyme. Boil until cream has reduced and thickened about 5 minutes. Season to taste. Slice beef into ½" slices - pour sauce over and serve. Serves 6. (#6 tenderloin - 2 pieces - serves 12 - 14). Enjoy!

Granddaughter of Governor George T. Mickelson and Niece of Governor George S. Mickelson

BEER HALL PIE

George Mark Mickelson

1 cup Bisquick baking mix
⅓ cup milk
1 1 lb. pkg. ground beef
1 medium onion, sliced thin
1 tsp. salt
½ tsp. pepper

1 (15-oz.) can tomato sauce
2 tbls. Bisquick baking mix
2 eggs, slightly beaten
1 cup cottage cheese
paprika and parsley

Combine 1 cup Bisquick and milk, mix gently around a lightly floured board. Press into a 9" pie plate (greased). Heat skillet and sauté onion and beef until beef is brown and onion is tender. Stir in salt, pepper, tomato sauce, and 2 tbls. of Bisquick. Fill dough shell with meat mixture. Blend eggs with cottage cheese and pour over meat and onion. Bake at 350° for 30 minutes. Sprinkle with paprika and garnish with parsley. Per serving: 425 calories: 28.1 Fat 22.3 protein 21.6 carbohydrate; 130 cholesterol; 1095 sodium.

Son of Governor George S. Mickelson and Grandson of Governor George T. Mickelson

BISCUIT PIZZA BAKE

Deb Vedvei

1 lb. ground beef
2 (12-oz.) tube refrigerated
  buttermilk biscuits
1 (15-oz.) can pizza sauce
1 cup chopped green pepper
½ cup chopped onion
1 (4-oz.) can mushroom stems
  and pieces, drained

1 (3-½-oz.) pkg. sliced
  pepperoni
1 cup (4 oz.) shredded
  mozzarella cheese
1 cup (4 oz.) shredded cheddar
  cheese

In a skillet, cook beef over medium heat until no longer pink. Meanwhile quarter the biscuits; place in a greased, shallow 3 quart baking dish. Top with pizza sauce. Drain beef, sprinkle over biscuits and sauce. Layer with green pepper, onion, mushrooms, pepperoni, and cheeses. Bake uncovered at 350° for 25 - 30 minutes or until cheese is melted. Let stand for 5 - 10 minutes before serving.

Sister-in-law of Governor M. Michael Rounds

85104-07

BISTRO CHICKEN

Sarah Adam Axtman

2 tbls. unsalted butter
4 (8-oz.) skinless, boneless
  chicken breasts, slightly
  pounded and flattened
fine sea salt
freshly ground pepper
3 tbls. chopped shallots
½ cup Kentucky bourbon

½ cup dry white wine
3 tbls. Dijon mustard
1-½ cups homemade chicken
  broth or store-bought low
  sodium chicken broth
½ cup heavy cream
3 tbls. minced fresh chives

Heat the butter in a wide, heavy-bottomed sauté pan until it begins to melt and foam. Season the chicken with salt and pepper. Add the breasts to the pan and brown them on one side, 6 to 8 minutes. Turn them over and cook them until well browned on the other side, about 6 more minutes. The chicken is done when firm to the touch and the juices run clear. Transfer the chicken to a plate and cover with foil to keep warm. Add the shallots to the same pan and sauté until softened but not browned, about 2 minutes. Lower the heat, move the pan away from the flame, lean away and carefully pour in the bourbon, taking care not to let it flame. Return the pan to the stove and let the bourbon evaporate over low heat. Add the wine to the pan, raise the heat to high, and bring it to a boil. Whisk in the mustard and let reduce for 1 minute. Pour in the broth and cook for 2 to 3 minutes more. Stir in cream and bring just to a boil. Stir in the chives. Return the chicken breasts to the pan and simmer gently until the stock has reduced and thickened slightly, 4 to 5 minutes. To serve, put 1 chicken breast in the center of each plate and spoon the sauce over the top. Delicious with mashed potatoes, rice or noodles. Makes 4 servings.

Granddaughter of Governor George T. Mickelson and Niece of Governor George S. Mickelson

BONNIE'S CRANBERRY PHEASANT

Bonnie Untereiner Bjork
Former Governor's Cabinet

Pheasant breasts
1 can whole cranberry sauce

1 cup Zesty Italian Dressing
1 pkg. onion soup mix

Place pheasant breasts in glass baking dish. Cover with the cranberry sauce, Zesty Italian Dressing, and onion soup mix mixture. Bake at 350° for 30 minutes.

Note: Chicken breasts may also be used.

BRAISED SOUTH DAKOTA PHEASANT

Joseph 'Frank' Foss

2 South Dakota Pheasants
1/2 - 3/4 cup flour
1 tbls. paprika
1/4 tsp. salt

1/4 tsp. pepper
1 - 2 tbls. butter
1 - 2 tbls. oil
1/2-1 cup flour

Preheat oven to 250°. Remove breast and thigh meat from bone. Mix flour, paprika, salt, and pepper in a large Ziploc bag. Shake pieces of pheasant in bag to coat with mixture. Shake off excess mixture. Heat butter and oil in frying pan. Sauté on all sides until golden brown. Remove to baking dish (11 x 13). Stir water into pan to loosen drippings and pour over pheasant. Cover with foil and bake at 250° for at least 6 hours or tender. Can be served with mashed potatoes. My wife fixes our pheasant this way and it is my favorite. There is no cream of mushroom soup involved.

Son of Governor Joe Foss

BREADED RANCH CHICKEN

Tim Reisch
Governor's Cabinet

1/2 cup crushed cornflakes
1/2 cup grated Parmesan cheese
1 envelope ranch salad dressing
  mix

4 boneless, skinless chicken
  breast halves
1/4 cup butter, melted
1/4 tsp. lemon juice

In shallow bowl, combine the cornflakes, cheese, and salad dressing mix. Brush chicken with butter and lemon juice mixture, then roll in cornflake mixture to coat. Place in a greased baking dish. Bake uncovered at 375° for 40 minutes or until chicken juices run clear.

BROILED STEAK

Governor Peter Norbeck

Have ready a 2" steak at room temperature. Pre-heat broiler and grease broiler tray. Place steak on center of tray and put 3 inches from fire, leaving broiler door open 3 inches. Broil until top of steak is brown, season well, turn and broil other side until brown. Spread with butter, garnish with parsley, and serve on hot platter. It will take from 20-30 minutes, depending on degree of rareness.

Recipe submitted by daughter Nell Wegner

85104-07

BROOKE'S CHICKEN ENCHILADAS

Deb Bowman
Governor's Cabinet

¼ cup chopped pecans
½ cup chopped onion
2 tbls. margarine or butter
¼ tsp. ground cumin
12 7" flour tortillas
1 (10.75 -oz.) can condensed cream of chicken or cream of mushroom soup
1 cup milk
1 (4-oz.) can diced green chili peppers (mild)

1 (3-oz.) pkg. cream cheese, softened
1 tbls. milk
2 cups chopped, cooked chicken
1 (8-oz.) carton dairy sour cream
¾ cup shredded Monterrey Jack or Cheddar cheese
2 tbls. chopped pecans

In a skillet, cook ¼ cup of the pecans and the onion in butter or margarine over medium heat till onion is tender and pecans are lightly toasted. Remove skillet from heat and stir in 1 tbls. of the canned green chili peppers. In a medium mixing bowl, combine softened cream cheese, 1 tbls. milk and cumin; add nut mixture and chicken and stir until combined. Spoon about 3 tbls. of the chicken mixture onto each tortilla near an edge; roll up. Place filled tortillas, seam sides down in a greased 3-quart rectangular baking dish. In a medium mixing bowl, combine soup, sour cream, the 1 cup milk, and remaining canned chili peppers. Pour the soup mixture evenly over the tortillas in the baking dish. Cover with foil and bake in a 350° oven for about 35 minutes or until heated thoroughly. Remove foil, sprinkle enchiladas with Monterey Jack cheese and 2 tbls. pecans. Return to oven and bake about 5 minutes more or until cheese melts. Serves 6.

Note: For a lower fat dish: prepare as directed, but use fat-free cream cheese (4 oz.), reduced-sodium soup, fat free sour cream, skim milk, and reduced fat Monterey Jack cheese.

BUFFALO CURRY WITH TOMATO CHUTNEY AND RAITA

Marcia Donnan Mitchell
Former Governor's Cabinet

2 medium onions, chopped
½ cup oil
1 tsp. salt
flour sufficient for light dusting
1-½ lbs. buffalo, cut into 1 inch
  pieces
2 tbls. curry powder
½ tsp. fenugreek
½ tsp. turmeric

1 clove garlic, chopped
1 stick cinnamon
1 small spray parsley, chopped
1 green apple, peeled, cored,
  sliced
½ cup grated coconut
1 cup sliced tomatoes
¾ cup stock or water
½ tsp. salt

In a heavy pan with a tight-fitting lid, cook onions in oil until soft and beginning to brown. Remove onions to bowl. Lightly salt meat and dust with flour, brown in same pan. Reduce heat to low, add curry powder, fenugreek, turmeric, garlic, cinnamon, parsley, apple, coconut, tomatoes, water, and salt. Stir well. Return cooked onions to pan. Cover and simmer until the meat is very tender. Remove cinnamon stick. (Cooking time will vary, approximately 1 hour. Do not over cook). Serve with Tomato Chutney and Raita.

Tomato Chutney:

1 tbls. shortening or salad oil
1 small red chili pepper,
  crumbled
½ tsp. cumin seeds
¼ tsp. nutmeg
¼ tsp. mustard seed

4 medium tomatoes, peeled,
  sliced very thin
½ lemon
⅓ cup raisins (1-½ oz. pkg.)
½ cup sugar

Heat shortening or oil in medium saucepan. Add crumbled chili pepper, cumin seed, nutmeg, and mustard seed. When seeds start to jump, add tomatoes. Quarter lemon half and place on top (do not remove). Simmer, stirring frequently, for 15 min. Stir in raisins and sugar. Simmer again, stirring frequently, until thickened, about 30 minutes. Makes two cups.

Raita:

1 large cucumber, seeded,
  peeled and finely grated
3 cups plain yogurt
½ medium onion, coarsely
  chopped

1 tsp. salt
1 tsp. cumin seed

Grate cucumber into yogurt, add onion and salt. Heat cumin seeds in a dry, heavy saucepan until they start jumping. Remove from heat and crush seeds to a fine powder. Just before serving, stir in toasted cumin.

85104-07

CASSEROLED PHEASANT

First Lady June Foss

Cut pheasant in serving pieces - wash and drain. Mix about 1 cup flour, 1 teaspoon salt, pepper in a paper bag. Shake each piece or 3 or 4 together until well coated. Heat cooking oil in heavy fry pan. Do not get it to the smoking point. Gently brown pieces and lay in casserole (better if casserole is quite heavy). Pour off oil except for 3 or 4 tbls. Add remaining flour in sack (about 4 or 5 tablespoons) to oil and stir scraping brown from bottom of pan. Add 2 to 3 cups hot water stirring vigorously to make a thin gravy. Canned milk or sour cream can be added if desired. A bit of onion salt is good if you desire. Add salt and pepper to taste. Otherwise pour 3 to 4 cups gravy over pheasant. Cover and bake at 300° for at least 2 hours depending on size and age of pheasant. Take cover off last half hour to let bird brown.

Recipe submitted by daughter Mary Joe Foss Finke.

CEDAR PLANKED SALMON WITH SPICED CRANBERRY RELISH

Cade and Michelle Caldwell

**1 untreated 6 x 12" cedar plank
or shingle**

Soak cedar plank or shingle in water or wine for 1 - 2 hours.

Relish:

**1 cup Ocean Spray cranberry
juice cocktail**
**¾ cup Craisins original
sweetened dried cranberries**

¼ cup finely chopped onion
1 tsp. orange peel
¾ tsp. five-spice powder

Combine all ingredients in medium saucepan. Cook over medium heat until mixture boils, stirring occasionally. Reduce heat; simmer 6 - 8 minutes or until onion is tender and mixture thickens. Cool.

Marinade:

**2 tbls. soy sauce
2 tbls. orange juice
1 tsp. honey**

**1-¼ lb. salmon filet, ¾ - 1-½"
thick**

Combine soy sauce, orange juice and honey in shallow dish, add salmon, skin side up. Cover; refrigerate 30 minutes. Heat grill. Place salmon skin side down on plank; place on grill. Grill for 20-30 minutes or until flesh is opaque and flakes easily with fork. Place salmon on serving platter and cut into 4 pieces. Serve with relish.

CHEESE AND HOT PEPPER CHICKEN

Mary Farrar Turner

1 tbls. salt
1 tsp. onion powder
1 tsp. garlic powder
1 tsp. dry mustard
1 tsp. ground red pepper
  (preferably cayenne)

½ tsp. white pepper
½ tsp. ground cumin
½ tsp. black pepper
½ tsp. dried thyme leaves
½ tsp. oregano leaves
¼ tsp. ground cinnamon

Thoroughly combine the seasoning mix ingredients in a small bowl, breaking up any mustard lumps. Combine 1 tbls. of the mix with the flour in a plastic or paper bag and set aside.

1-¼ cups all-purpose flour
2 2-½ - 3 lb. chickens, cut in 16
  pieces and at room
  temperature
vegetable oil for frying
2-⅔ cups chopped green bell
  peppers, in all
2 cups chopped onions
1 cup chopped green chilies, in
  all
2 bay leaves
2 tsp. salt
2 tsp. minced garlic
1-½ tsp. ground red pepper
  (preferably cayenne)

¾ tsp. white pepper
¾ tsp. black pepper
2 tbls. finely chopped jalapeño
  peppers
4 cups basic chicken stock (in
  all)
1-½ cups heavy cream
1 cup dairy sour cream
1-½ cups grated Monterey Jack
  Cheese or other white non
  processed cheese
1-½ cups grated cheddar
  cheese
4 cups hot cooked rice

Remove any excess fat from chicken pieces. Sprinkle the remaining seasoning mix evenly on the chicken, patting it in by hand. Dredge chicken in the seasoned flour. Reserve leftover flour. Heat ½ inch of oil in a large skillet (I find this dish tastes significantly better if you don't use a nonstick type skillet) to 350°. Fry the chicken in batches, large pieces and skin side down first, just until light brown and crispy, about 2-4 minutes per side. (Lower heat if drippings in pan start to brown; you will use the drippings in the cream sauce, and you need them to remain light in color and taste so they won't dominate the cheese, peppers and cream flavors.) Drain on paper towels. Carefully pour the hot oil into a glass measuring cup, leaving as much sediment as possible in the skillet; return ½ cup hot oil to the skillet. Add 2 cups of the bell peppers, the onions and ⅔ cup of the green chilies; turn heat to high and stir well to mix vegetables with the sediment on the pan bottom. Cook until onions start to brown, about 6-8 minutes, stirring occasionally. Add the bay leaves, salt, garlic, and the red, white and black peppers; stir well. Then sprinkle 3 tbls. of the reserved flour on the vegetable

(continued)

mixture and stir thoroughly. Stir in the jalapeño peppers and cook about 2 minutes, stirring occasionally (lower heat if sticking excessively). Stir in 1 cup of the stock and scrape pan bottom well. Stir in 2 cups more stock and stir. Remove from heat. Place the chicken in a 5-²/₃ quart saucepan or large Dutch oven. Add the vegetable mixture and the remaining 1 cup stock to the chicken; stir well. Bring to a boil and then simmer over low heat for 15 minutes, stirring occasionally and being careful not to let mixture scorch. Add the remaining ²/₃ cup bell peppers, ¹/₃ cup green chilies, the cream, and sour cream. Bring to a boil over medium heat, stirring fairly constantly. Then stir in the cheeses and cook just until cheese melts, stirring constantly. Serve immediately, allowing about ¹/₂ cup rice and 2 pieces of chicken per serving, topped with ²/₃ cup sauce. (Leftover sauce is wonderful over vegetables.)

Daughter of Governor Frank Farrar

CHEESY MOSTACCIOLI

Deb Hall
Former Governor's Staff

1 (16-oz.) pkg. mostaccioli
  pasta, cooked
1-¹/₂ lbs. ground beef, browned
  and drained
1 (11-oz.) can cheddar cheese
  soup
1 tsp. ground black pepper
1 tsp. Italian seasoning
1 (30-oz.) jar spaghetti sauce
3 cups shredded mozzarella
  cheese

Preheat oven to 400°. Combine pasta, meat, soup, and spaghetti sauce. Add pepper, seasoning, and 2 cups of the mozzarella cheese. Mix to combine. Place in baking bowl. Sprinkle remaining cheese on top. Bake for 25 minutes. Yield: 8-10 servings.

CHICKEN A LA KING

First Lady Mary Dean Janklow

2 (6-oz.) cans sliced
  mushrooms, drained (reserve
  ¹/₂ cup liquid)
1 cup diced green pepper
1 cup butter or margarine
1 cup flour
2 tsp. salt

¹/₂ tsp. pepper
2 cups light cream or half & half
2-¹/₂ cup chicken broth
4 cups cut-up cooked chicken
2 (4-oz.) jars pimento, drained
  and chopped
¹/₂ pkg. frozen peas (1 cup)

In large sauce pan, cook and stir mushrooms and green peppers in butter for 5 minutes. Stir in flour, salt and pepper. Cook over low heat, stirring constantly, until bubbly. Remove from heat, stir in cream, broth, and reserved mushroom liquid. Heat, stirring constantly, until sauce boils. Boil and stir 1 minute. Stir in chicken, pimentos, and peas; heat until hot. Serve over egg noodles or biscuits. Makes 12-14 servings.

CHICKEN A LA KING

Deb Hall
Former Governor's Staff

1 (4-oz.) can sliced mushrooms,
  drained (save liquid)
1 green pepper, cut up (¹/₂ cup)
¹/₂ cup margarine or butter
¹/₂ cup flour
1 tsp. salt

¹/₄ tsp. pepper
1-¹/₂ tsp. chicken bouillon
1-¹/₂ cups milk
1-¹/₄ cups hot water
2 cups chicken or turkey
1 tsp. pimento (optional)

Cook and stir mushrooms and green pepper in margarine over medium heat. Cook 5 minutes; remove from heat. Blend in flour, salt and pepper. Cook over low heat, stirring constantly until mixture is bubbly, remove from heat. Stir in bouillon, milk, water, and mushroom liquid. Heat to boil. Stir in chicken or turkey. Heat until meat is hot or warm. Serve over noodles, rice or mashed potatoes.

85104-07

CHICKEN AND BROCCOLI CASSEROLE

Jackie Rounds

1-½ lbs. chicken breast, cubed
1 cup chopped broccoli
2 (10-oz.) cans cream of chicken
  soup
2 (10-oz.) cans cream of
  mushroom soup

1 can water
½ cup cheddar cheese
2 pkg. Ritz crackers, crushed

Preheat oven to 375°. In frying pan, cook chicken thoroughly. In large bowl, mix soups, water, and broccoli together; add cooked chicken and spread in 9 x 13 baking dish. Top with crushed Ritz crackers and cheese. Bake at 375° for 1 hour.

Sister-in-law of Governor M. Michael Rounds

CHICKEN BISCUIT STEW

Lynnette M. Hauschild Eckert
Governor's Staff

¼ cup Parkay margarine
⅓ cup flour
½ tsp. salt
dash pepper
1 (10¾-oz.) cans condensed
  chicken broth
¾ cup milk
2 cups cubed cooked chicken

⅓ cup chopped onion
1 cup cooked peas, drained
1 cup cooked whole baby
  carrots, drained
1 can (10 biscuits) Pillsbury
  refrigerated buttermilk or
  country style biscuits,
poppy seed, if desired

Heat oven to 375°. In oven proof 10" skillet, melt margarine, blend in flour, salt, and pepper. Add chicken broth and milk. Cook, stirring constantly until thickened. Add chicken, onion, peas, and carrots, simmer until hot and bubbly. Separate dough into 10 biscuits. Arrange biscuits over hot chicken mixture. Sprinkle with poppy seeds. Bake at 375° for 20 - 25 minutes or until the biscuits are golden brown. Makes 5-6 servings.

CHICKEN BREASTS STUFFED WITH SPINACH AND RICOTTA

Recipe Box at the
Governors Residence

4 bone in chicken breasts
(about 12 oz. each)
1 (10-oz.) pkg. frozen chopped
spinach (thawed)

½ cup Ricotta cheese
2 cloves garlic, finely minced
tsp. coarse salt
tsp. ground black pepper

Preheat oven to 425°. Drain thawed spinach; transfer to a large bowl. Add Ricotta cheese, garlic, 1 tsp. salt, and ¼ tsp. pepper; stir well to combine. Stuff chicken with filling; (to stuff the chicken - place chicken on a clean work surface, with your fingers loosen the skin and place a quarter of the filling underneath the skin of each breast; with one hand on top of chicken breast and the other keeping opening closed, press filling evenly to edges),season chicken generously with salt and pepper. Place on a rimmed baking sheet; roast until chicken is cooked through, 25 to 30 minutes.

CHICKEN BURRITOS

Chris & Lindsay Rounds

1 small onion, chopped
2 small garlic cloves, minced
2 tsp. vegetable oil
12 oz. chicken breasts, cut in 2"
strips
1 (12-oz.) can black beans,
rinsed & drained

1-½ cups salsa
½ tsp. chili powder
6 8" whole-wheat tortillas
¾ cup shredded cheddar
cheese
½ cup nonfat sour cream

In a large skillet, sauté chopped onion and minced garlic in oil over medium-high heat until onion is translucent. Add chicken strips, cook 5 minutes or until no longer pink. Stir in beans, ½ cup salsa and chili powder; cook 3 minutes longer. Warm tortillas. Spoon ½ - ¾ cup filling into each tortilla, top with 1 tbls. cheese. Fold into a burrito. Serve with salsa, cheese and sour cream as toppers. Time: 30 minutes. Makes 6 low-fat burritos.

Son and Daughter-in-Law of Governor M. Michael Rounds and First Lady Jean Rounds

85104-07

CHICKEN CORDON BLEU

Recipe Box at the
Governors Residence

4 skinless, boneless chicken breast halves
4 slices cooked ham
1/2 cup seasoned bread crumbs

6 slices Swiss cheese
1/4 tsp. salt
1/8 tsp. ground black pepper

Preheat over to 350°. Coat a 7 x 11 inch baking dish with nonstick cooking spray. Pound chicken breasts to 1/4 inch thickness. Sprinkle each piece of chicken on both sides with salt and pepper. Place 1 cheese slice and 1 ham slice on top of each breast. Roll up each breast, and secure with a toothpick. Place in baking dish, and sprinkle chicken evenly with bread crumbs. Bake for 30-35 minutes, or until chicken is no longer pink. Remove from oven, and place 1/2 cheese slice on top of each breast. Return to oven for 3-5 minutes, or until cheese has melted. Remove toothpicks, and serve immediately.

CHICKEN FOR A CROWD

Ellen Javernick

24 pieces chicken (skinless breasts)
2 cups flour
2 tsp. paprika

2 tsp. garlic salt
2 tsp. coarse pepper
juice of 1 lemon
oil to combine with lemon

Combine flour, paprika, garlic salt, and pepper in a brown paper bag. Shake the chicken pieces in the flour mixture until well coated. Arrange in 9 x 13 inch baking pans. Combine lemon juice and enough oil to fill 1 cup. Drizzle over the chicken. Refrigerate overnight. Bake 15 minutes at 450°. Reduce heat to 350°, and continue baking for 30 minutes (final cooking depends on size of pieces).

Granddaughter of Governor Harlan Bushfield

CHICKEN FRIED RICE

Janie Beeman
Former Governor's Staff

1 cup cut up uncooked chicken
1 tbls. Accent
2 - 4 cloves garlic
1 cucumber, peeled and cut up
1 bunch green onions, sliced
1 broccoli floweret head, cut
  into small pieces

1 small can mushrooms or
  equivalent fresh mushrooms
2 cups cooked rice
soy sauce
olive oil
salt and pepper
2 eggs

At least 3-4 hours prior to preparing the dish, cook the rice according to the instructions and then it needs to be totally cooled. That's what keeps it from getting mushy! Cut up the chicken and in a dish, combine with the Accent and 1-2 tbls. soy sauce. Set aside. In wok or stir-fry pan, put 1-2 tbls. oil; stir-fry the garlic until lightly browned (about 1-2 minutes), then add the cucumber, onions, broccoli, mushrooms (sometimes I have sliced up a couple of carrots and/or green peppers) until tender but firm. Remove from pan and set aside. Add to the pan the chicken mixture and stir-fry until cooked (no pink centers). When the chicken is cooked, add to that the rice mixture. Stir-fry that and add soy sauce, salt and pepper to taste. Stir-fry that for a couple of minutes until the rice is warming up, then add the vegetable mixture. Stir-fry that so that everything is mixed together. Then make a hole in the middle of the mixture, all the way to the bottom of the pan. Add the 2 eggs. Let them cook in the middle for a couple of minutes, then stir-fry the whole mixture together until the egg basically cooks and gets absorbed into the rice mixture.

Note: For rice - I use Uncle Ben's regular rice because it doesn't get mushy so fast. For olive oil - you can also use whatever kind of cooking oil you normally use. I also add red pepper flakes because I like spice.

85104-07

CHICKEN HOT DISH

Susan Stoneback
Former Governor's Staff

2 cups chopped cooked chicken
(or more)
1 cup chopped cooked broccoli
(or more)
1 (10-oz.) can cream of chicken
soup
¼ cup chopped onion
¼ cup mayonnaise
1-½ tsp. Worcestershire sauce
dash curry powder (to taste; at
least ⅛ tsp.)

½ cup shredded Cheddar
cheese
1 can refrigerator biscuits (10
count can, separated and cut
each in half)
¼ cup sour cream
1 egg
1 tsp. celery seed
½ tsp. salt

Preheat oven to 375°. Combine the cooked chicken, the broccoli, the soup, onion, mayonnaise, Worcestershire sauce, and curry powder in 1-½ quart casserole dish. Mix well, then bake for 20-25 minutes until bubbly. Sprinkle the top with cheese. Arrange biscuits, cut side down, around the edge of the casserole. Combine sour cream, egg, celery seed, and salt in a bowl - blending well. Spread over the biscuits. Bake 25-30 minutes until golden brown.

Note: This recipe requires some forethought, but if you like chicken with a touch of curry, it's worth the effort. The recipe makes 6 servings, but it is easily expandable by increasing the chicken or broccoli.

CHICKEN LASAGNA FLORENTINE

Dr. Howell W. Todd
Former Governor's Cabinet

9 lasagna noodles
3 large chicken breasts
2 (15-oz.) jars Bertolli Garlic
Alfredo sauce
1 cup roasted sweet peppers,
chopped
3 tbls. lemon juice

½ tsp. pepper
1 (10-oz.) pkg. frozen chopped
spinach, thawed and squeezed
in paper towel
1 cup shredded Kraft Italian
blend cheese

Cook lasagna noodles according to package directions. Drain, rinse with cold water, and drain again. Dice chicken breasts and sauté in olive oil until done. Mix chicken with remaining ingredients. Spray or oil a baking dish of sufficient size to use three noodles. Layer noodles on bottom and spread a third of the chicken/spinach mixture. Layer noodles again topped by another third of the chicken/spinach mixture. Layer noodles again and use remaining chicken/spinach mixture. Cover with foil and bake 50 minutes at 325°. Uncover, sprinkle cheese on top, and continue baking for another 5 - 7 minutes until cheese is melted and slightly browned.

CHICKEN PARMESAN

First Lady Mary Dean Janklow

2-2-1/2 lbs. boneless chicken
  breasts
1/4 cup flour
1/4 tsp. pepper
3 tbls. oil
1 1 lb. can whole tomatoes (cut
  up)

1/3 cup Heinz 57 sauce
1/3 cup grated Parmesan cheese
1 tbls. sugar
1/4 tsp. oregano leaves (crushed)
1/4 lb. mozzarella cheese

Coat chicken with mixture of flour, salt, and pepper and brown well in the oil. Place chicken in 12 x 7 inch baking dish. Blend the remaining flour mixture with the tomatoes, Heinz 57, Parmesan cheese, sugar and oregano leaves. Pour over chicken. Cover with tin foil and bake in 350° oven for 30 minutes. Remove cover and top with mozzarella cheese (do not recover). Bake for an additional 25 - 30 minutes or until the chicken is tender and cheese is nice and bubbly. Skim off any excess fat from the sauce. Serve with hot linguine pasta.

CHICKEN POT PIE

First Lady Jean Rounds

3-4 boneless chicken breasts
2 cans mixed vegetables,
  drained
2 cans cream of mushroom
  soup

1 cup chicken broth
1 cup milk
1/2 cup margarine, melted
1-1/2 cups Bisquick

Cook chicken breasts. Cut into bite-sized pieces and put in bottom of 9x13 inch baking dish. Pour mixed vegetables over chicken. Mix together cream of mushroom soup and chicken broth. Pour over meat and vegetables. Mix together milk, margarine, and Bisquick. Pour over top. Bake for 1 hour and 20 minutes at 350° until the crust is golden brown.

CHICKEN POT PIE

Ron Zylstra
Former Governor's Staff

1 cup cooked, diced chicken
1 cup diced, cooked potatoes
1/2 cup frozen peas
2 cups shredded cheddar
  cheese

1 cup frozen corn
1 can cream of celery soup
1 can cream of chicken soup
1 cup milk/broth
2 pie crusts

Mix all together, pour into pie crust shell, and top with crust. Bake at 425° until brown and bubbly.

85104-07

CHICKEN TETRAZZINI

Mary Joe Foss Finke

2-3 cups cooked chicken
  breasts. chopped
1 onion chopped
2 red or green peppers,
  chopped
1 lb. mushrooms, sliced
  (optional)

8 oz. spaghetti, cooked
1 stick butter
¾ cup flour
1 qt. whole milk
1 lb. Kraft Old English or sharp
  cheddar cheese
dash Tabasco sauce

Sauté onion, peppers, and mushrooms. Boil spaghetti and drain. Make white sauce - melt butter, add flour, stir, add milk, and cook over medium heat, stirring constantly until thick. Remove from heat and add Tabasco sauce and cheese-stir until smooth. Mix chicken, sautéed veggies, and spaghetti. Stir in cheese sauce. Pour into greased 11 x 14 inch casserole. Bake at 350° uncovered 40-60 minutes until bubbly and light brown. May freeze - do not thaw before baking.

Daughter of Governor Joe Foss

CHILE CHICKEN

Jason Dilges
Governor's Staff

4 chicken breasts
½ cup green chilies, diced
1 can cream of chicken soup
1 can cream of mushroom soup
1 cup cheddar cheese, shredded
1 cup milk

1 medium onion, chopped
2 tbls. oil
½ cup chicken broth
8 soft flour tortillas
paprika

Sauté onion in oil. While sautéing onion, cut chicken into pieces. Add chicken to onion. Add soup and stir. Blend in milk and cheese and heat until cheese melts. Add broth and chilies. Continue to cook until chicken is done and all ingredients are blended well. Cut tortillas into strips. In 9 x 13 inch pan, layer tortillas, chicken and sauce. Repeat. Top with tortillas and sauce. Sprinkle with paprika. Bake at 325° for 45 minutes to 1 hour. Let stand for 10 minutes and then serve by cutting into pieces.

CHILI RELLENOS CASSEROLE

Susan L. Walker
Former Governor's Cabinet

½ tbls. butter or margarine
1 cup half & half
2 eggs
⅓ cup flour
1 (7-oz.) can whole green chilies

1 8 oz. Monterey Jack cheese, grated
1 8 oz. cheddar cheese, grated
1 (8-oz.) can tomato sauce

Grease casserole dish with butter. Beat half & half with eggs and flour until smooth. Seed and drain chilies. Mix grated cheeses. Reserve half for top. Alternate layers of cheese, chilies, and egg mixture in 1-½ quart casserole. Pour tomato sauce over top and sprinkle with remaining cheese. Bake at 350° for 60 minutes. Salt and pepper to taste. Serve with salsa. Serves 4.

Note: You will think there are several eggs in this! It makes a great breakfast egg casserole accompanied with meat or enjoy as a meatless dinner. I've been asked for the recipe every time I serve it to guests.

COFFEE CRUSTED TENDERLOIN (BEEF, PORK, OR ELK)

Kevin Forsch
Governor's Staff

1 2 lb. tenderloin
⅛ cup ground coffee
¼ cup brown sugar
2 tbls. chili powder
2 tbls. paprika

2 tsp. ground sage
1 tsp. onion powder
¼ tsp. cayenne
red onion, quartered

Preheat oven to 500°. In a small bowl, combine coffee, brown sugar, chili powder, paprika, sage, onion powder, and cayenne. Rub mixture into meat. Let stand for 15 minutes. Place meat on a rack in a roasting pan and place red onions in pan around meat. Do not cover. Place in oven and turn oven down to 400°. Roast meat for 30 to 40 minutes or until internal temperatures of the tenderloin reach 130 - 145°. Remove from oven and let set for 10 minutes.

85104-07

COLORFUL CHICKEN CROISSANTS

Rick Melmer
Governor's Cabinet

2 cups cooked chicken, cut up
¼ cup diced celery
¼ cup craisins
¼ cup sliced almonds
¾ cup mayonnaise

2 tbls. chopped red onion
¼ tsp. salt
¼ tsp. pepper
4 croissants

Mix together. Spread on croissants.

COWBOY BEEF STEW

Governor Walter Dale Miller

1-½ lbs. road kill (if available) or
  round steak
1 cup flour
1-½ tsp. salt
½ tsp. ground pepper
1 tbls. beef bouillon granules
3 tbls. olive oil
1 medium onion, chopped
2 tbls. butter
2 tbls. brown sugar

1 large can stewed tomatoes,
  puréed
1 pkg. McCormick Stew
  Seasoning (add dry mixture)
1 can beef broth
4 medium red potatoes, cubed
3 medium rutabagas, cubed
6 carrots, cut into chunks
1 stalk celery, cut into chunks
2 cups cabbage, shredded

Cut meat into bite size pieces. Cover meat with flour, salt and pepper
and bouillon, stir until meat is well coated. Heat olive oil in large skillet.
Sauté onion until transparent, do not brown. Remove from skillet and
set aside. Add butter to the skillet, brown meat and flour mixture until
meat is medium rare. Add onion, brown sugar, stewed tomatoes, beef
broth and stew seasoning. Cover and simmer until gravy thickens. Add
potatoes, rutabagas, carrots, and celery. Cook in a slow cooker for 8 -
10 hours. Add cabbage to last hour of cooking time.

CREAMED CHICKEN BREASTS

Darrell Butterwick
Former Governor's Cabinet

5 boneless chicken breasts,
  halved
2 cans cream mushroom soup,
  undiluted

1 pint sour cream
2 jars dried beef

In 9 x 13 inch baking dish, layer bottom of pan with dried beef; lay
cleaned and patted dry chicken breasts flat. Set aside. In separate bowl
whisk together 2 cans soup and sour cream. Pour mixture on top of
chicken. Bake uncovered at 250° for 2 hours. Serve with side of rice.
Makes 10 servings.

CROCKPOT CHICKEN WITH MUSHROOM SAUCE

Harla Jessop
Former Governor's Staff

4 boneless skinless chicken breast halves
2 tbls. butter or margarine
1 (10¾-oz.) can condensed cream of mushroom soup
1 cup sour cream
1 (4-oz.) can mushrooms, drained

¼ cup white wine or chicken broth
½ tsp. garlic powder
½ tsp. salt
½ tsp. pepper

In a skillet, brown chicken on both sides in butter and placed in crock pot. In a bowl, combine the soup, mushrooms, wine or broth, garlic powder, salt, and pepper. Pour over the chicken. Add the sour cream about the last ½ hour. Bake in crock pot 4-5 hours. Serve over noodles or rice.

DAVE VOLK'S SMOTHERED CABBAGE

Dave Volk
Former Governor's Cabinet

1 tbls. olive oil
2 cups chopped yellow onions
1-½ cups chopped tasso (spicy cured ham) or kielbasa
1-½ cups chopped pickled pork or smoked ham butt
2 tbls. roasted garlic
1 tsp. Creole seasoning

2 lbs. green cabbage, trimmed, quartered, cored and sliced thin
salt to taste
½ tsp. freshly ground pepper
¼ tsp. crushed red pepper flakes
2 tbls. unsalted butter

Coat the bottom of a heavy pot with oil. Add onions and cook at medium-low heat, stirring occasionally, until onions begin to caramelize. Add tasso, pickled pork, garlic and Creole seasoning. Add cabbage and stir briefly. Add salt, pepper, pepper flakes and 3 cups of water. Bring to a simmer, cover the pan and cook over low heat for 45 minutes or until cabbage is tender. Uncover and stir in butter before serving.

85104-07

DORITOS CASSEROLE

Corrie Holt

1 lb. hamburger
1 small can chopped green chili peppers
1 can enchilada sauce

1 can cream of mushroom soup
1 can cream of chicken soup
1 pkg. Doritos
8 oz. Monterey Jack cheese

Brown hamburger - stir until crumbly. Pour off grease. Add green chili peppers, enchilada sauce, mushroom soup, cream of chicken soup. Mix well. Cook until bubbly. Spread Doritos in a baking dish. Spoon soup mixture oven Doritos. Top with cheese. Bake at 400° until cheese melts.

Niece of First Lady Jean Rounds

EASY LASAGNA

Jackie Rounds

2 lbs. ground beef
3 (28-oz.) jar spaghetti sauce
1-1/2 cups water
1-3/4 cup (15 oz.) cottage cheese
2 cups shredded mozzarella cheese (8 oz.)

1/2 cup grated Parmesan
2 eggs
1 pkg. lasagna noodles uncooked (8 oz.)

Preheat oven to 350°. Brown beef in frying pan, then add spaghetti sauce and water; simmer for 10 minutes. In large bowl stir 1/2 of the mozzarella cheese, all the Parmesan cheese, and all eggs together. In 9 x 13 inch baking dish, layer bottom with 1-1/2 cups of the meat sauce, layer meat sauce with uncooked lasagna noodles, add another layer of meat sauce. Now add half the cheese filling, add layer of noodles, then a layer of meat sauce. Add rest of cheese filling, another layer of noodles and rest of meat sauce. Top with rest of mozzarella cheese. Cover with foil and bake for 45 minutes. Uncover and bake for another 15 minutes.

Sister-in-law of Governor M. Michael Rounds

EGG ROLLS

Janie Beeman
Former Governor's Staff

1 pkg. egg roll skins
1 egg white
soy sauce
6 cups shredded cabbage
 (about 1 head)
6 cups thinly sliced celery
 (about 1 pkg.)

1 lb. sausage
1 bunch green onions, sliced
 (use white and green parts)
3 - 4 cloves garlic
2 cans small or broken shrimp,
 drained

Boil cabbage and celery together in large pot. Totally cover with water. Cook until they start to look clear and get tender. Drain water and set aside. Fry sausage, onions, and garlic together. After cooked, add the shrimp. Drain grease. Combine all cooked items in large pan and add soy sauce to taste. Fill skins and fold according to package. What I found to work best when cooking these is to use an electric skillet. Fill the skillet half full of whatever kind of frying oil you use. When oil is hot, lay filled egg roll skins in the pan and fry. You will need to turn them over once. They are done when the skins are golden brown. Take them out, lay them on paper towels to drain, and cook the next batch. This mixture freezes well. Also, cooked egg rolls freeze well.

85104-07

EGG ROLLS WITH SHRIMP AND PORK

Steve Wegman
Former Governor's Staff

½ lb. fresh bean sprouts or 1 lb. can of bean sprouts
½ lb. raw shrimp in their shells
3 tbls. oil
½ lb. lean boneless pork, finely ground
4 cups finely chopped celery
2 - 3 lbs. fresh mushrooms, cut in ¼" slices (about ½ cup)
1 tbls. soy sauce
1 tbls. Chinese rice wine, or dry sherry

2 tsp. salt
½ tsp. sugar
1 tbls. cornstarch, dissolved in 2 tbls. cold chicken stock, fresh or canned, or cold water
2 cups flour
½ tsp. salt
¾ cup cold water
1 egg, lightly beaten
3 cups peanut oil, or flavorless vegetable oil

Prepare ahead: Rinse bean sprouts in pot of cold water and discard any husks that float to the surface. Drain and pat dry with paper towels. To crisp canned bean sprouts, rinse them under running water and refrigerate them in a bowl of cold water for at least 2 hours. Drain and pat them dry before using. Shell the shrimp. With a small, sharp knife, devein them by making a shallow incision down their backs and lifting out the black or white intestinal vein with the point of the knife. Using a cleaver or large knife, cut the shrimp into a fine dice. To make the filling: Set a 12" wok of 10" skillet over high heat for 30 seconds. Pour in 1 tbls. oil, swirl it about in the pan and heat for another 30 seconds, turning the heat down to moderate if the oil begins to smoke. Add the pork and stir fry for 2 minutes, or until it loses its reddish color. Then add the wine, soy sauce, sugar, shrimp and mushrooms, and stir fry for another minute, or until the shrimp turns pink. Transfer the entire contents of the pan to a bowl and set aside. Pour the remaining 2 tbls. oil into the same wok or skillet, swirl it about in the pan and heat for 30 seconds, turning the heat down to moderate if the oil begins to smoke. Add the celery and stir fry for 5 minutes, then add the salt and bean sprouts and mix thoroughly together. Return the pork and shrimp mixture to the pan, and stir until all the ingredients are well combined. Cook over moderate heat, stirring constantly, until the liquid starts to boil. There should be about 2-3 tbls. of liquid remaining in the pan. If there is more, spoon it out and discard it. Give the cornstarch mixture a quick stir to recombine it, and add it. To make the wrappers: Sift flour and salt into a large mixing bowl. With a large spoon or your hands, gradually combine the flour and dough in the bowl for 5 minutes, or until it is smooth, then cover the bowl with a dampened cloth and let it rest for 30 minutes. Turn the dough out on a lightly floured surface and firmly roll it out until it is no more than 1/16" thick. With a cookie cutter, pastry wheel or sharp knife, cut the dough into 7" squares. When you have finished, there should be 16 squares.

(continued)

To assemble: For each egg roll, shape about ¼ cup of the filling with your hands into a cylinder about 4" long and 1" in diameter, and place it diagonally across the center of a wrapper. Life the lower triangular flap over the filling and tuck the point under it, leaving the upper point of the wrapper exposed. Bring each of the two small end flaps, one at a time, up to the top of the enclosed filling and press the points firmly down. Brush the upper and exposed triangle of dough with lightly beaten and then roll the wrapper into a neat package. The beaten egg will seal the edges and keep the wrapper intact. Place the filled egg rolls on a plate and cover them with a dry kitchen towel. If they must wait longer than about 30 minutes before being fried, cover them with plastic wrap and place them in the refrigerator.

To cook: Set a 12" wok or heavy deep-fryer over high heat, add 3 cups of oil and heat it until a haze forms above it or reaches a temperature of 375° on a deep-frying thermometer. Place 5 or 6 egg rolls in the hot oil and deep-fry them for 3-4 minutes, or until they have become golden brown and are crisp. Transfer the egg rolls to a double thickness of paper towels and let the oil drain off while you deep-fry another batch of 5 or 6. Serve the rolls as soon as possible, arranged attractively on a large heated platter. If necessary, the egg rolls can be kept warm for an hour or so in a preheated 250° oven, or they can be reheated for about 10 minutes in a 450° oven. To make spring rolls: Substitute 1 pound fresh, ready-made spring-roll wrappers for the egg-wrappers. Prepare the filling according to the recipe already given, then assemble the rolls and deep-fry them as described above. Because preparing spring-roll wrappers from scratch is so demanding and precise a culinary operation, even the fussiest Chinese cook prefers to use the ready-made variety.

Note: One pound ready-made egg-roll wrappers may be substituted for homemade wrappers.

EMERGENCY STEAK

Ida Covey

1 lb. hamburger
1 tbls. onion (minced)
½ cup milk
¼ tsp. pepper

1 tsp. salt
1 cup Wheaties (after being crushed) or ¼ cup bread crumbs

Pat into shape of T-bone steak, about 1 inch thick. May be broiled or grilled until well done.

Granddaughter of Lieutenant Governor Hyatt Covey

85104-07

ENCHILADA HOT DISH

Joyce Rounds (1933 - 1987)

1½ lbs. ground beef
1 small onion
1 (20-oz.) can refried beans

1 (15-oz.) can enchilada sauce
1 cup shredded cheddar cheese
1 bag nacho chips

Preheat oven to 350°. Brown hamburger and add onion. Drain mixture. Stir in refried beans and enchilada sauce. In a lightly greased 2 quart casserole dish, layer ½ of the following: crushed nacho chips, hamburger mixture and cheese. Repeat layers. Bake for 30 - 40 minutes.

Mother of Governor M. Michael Rounds

FABULOUS FAJITAS

Recipe Box at the
Governors Residence

2 green bell peppers, sliced
1 red bell pepper, sliced
1 onion, thinly sliced
1 cup fresh sliced mushrooms
2 cups diced, cooked chicken or
  beef

1 pkg. dry Italian Salad Dressing
  Mix
10 12" flour tortillas

Cut peppers and onion into thin slices - do not dice, leave slices long and thin. Sauté peppers and onion in a small amount of oil until tender. Add mushrooms and chicken. Continue to cook on low heat until heated through. Stir in dry salad dressing mix and blend thoroughly. Warm tortillas and roll mixture inside. If desired, top with shredded cheddar cheese, diced tomato and shredded lettuce.

FAMILY-STYLE BEEF ENCHILADAS

Patricia Van Gerpen
Former Governor's Cabinet

3 10" flour tortillas
1 lb. ground beef
1 small onion, chopped
1 tomato, chopped
1 clove garlic, minced
1/3 cup plus 2 tbls. picante
   sauce
1/2 tsp. ground cumin

1/4 tsp. salt
1/4 tsp. sliced green onions
3/4 cup shredded Mexican-style
   or cheddar cheese
1 cup sour cream (optional)
1/4 cup ripe black olive slices
   (optional)

Brown beef with onion and garlic and drain. Stir in 1/3 cup picante sauce, cumin and salt. Simmer on stovetop for 5 minutes, stirring. Remove from stove and stir in tomato and green onions. Place one tortilla in round oven baking dish and top evenly with half the meat mixture and 1/4 cup cheese. Repeat the same steps with second tortilla. Top with third tortilla. Sprinkle with remaining cheese and drizzle the top with 2 tablespoons picante sauce. Bake for 15 minutes at 350°. Top with sour cream and onions, if desired, and serve.

FANCY PHEASANT

Rachel Hansen Kippley
Former Governor's Staff

2 pheasant breasts
onion
1 can mushrooms
1 can cream of chicken soup

1 pkg. onion soup mix
splash of Boone's Mountain
   Berry Wine

Lay pheasant breast halves in bottom of 9 x 13 inch pan. Cover with remainder of ingredients, making sure pheasant is completely covered. Bake at 250° for 3 - 4 hours. Serve over rotini pasta.

85104-07

FARRAR PHEASANT FANTASY

Karon Schaack
Former Governor's Cabinet

4-6 pheasant breasts
oil to brown breasts in
1 cup water
1 cup smoked long grain rice
  (or 1 pkg. brown 'n wild rice)

1 can cream of celery soup
1 cup chicken broth
1 can cream of chicken soup
1 tbls. minced parsley
1/2 cup slivered almonds

Brown breasts in a small amount of cooking oil over medium heat. Remove breast; add 1 cup hot water to the drippings and scrape. Cook, stirring to blend and add 1 cup broth. Grease a large casserole or Pyrex pan. Spread dry rice on bottom, spoon on both soups (undiluted) over the rice in layers. If using packaged rice mix, sprinkle the herb packet over the soup layers. Pour broth mixture from frying pan over all evenly. Lay browned breasts on top of layers. Cover casserole or use several thickness of aluminum foil to cover tightly. Bake in pre-heated oven at 350° for 1-1/2 hours. Uncover and brown for another 30 minutes. If it appears the breasts are drying, add a bit more water. Sprinkle parsley and almonds over the top the last 30 minutes.

FAST FAMILY FAJITAS

Kris Ingram
Governor's Staff

1 medium green bell pepper
1 medium red bell pepper
4 boneless, skinless chicken
  breasts
2 tsp. vegetable oil
1 clove garlic, pressed

1 envelope onion soup mix (1
  oz.)
1/2 cup water
1/2 cup salsa
12 (7-8 inch) flour tortillas,
  warmed

Cut bell peppers into 1/2 inch strips. Cut chicken crosswise into thin strips. Heat 1 teaspoon oil and chicken in skillet over med-high heat. Fry this for 3-4 minutes. Remove from skillet; set aside. Add remaining oil, bell peppers and garlic; fry 1 - 2 minutes until vegetables are tender. Add chicken, onion soup mix, water and salsa to bell pepper mixture. Cook and stir 2-3 minutes or until heated through. To serve, place chicken mixture in center of warm tortillas. Serve with toppings, if desired.

FETTUCCINI ALFREDO

Jim Hagen
Former Governor's Cabinet

1 stick butter
1 carton half & half
1 heaping cup Parmesan cheese
1 tbls. parsley

salt & pepper
garlic powder
1 (16-oz.) box fettuccini noodles

Melt butter. Add half & half and cheese, parsley, and seasonings. Stir over low heat. Serve over hot fettuccini noodles.

FRESH POLISH SAUSAGE

Kathy Adam Bykowski

2 pt. hog casings
13 lbs. pork shoulder (not too fat, cut in pieces)
3 cloves fresh garlic
1 tbls. salt
1 tbls. sugar

1 tbls. marjoram
1 tbls. Accent
1 tbls. pepper
1/4 cup salt
2 cups water

Cut garlic in small pieces and mash salt and garlic together real good. Sprinkle garlic and salt over the meat. Add sugar, marjoram, Accent, pepper, water, and 1/4 cup salt. Mix well. Stuff into casings. Slow boil until done (internal temp 170°). For dinner, complement with buttered mashed potatoes, sauerkraut, corn, and fresh bread.

Granddaughter of Governor George T. Mickelson and Niece of Governor George S. Mickelson

85104-07

GLAZED PORK ROAST

Dean Anderson
Former Governor's Cabinet

4 - 5 lb. pork loin roast
salt
pepper
²/₃ packed cup brown sugar

2-¹/₂ tsp. dry mustard
2 tbls. cornstarch
2 cups apricot nectar
4 tsp. cider vinegar

Rub roast well with salt and pepper; score fat on roast in a diamond pattern. Place roast, fat side up, on a rack in an open roasting pan. Roast meat in a slow to moderate oven (325° - 350°). About ¹/₂ hour before roast is done, mix brown sugar, mustard, and cornstarch in a saucepan. Stir in apricot nectar and cider vinegar. Place over medium heat and cook, stirring constantly, until slightly thickened. Remove roast from oven and spoon about ¹/₂ cup glaze over it (reserve rest of glaze). Replace meat in oven until done. Remove roast from oven 20 minutes before serving for easier carving. Serves 8. Apricot Sauce: Mix about 3 tablespoons brown drippings from roast with remaining apricot glaze. Heat and serve as a sauce to spoon over the roast pork.

Note: This roast is a tradition in the Anderson family, served every year for their Christmas Day dinner.

GOLUMPKI (POLISH STUFFED CABBAGE)

Kathy Adam Bykowski

1 large head cabbage (16 leaves)
2 lbs. raw ground beef
2 tsp. salt

½ tsp. pepper
4 tbls. diced, minced onion
2 cups freshly cooked rice
2 eggs

Combine mixture ingredients together well. Boil the head of cabbage after coring it, just to loosen the leaves for about 3 to 5 minutes. Take 1 leaf out at a time and fill it with approximately 2 tablespoons of rice-meat mixture. Fold it over horizontally and then bring in the sides of leaf to make a pocket.

Sauce:

2 (10¾-oz.) cans condensed tomato soup (Campbell's)
2 cans water (use Campbell's cans)

1 tbls. brown sugar

In pressure cooker: Place the Golumpki on the cooking rack. Blend tomato soup and water together and pour over the Golumpki. Sprinkle brown sugar on top. Close lid. Cook for 10 minutes after control jiggles. Cool pan and reduce pressure. Remove Golumpki and keep warm. Thicken sauce for gravy. In casserole dish or roasting pan. Arrange in dish or pan, pour sauce over Golumpki and sprinkle with brown sugar. Bake at 350° for about an hour until internal temperature reaches 160°. To complete dinner, complement with sides of white rice, green beans and fresh bread. Use sauce as gravy for Golumpki and rice.

Granddaughter of Governor George T. Mickelson and Niece of Governor George S. Mickelson

GOOSE LEGS DELIGHT

Steve Pirner
Governor's Cabinet

legs/thighs from wild Canadian geese

water
barbeque sauce

Many people clean Canadian geese by breasting them. However, if you are not taking a few extra minutes to save legs/thighs too, you are missing the best part of the goose. To cook, leave the leg and thigh together, soak overnight in cold salt water, and drain. Add just enough water to cover the bottom of your crock pot, add the legs/thighs, and lightly drizzle just a little barbeque sauce on each piece. Set your crock pot on high and cook for four hours, then cook another four hours on low. There is just enough fat in the legs and thighs to make them moist and tender.

85104-07

GOULASH/JO-BOB CASSEROLE

Jennette Crawford Lusk

1 pkg. spaghetti
1 qt. water
1 can tomatoes
½ tsp. salt
3 tbls. butter

3 medium onions, chopped
2 green bell peppers, chopped
1 can mushrooms
3 tbls. parsley, chopped
1 tbls. Worcestershire sauce

Combine spaghetti, water, tomatoes and salt in large pot. Cook slowly until spaghetti is done. Fry in butter, the onions, peppers, mushrooms and parsley. Combine with spaghetti mixture and season with Worcestershire sauce. Bake 45 minutes at 350°.

Daughter of Governor Coe I. Crawford, Recipe submitted by Vicki Coe Lusk, Jeanette's daughter.

GREEK LEMON CHICKEN

Karon Schaack
Former Governor's Cabinet

6 whole large chicken breasts,
  boned & skinned
3 tbls. olive oil
2 tbls. butter
2 tbls. flour
½ tsp. salt
2 tsp. prepared mustard
1 cup milk
2 egg yolks
freshly grated peel of 1 lemon

1 tsp. fresh lemon juice
1 tsp. dried dill weed
¼ cup sour cream
¼ cup butter, melted
½ cup crumbled feta cheese
1 lb. angel hair pasta, cooked al
  dente and kept warm
½ cup shredded muenster
  cheese

Marinade:

1 cup fruity white wine
¼ cup olive oil
¼ cup fresh lemon juice
1 tsp. freshly grated lemon peel

1 tsp. salt
1 tsp. freshly ground black
  pepper
3 cloves garlic, crushed

Makes 6 - 8 servings. In a bowl, combine all marinade ingredients. Pound chicken breasts slightly and place in shallow casserole or in plastic zip-lock bag, and cover with marinade. Refrigerate for up to 12 hours. Discard marinade. Heat oil in skillet and sauté chicken until tender. Slice and set aside. In heavy saucepan, melt 2 tbls. butter; blend in flour and salt to create a roux. Add mustard and slowly add milk, stirring constantly until thick and smooth. In small bowl, mix egg yolks, lemon peel, and lemon juice together. Whisk a small amount of roux into egg mixture. Then whisk egg mixture into roux and bring to a gentle boil. Remove from heat and add dill and parsley. When parsley wilts, stir in sour cream. Add ¼ cup butter, ¾ cup of the egg sauce and feta cheese to cooked pasta; stir well. Place in greased 9 x 13 inch baking pan, and top with sliced chicken breasts, remaining sauce, and Muenster cheese. Broil until cheese is golden.

GRILLED ROSEMARY LEMON CHICKEN BREASTS

Dale Bertsch
Governor's Staff

4-6 skinless, boneless chicken
  breasts
½ cup fresh rosemary, chopped
juice of three lemons

8 cloves garlic
⅔ cup olive oil
¼ tsp. salt
¼ tsp. pepper

Place rosemary, lemon juice, garlic cloves, olive oil, salt, and pepper in food processor. Process until smooth. Place breasts in Ziploc bag. Pour processed ingredients into bag. Marinate in refrigerator for 2 to 4 hours. Remove from marinade and grill.

85104-07

GRILLED SALMON & MANGO SALSA

*Recipe Box at the
Governors Residence*

4 6-8 oz. fresh or frozen salmon
  fillets (with skin, 1" thick)
2 tbls. sugar
1-1/2 tsp. finely shredded lime
  peel
3/4 tsp. salt
1/4 tsp. ground red pepper
1 large ripe mango, peeled,
  seeded, and cut into thin bite-
  size strips

1/2 of a medium cucumber,
  seeded and cut into thin bite-
  size strips
2 green onions, sliced
3 tbls. lime juice
1 tbls. snipped fresh cilantro or
  2 tsp. snipped fresh mint
1 small fresh jalapeño pepper,
  seeded and chopped
1 clove garlic, minced

Thaw fish, if frozen. Rinse fish, then pat dry. Place fish, skin sides down, in a shallow pan. For rub, in a small bowl, stir sugar, lime peel, 1/2 tsp. of the salt and the red pepper. Sprinkle rub evenly over fish; rub in with your fingers. Cover and marinate in the refrigerator 4-24 hours. Meanwhile, for salsa, in a medium bowl, combine mango, cucumber, green onions, lime juice, cilantro, jalapeño pepper, garlic, and the remaining 1/4 tsp. salt. Cover and refrigerate until ready to serve. In a grill with a cover, arrange medium-hot coals around a drip pan. Test for medium heat above the pan. Place fish, skin sides down on the greased grill rack over the drip pan, tucking under any thin edges. Cover and grill for 14-18 minutes or until fish flakes easily with a fork. If desired, remove skin from fish. Serve the fish with salsa. Makes 4 servings.

GRILLED SHRIMP

David Mickelson

1 cup white wine vinegar
1/2 cup chili sauce
2 cloves garlic, minced
1/4 cup vegetable oil
2 tbls. Worcestershire sauce
2 tsp. Tabasco

1/4 cup apple juice
1/4 packed cup brown sugar
1/2 tsp. salt
1/2 tsp. cayenne pepper
2-3 lbs. medium shrimp,
  shelled & deveined

Combine all ingredients into large bowl and blend. Add shrimp and marinate 2-4 hours. Place shrimp on skewers. Cook on greased grill 4-6 minutes.

Son of Governor George S. Mickelson

GRILLED STEAK AND ASPARAGUS SALAD

Craig Johnson
Former Governor's Staff

½ cup light olive oil vinaigrette dressing
⅓ cup A-1 Steak Sauce
1 lb. beef steak (should be a tender cut or tenderized)
1 bunch fresh asparagus (can use 10 oz. pkg. of frozen spears), cooked and cooled

½ cup thinly sliced red bell pepper
8 large green or red lettuce leaves
1 tbls. toasted sesame seeds

In a small bowl, blend vinaigrette and steak sauce. Pour marinade over steak in non-metal dish. Cover, refrigerate 1 hour. While steak is in marinade, steam or grill asparagus till just tender, let cool. Slice red pepper thin. Toast sesame seeds. Take steak out of marinade and grill till medium done. Grill slowly, turning steak often. When steak is done, thinly slice across grain (muscle strands). Heat to a boil remaining marinade. While the marinade is heating up, arrange lettuce leaves on plate, add asparagus, pepper and steak.

HAMBURGER AND RICE HOT DISH

Joseph 'Frank' Foss

1 lb. ground beef
1 (10¾-oz.) can cream of chicken soup
1 (10¾-oz.) can cream of mushroom soup
1 cup fine cut celery (optional)

1 small onion, chopped
3 tbls. soy sauce
½ cup uncooked rice
1½ cup boiling water
1 can chow mein noodles (optional)

Brown hamburger, celery and onion - drain off fat. Add chicken and mushroom soups, rice, and soy sauce to hamburger. Mix it all together. Put in greased 2½ qt. casserole dish. Add boiling water just before putting in oven. (Don't mix water in meat mixture, just pour it on top). Bake for 1 hour at 350°. Add chow mein noodles over top and bake another ½ hour.

Son of Governor Joe Foss

HOBO CASSEROLE

Steve Wegman
Former Governor's Staff

2 (10-oz.) pkgs. chopped
 broccoli
1 cup rice (Minute Rice)
2 tbls. melted butter
½ cup celery
½ cup onion

1 (8-oz.) jar Cheez Whiz
1 can water chestnuts, sliced
 and rinsed
1 can cream of mushroom soup
1 soup can of water
Parmesan cheese

Mix all ingredients together. Bake in a 9 x 13 inch pan at 350° for 1 hour. The last 15 minutes of baking, sprinkle Parmesan cheese over casserole. Makes 8-12 servings.

HUNTER'S CHICKEN/PHEASANT

Anne Farrar

1 cup dried porcini mushrooms
2 tbls. olive oil
1 tbls. butter
4 chicken pieces on the bone,
 skinned
1 large onion, thinly sliced
1 (14-oz.) can chopped tomatoes
⅔ cup red wine

leaves of one sprig of fresh
 rosemary, finely chopped
1-¾ cups fresh field
 mushrooms, thinly sliced
salt and freshly ground pepper
fresh rosemary sprigs to
 garnish
chopped garlic

Put the porcini mushrooms in a bowl, add one cup warm water and soak for 20-30 minutes. Remove from the liquid and squeeze the mushrooms over the bowl. Strain the liquid and reserve. Finely chop the mushrooms. Heat the oil and butter in a large flame proof casserole on stove top until foaming. Add the chicken. Sauté over medium heat for 5 minutes or until golden. Remove and drain on paper towels. Add onion and chopped porcini mushrooms to the pan; cook gently, stirring frequently for 3 minutes until onion is softened but not browned. Stir in the chopped tomatoes, wine, and reserve mushroom soaking liquid. Then add crushed garlic and chopped rosemary with salt and pepper to taste. Bring to a boil, stirring frequently. Return chicken to the pan and coat with sauce in the pan, cover and simmer gently for 30 minutes. Add fresh mushrooms and stir well to mix into sauce. Continue simmering gently for 10 minutes or until chicken is tender. Taste for seasoning. Serve hot with mashed potatoes or polenta. Garnish with rosemary.

Daughter of Governor Frank Farrar

ITALIAN BEEF FOR SANDWICHES (CHICAGO FAVORITE)

Kathy Adam Bykowski

10 lbs. top round roast
Spice mix:

2 parts oregano
1 part basil

Lawry's seasoned salt
pepper
garlic powder

1 bottle garlic cloves

1 part thyme
sprinkle marjoram

6 cans beef consomme
1 onion
2 bell peppers

Make holes with knife about a ½-inch deep into roast. Push spice mixture in holes, then shove garlic clove in on top of the mixture. Do this liberally all over the roast. Put Lawry's salt, pepper, and garlic powder all over on the outside of roast. I'm very liberal with the spices. To me, the more spices the better. Put in deep roaster pan with a couple of inches of water. Cover and cook at 450° for 1 hour. Take out and add consomme and 3 cans of water. Add sliced onion and bell peppers. Cover and cook about 8 minutes per pound. After ¾ cooking time, flip roast over and continue cooking. When done, cool immediately and chill over night. Slice beef very thin and store in the beef au jus gravy. Extra Peppers: Cut bell peppers and onions. Combine with water and put into a big fry pan. Add garlic powder, paprika, and a ladle of the beef au jus gravy. Add 1 tablespoon of red wine vinegar. Cook al dente. When ready to serve, simmer meat in au jus gravy on top of stove for about an hour. Make sure meat is covered in gravy. Serve hot on Italian or French bread (cut thin loaves about 6 inches). Spoon au jus on bread to moisten, then pile meat on high.

Granddaughter of Governor George T. Mickelson and Niece of Governor George S. Mickelson

Note: This classic is traditionally served with your extra peppers and options on top. Some like hot Gardinera mix in place of the peppers. Serve with potato chips and a Coke!

85104-07

JAMBALAYA

Tim Reisch
Governor's Cabinet

1-½ lbs. Italian Sausage
1 (12-oz.) jar salsa (or 16 oz.)
1 can chili beans
1 can red beans

3 cups Uncle Ben's Rice
chicken breasts, optional
2 cans whole kernel corn

Cut Italian sausage into ½ - ¾" chunks while still partially frozen. Brown until fully cooked. Add jar of salsa, chili beans, and red beans, bring to a boil. Add Uncle Ben's rice (uncooked), and 5 cups water. Bring to a boil and reduce to simmer for 20 minutes until rice is fully cooked. If it is not spicy enough for you, add hot sauce and/ or chili powder to taste. Add 2 cans of kernel corn just before serving.

Note: Optional: 2 chicken breasts, cut up and browned, can be used instead of Italian sausage.

JAMBALAYA

Mardell Davis
Governor's Staff

1 tbls. oil
2 lbs. kielbasa sausage cut into
  1-inch pieces
1 lb. boneless chicken breasts
  cut into strips
1 large onion
3 to 4 cloves garlic, crushed
2 green bell peppers, chopped
2 stalks celery, sliced

5 cups water
2 tsp. salt
½-1 tsp. cayenne pepper
1 (6-oz.) can tomato paste
2 bay leaves
3 cups uncooked long grain rice
2 lbs. medium-sized uncooked
  shrimp, peeled

Heat oil in 6-quart Dutch oven over medium heat. Add sausage, chicken, onion, garlic, peppers, and celery. Cook until chicken is no longer pink, stirring occasionally. Stir in water, salt, cayenne, tomato paste, and bay leaves. Bring to a boil; stir in rice and shrimp. Reduce heat to simmer. Cover and cook 25-30 minutes or until rice is tender and fluffy, stirring frequently. To serve, remove bay leaves; garnish as desired. Makes 12 (1-⅓ cup) servings.

JAMBALAYA

Bill Even
Governor's Cabinet

1 lb. Kielbasa or Polish
  Sausage, cut into ½ inch
  slices
1 lb. boneless skinless chicken
  breast, cubed
1 large onion, chopped
½ cup celery
½ cup chopped green pepper
4 cloves garlic, minced
2 tbls. butter

1 (14-½-oz.) can diced
  tomatoes, drained
1 (6-oz.) can tomato paste
½ tsp. hot pepper sauce
¼-½ tsp. cayenne pepper
⅛ tsp. garlic powder
½ lb. uncooked medium shrimp,
  peeled and deveined
hot cooked rice (optional)

In a Dutch oven or large sauce pan, sauté the sausage, chicken, onion, celery, green pepper, and garlic in butter until chicken is browned. Stir in tomatoes, tomato paste, and seasonings. Bring to a boil. Reduce heat; cover and cook 6-8 minutes or until chicken is no longer pink. Stir in shrimp, cover, and simmer for 4 minutes or until shrimp turns pink. Serve over rice.

Note: Can be frozen for 2 months.

85104-07

KASE KNEPFLA

Steve Pirner
Governor's Cabinet

3 cups flour
1 cup warm water
2 tbls. oil

2 egg whites, beaten until frothy
$1/2$ tsp. salt

Combine ingredients and knead well until dough feels elastic-like. Roll out until thin and cut into rectangles.

Cheese Filling:

$1/2$ tsp. salt
2 (12-oz.) pkg. dry curd cottage cheese

2 egg yolks

Combine ingredients and place rounded tbls. on half of each rectangle. Moisten dough around cheese with water, fold other half of rectangle over cheese, and seal by pressing dough together with fork. Carefully drop into boiling salt water. Gently boil uncovered for 35 minutes and drain.

Meat Sauce:

1 onion
3 lbs. hamburger
salt and pepper to taste

1 (16-oz.) can tomato sauce
$3/4$ cup water
flour to thicken if needed

Brown hamburger with chopped onion, add tomato sauce and water, simmer for 45 minutes, thicken with flour if needed. Serve separately so meat sauce can be spooned over cheese pods.

LASAGNA

First Lady Jean Rounds

1 lb. hamburger
1 tbls. basil
1 1 lb. can tomatoes
1 clove garlic (or garlic powder)

1-½ tsp. salt
2 (6-oz.) cans tomato paste
1 (10-oz.) pkg. lasagna noodles

Brown meat, drain. Add remaining ingredients. Simmer, uncovered for 30 minutes. Cook lasagna noodles until tender. Drain. Rinse in cold water.

Cottage Cheese Mixture:

3 cups cottage cheese
2 tbls. parsley flakes
2 tsp. salt
½ cup Parmesan cheese

2 eggs, beaten
½ tsp. pepper
1 lb. shredded Mozzarella
  cheese

Mix all ingredients together. Put ½ of noodles in 9 x 13 inch pan. Spread with half the cottage cheese mixture, add half the meat sauce, and top with ½ lb. grated mozzarella cheese. Repeat layers. Bake at 375° for 30 minutes. If you refrigerate and bake later, decrease temperature to 350° and bake for 45-55 minutes.

85104-07

LASAGNA

Jason Dilges
Governor's Staff

12 lasagna noodles
1 cup mozzarella cheese,
 shredded

1 cup American cheese,
 shredded
Parmesan cheese

Cook the lasagna noodles, drain and cool.

Sauce:

2 lbs. hamburger
½ medium onion, chopped
2 (15-oz.) cans tomato sauce
2 (6-oz.) cans tomato paste

1 tsp. garlic powder
3 - 4 bay leaves
salt and pepper
2 cups water

In large pot on stove, brown the hamburger and drain. Add the onion, tomato sauce, tomato paste, garlic powder, bay leaves, water and salt and pepper to taste. Simmer 1 hour. Remove bay leaves. While sauce is simmering, make filling.

Filling:

1 (12-oz.) container cottage
 cheese

2 eggs, beaten
salt and pepper

Mix together the cottage cheese, eggs, salt, and pepper. In 9 x 13 inch pan, spoon small amount of sauce. Place four cooked noodles over sauce. Cover with sauce. Spread ½ of filling over sauce. Then place four noodles, cover with sauce, spread remaining filling. Cover with ½ the mozzarella and American cheese. Place remaining four noodles, cover well with remaining sauce. Top with remaining cheese. Sprinkle Parmesan cheese on top. Bake 30 minutes at 350°. Let stand 5-10 minutes before serving.

LASAGNA (NO BOIL)

Lance Burma

1 pkg. lasagna noodles (no boil)
1 (28-oz.) jar Prego Traditional
  Spaghetti Sauce
1 (14-oz.) jar Prego Traditional
  Spaghetti Sauce
1 lb. lean ground beef

1 pkg. Hormel sliced pepperoni
1 medium cottage cheese (2%)
2 cups shredded cheddar
  cheese
2 cups mozzarella cheese

Brown ground beef and drain fat. Mix with spaghetti sauce. Set aside. Spray 13 x 9 pan with non stick spray. Place one layer uncooked noodles in pan. Spread spaghetti sauce generously over noodles. Top with 10-12 pepperoni slices, spread several spoonfuls of cottage cheese; then sprinkle both types of shredded cheese generously. Repeat layer. On third layer, omit the cottage cheese. Bake in 350° oven for 1 hour. Let sit for 10 minutes or so before cutting.

Grandson of Governor Walter Dale Miller

LEMON-GARLIC CHICKEN BREAST

Karl Adam

6 chicken breast filets
1/2 cup melted butter
1 small clove of garlic, crushed
3/4 cup dry bread crumbs
1/2 cup grated Parmesan cheese
1 1/2 tsp. minced parsley

1 tsp. salt
pepper to taste
2 tbls. melted butter
juice of 1 lemon
paprika to taste

Rinse chicken and pat dry. Dip in mixture of 1/2 cup butter and garlic. Coat in mixture of bread crumbs, Parmesan cheese, parsley, salt, and pepper. Arrange in nonstick baking pan. Drizzle with 2 tbls. butter and lemon juice. Sprinkle with paprika. Bake at 325° for 50 minutes or until chicken is tender.

Grandson of Governor George T. Mickelson and Nephew of Governor George S. Mickelson

85104-07

LITTLE CHEDDAR LOAVES

Cleo Shroyer
Governor's Staff

1-1/2 lb. hamburger
3/4 cup oatmeal
1 tsp. salt

1/2 cup cheddar cheese
1 egg
3/4 cup milk

Combine all ingredients and shape into 6 small loaves. Place in shallow baking pan. Combine 1 tbls. brown sugar, 1 tbls. mustard, and 1/3 cup ketchup. Spread even amounts on top of each meat loaf and bake at 350° for 45 minutes to 1 hour.

MARINATED FLANK STEAK

Amy Mickelson Brecht

2 flank steaks
1/2 cup olive oil
1/4 cup soy sauce
3 tbls. balsamic vinegar
1/4 cup lemon juice
3 tbls. honey
1 clove garlic, minced

1/2 tsp. ginger
1 1/2 tsp. salt
1 tsp. sugar
2 tbls. grated onion
1/2 tsp. dry mustard
1 tsp. fresh ground pepper

Combine all marinade ingredients in a food processor and blend. Place flank steak in a bag and cover with marinade. Let steak marinate overnight. Broil or grill 3 - 6 minutes per side. Remove from heat and slice thinly diagonally across the grain.

Daughter of Governor George S. Mickelson and Granddaughter of Governor George T. Mickelson

MARYLAND CRAB SHELLS

Richard Benda
Governor's Cabinet

24 - 30 jumbo shells
1 (12-oz.) pkg. crab meat
1 tbls. green pepper, finely chopped
1 tbls. red onion, finely chopped
3 tbls. margarine, divided
1/2 tsp. pepper

1 tsp. Old Bay seasoning
1 egg, beaten
2 cups skim milk, divided
1/2 cup low-fat mayonnaise
2 tbls. flour
1/2 cup grated Parmesan cheese

Preheat oven to 350°. Cook pasta according to package directions. While pasta is cooking, sauté green pepper and onion in 1 tsp. melted margarine until tender. Combine the crab meat, spices, egg, 2 tbls. milk, vegetables, and mayonnaise. Spoon mixture into shells. Spray the bottom of a 9 x 13 inch casserole dish with cooking spray, place stuffed shells in dish in a single layer. Melt 2 tbls. of margarine in saucepan. Over low flame, stir in flour with a wire whisk and gradually add 1-1/2 cups of milk. When sauce is smooth, stir in Parmesan cheese. Drizzle sauce over shells. Sprinkle top with Old Bay seasoning. Bake for 30 minutes or until bubbling.

MEAT CROQUETTES

First Lady Mary E. Elrod

3 cups chopped meat
2 eggs, well beaten
salt

pepper
juice half lemon

Mix with white sauce made as follows: Rub together a large tbls. flour with 1 tbls. butter, add small cup milk, and cook until thick, stirring constantly; make croquettes into cylinders, roll in bread crumbs and fry in deep fat.

Note: Recipe submitted by Ailene R Luckhurst, Clark County Historical Society.

85104-07

MEATBALLS

Deb Vedvei

1 lb. hamburger
½ cup milk
1 cup soft bread crumbs
1 tsp. salt
½ cup pepper
onion

1-½ tbls. Worcestershire sauce
¼ cup vinegar
3 tbls. brown sugar
½ cup ketchup
½ cup water

Mix together hamburger, milk, bread crumbs, salt, pepper, and onion. Form into balls and put in a pan. Next mix Worcestershire sauce, vinegar, brown sugar, ketchup, water, and pour over top. Bake 1 hour at 350°.

Sister-in-Law of Governor M. Michael Rounds

MEATBALLS & GRAVY (OLD FASHIONED - DELICIOUS)

Dar Baum
Former Governor's Cabinet

Meatballs:

2 lbs. hamburger
3-4 slices bread
¼ cup grated onion
½ tsp. salt

½ lb. pork sausage
2 eggs
1½ tsp. nutmeg
¼ tsp. pepper

Place bread in small amount of water and crunch with hand just until moist. Set aside. Using hands, mix hamburger, sausage, eggs, onion, nutmeg, salt, and pepper in large mixing bowl. Mix in moist bread. Form into 2" balls and fry in covered pan, reserving drippings (can be microwaved on high). Drain. Place in large casserole or roaster.

Gravy:

Pan drippings
1 cup flour
6 tbls. Tone's gravy mix

3 cups water, divided
1 cup beef broth

In fry pan, bring drippings to boil. Add flour and 1 cup water. Bring to boil. Add beef broth, 2 cups water, and gravy mix. Stir just until boiling and pour over meatballs. Bake at 350° for ½ hour to 45 minutes. Just before serving, add gravy mix to meet your family's desired gravy thickness.

MEDITERRANEAN SPAGHETTI

Mike Mueller
Former Governor's Staff

½ lb. lean ground beef
1-½ tsp. dried oregano
2 cups chopped onion
  (optional - if left out, increase
  to 1 lb. ground beef)
2 cloves garlic, minced
½ cup dry red wine
¼ cup water
¾ tsp. ground cinnamon
½ tsp. salt
⅛ tsp. ground nutmeg (optional)
⅛ tsp. pepper
1 (14.5-oz.) can stewed
  tomatoes, undrained

¼ cup all-purpose flour
1 cup crumbled peppercorn feta
  cheese
2 cups 1% lowfat milk
2 tbls. grated Parmesan cheese,
  divided
1 large egg
2 tbls. breadcrumbs, divided
4 cups cooked spaghetti (about
  8 oz. uncooked pasta)
cooking spray

Preheat oven to 375°. Heat a large nonstick skillet over medium-high heat. Add the first 4 ingredients and sauté 5 minutes. Add the wine and next 6 ingredients (wine through tomatoes). Bring mixture to a boil; reduce heat, and simmer 10 minutes until thick. Combine the flour, milk and nutmeg in a medium saucepan, and bring to a boil. Reduce heat and cook for 7 minutes or until thick, stirring constantly. Remove milk mixture from heat. Stir in feta cheese, 1 tbls. Parmesan cheese, and egg. Sprinkle 1 tbls. breadcrumbs in a 2-quart casserole coated with cooking spray. Place 2 cups spaghetti in casserole, and top with 2 cups beef mixture and 1 cup sauce. Repeat layers. Combine 1 tbls. Parmesan cheese and 1 tbls. breadcrumbs, and sprinkle over the casserole. Bake for 30 minutes or until golden brown. Let stand for 5 minutes. Yield: 6 servings about 1-⅓ cups each.

MEXICAN DISH

Luz Naasz
Residence Staff

1 bag Frito corn chips
2 cans chili beans
2 cans creamed corn
1 small can green chilies
1 onion

2 cans cream of mushroom
  soup
1 cup sour cream
shredded cheese

In glass pan, layer ingredients starting and ending with corn chips. Cook at 350° for about 30 minutes. Can also add hamburger if desired.

85104-07

MOM'S BAR-B-QUES

Rob Skjonsberg
Governor's Staff

1 lb. hamburger
1 small onion
salt & pepper to taste
1 can tomato soup

$\frac{1}{2}$ cup ketchup
1 tbls. prepared mustard
$\frac{3}{4}$ cup brown sugar
$\frac{1}{4}$ cup water - if dry, add more

Brown hamburger and onion in large frying pan. Add salt & pepper, tomato soup, ketchup, mustard, brown sugar, and water. Lower heat and simmer for 15 minutes. Serve on hamburger buns.

MOM'S MEATBALLS

First Lady Jean Rounds

5 lbs. hamburger
5 cups fine bread crumbs
1-$\frac{2}{3}$ cups milk
1 cup chopped onion
5 eggs

7-$\frac{1}{2}$ tsp. salt (she uses $\frac{1}{2}$
  regular salt and $\frac{1}{2}$ Lawry salt)
$\frac{5}{8}$ tsp. pepper
1-$\frac{1}{4}$ tsp. nutmeg
2-$\frac{1}{2}$ tsp. dry mustard

Pour milk over bread crumbs until soaked. Mix rest of ingredients. Shape into balls, and brown in 10 tablespoons butter. Remove and use the juice to make gravy.

Gravy:

5 tbls. flour
5 cups hot water
5 tsp. beef base or 5 bouillon
  cubes

1 pt. cream

Add flour, hot water, and beef base or bouillon cubes to the juice, then add the cream. Cook until thick.

MUSTARD-GRILLED CHICKEN BREASTS

Doneen Hollingsworth
Governor's Cabinet

1 medium clove garlic
1 medium onion
1/4 cup parsley sprigs
1/4 cup Dijon-style mustard
1/4 cup lemon juice
1/4 cup olive oil

1 tsp. Worcestershire sauce
4 whole boneless chicken
  breasts, skinned & halved
1/2 tsp. salt
1/2 tsp. pepper

In food processor, mince garlic. Add onion and parsley; coarsely chop. Add mustard, lemon juice, oil, Worcestershire, salt and pepper; purée. In shallow baking dish, cover chicken with mustard mixture. Refrigerate covered for at least 2 hours. Prepare outdoor grill for cooking. Drain chicken, reserving marinade. Grill chicken about 5 minutes on each side, or until cooked through. In saucepan, simmer marinade 5 minutes; spoon some mixture over each piece of chicken.

NEVER FAIL ROAST TURKEY

Connie Tveidt
Governor's Staff

Turkey, any size, any brand
1 cup table salt
1 cup mayonnaise

Your favorite stuffing recipe
One or two brown grocery
  sacks

Optional step: Soak turkey overnight covered in water with 1 cup salt dissolved well. I use a 5 gallon round beverage cooler with approximately 3 gallons of water. This is a perfect way to complete the thawing of your turkey. You can put the lid on the cooler to keep the bird cool and add ice cubes if necessary. Rinse turkey well inside and out and place in greased roaster pan. Add stuffing. Smear entire turkey generously with 1/2 - 1 cup mayonnaise. Slide pan into brown sack and staple closed. I use a large pan that holds a 22 lb. turkey so I use two brown bags-sliding the pan into one from each end. (No stapling required and you can use toothpicks to keep the bag away from the bird.) Bake at 325° - 20 minutes per pound.

85104-07

NEW YORK SAUSAGE POTPOURRI

Steve Pirner
Governor's Cabinet

2 1 lb. pkgs. plain bratwurst
1 1 lb. pkg. cheese bratwurst
1 1 lb. pkg. jumbo hot dogs
1 1 lb. pkg. cocktail sausages
water
barbeque sauce

1 (8-oz.) pkg. shredded pizza
  cheese
$1/2$ green pepper
$1/2$ red pepper
1-3 jalapeño peppers

Grill bratwurst and hot dogs on outside gas grill under low heat until just barely done; let rest and then cut into bite sized slices. Add just enough water to crock pot to cover bottom; add grilled brats, hot dogs, and cocktail sausages; stir until mixed. Lightly apply your favorite barbeque sauce to the top layer in the crock pot. Chop or slice the green pepper, red pepper, and jalapeño peppers; sprinkle half over the top layer in the crock pot; add cheese; and then sprinkle remaining half of peppers over the cheese. Do not stir; cover and cook on high until cocktail sausages are hot and cheese is melted. Serve in crock pot to retain brightly colored topping. Everything will become mixed as sausage potpourri is spooned out.

NORWEGIAN BEEF ROAST

Mrs. Sissel Boe

8 pitted prunes or other dried
  fruit
2 cups hot tea
1 3 - 5 lb. pot roast
1 tsp. salt and pepper
$1/4$ tsp. ginger

2 tbls. lard
2 onions, sliced
1 large clove of garlic, minced
$1/2$ cup water
3 - 4 tbls. flour

Preheat oven to 325°. Cover prunes with hot tea and allow to soften, and cool. Melt lard in large Dutch oven. Rub both sides of meat with salt, pepper, and ginger. Sear in Dutch oven until both sides are brown and crusty, over medium-high heat. Remove prunes from tea; keep liquid. Cut prunes in half. Remove Dutch oven from heat and put onions and garlic on top of meat. Add prunes around meat and $3/4$ cup of the tea mixture. Mix remaining tea with water. Put roast in covered Dutch oven in oven and bake at least 2 hours. If roast gets dry, add more of the tea mixture. When roast is tender, make gravy out of broth and flour; mix and cook. Vegetables may be added the last hour of cooking or serve with baked potato. (The cold roast makes wonderful sandwiches.)

Mother of Governor Nils Boe

Note: Recipe submitted by Carol Mashek, Minnehaha County Historical Society

ONE POT DINNER IN SLOW COOKER

Bonnie Untereiner Bjork
Former Governor's Cabinet

1 lb. ground beef
³/₄ lb. bacon
1 cup onion, chopped
1 can butter lima beans
1 cup ketchup
2 (15-oz.) cans pork and beans

1 tsp. salt
1 dash pepper
¹/₄ cup brown sugar
1 tbls. liquid smoke
3 tbls. white vinegar

Brown and drain ground beef, bacon and onions. Combine all the other ingredients in 5 quart crock pot. Stir. Cover and cook on low 4-9 hours.

OVEN "FRIED" CHICKEN

Jim Hagen
Former Governor's Cabinet

¹/₄ cup flour
¹/₄ cup whole-wheat flour
¹/₂ tsp. garlic powder
¹/₄ tsp. pepper
¹/₈ tsp. marjoram
¹/₂ tsp. salt

2 egg whites
¹/₂ cup low fat buttermilk
4-¹/₂ cup cornflakes, crushed
4 tbls. sesame seeds
2 - 3 lbs. chicken

Preheat oven to 375°. Line a large baking pan with aluminum foil. Place the first 6 ingredients in a bowl. Mix well. Beat together the egg whites and buttermilk in another bowl. Place the cornflakes and sesame seeds in another bowl. Mix. Dip the chicken, one piece at a time, into the flour mixture, then into the buttermilk and then into the cornflakes/sesame mixture, coat evenly. Place the chicken in the baking pan and bake for about an hour depending on size of the chicken.

85104-07

PEAS, NOODLES, AND HAMBURGER

Bob Mercer
Former Governor's Staff

½ can peas
½ box rotini pasta
1 lb. hamburger

little salt
little butter

Brown the hamburger. At the same time, boil the water and get the rotini done. It is optional whether you want to drain the grease from the meat, depending how much flavor and how much fat you want. After draining the rotini, mix the noodles with the hamburger in the frying pan on low heat; add about ⅛ stick of butter, drain and add the peas; mix it around and let it warm on low heat, salt to taste. It's awfully plain, but it reheats easily.

Note: What do you do with the other half of the can of peas? The answer is: You make a double batch!

PENNE WITH CHICKEN

Jason Dilges
Governor's Staff

4 chicken breasts
1 box penne pasta
1 pkg. fresh mushrooms, sliced
8 slices prosciutto ham (Italian bacon), chopped
1 qt. cream

½ cup chicken stock
⅔ cup white wine
dried basil
salt and pepper
2 tbls. olive oil

Cut chicken into pieces and begin cooking in oil. Mix white wine and chicken stock in separate bowl. Slowly add wine/stock mixture to chicken as it cooks. Salt and pepper to taste. Add prosciutto, when cooked, add mushrooms. Cover chicken mixture with basil. When mushrooms soften, turn heat off and let chicken absorb juice for about 10 minutes. Return heat and add cream and cook until bubbling. Add cooked pasta and cover again with basil. Cook, stirring occasionally, until cream thickens. Serve.

PEPPER STEAK

John Cooper
Former Governor's Cabinet

2 lbs. round steak
2 cups chopped onion (small)
2 cloves garlic, crushed
2 tbls. olive oil
1 tsp. salt
1/2 tsp. celery salt
1/4 tsp. pepper

3-1/3 cup pear shaped tomatoes
1 beef bouillon cube
1 large thinly sliced green
  pepper
2 tbls. Worcestershire sauce
2 tbls. cornstarch

Trim fat from steak. Cut into thin strips. Brown meat, onion, and garlic in oil in large skillet. Add salt, celery salt, pepper, tomatoes, bouillon cube, and green pepper. Cover and simmer 30 - 45 minutes or until meat is tender. Combine cornstarch and Worcestershire sauce. Stir into meat mixture. Cook until thickened. Serve with cooked rice. Servings: 6

PEPPER STEAK WITH RICE

Recipe Box at the
Governors Residence

3 cups hot, cooked rice
1 tbls. paprika
2 cloves garlic, crushed
1 cup sliced green onions, incl.
  tops
1/4 cup water - extra may be
  added if needed
2 large fresh tomatoes, cut in
  eighths

1 lb. lean round steak
2 tbls. butter
1-1/2 cup beef broth
2 green peppers, cut in strips
2 tbls. cornstarch
1/4 cup soy sauce

While rice is cooking (not Minute Rice), pound steak to 1/4 inch thickness. Cut into 1/4 inch strips. Sprinkle meat with paprika and allow to stand while preparing other ingredients. Using a large skillet, brown meat in butter. Add garlic and broth. Cover and simmer 30 minutes. Stir in onions and green peppers. Cover and cook 5 minutes more. Blend cornstarch, water and soy sauce. Stir into meat mixture. Cook, stirring until clear and thickened, about 2 minutes. Add tomatoes, stir gently. Serve over rice.

85104-07

PHEASANT CASSEROLE

Doneen Hollingsworth
Governor's Cabinet

4 pheasant breasts
3 beaten eggs
3 cups chicken broth
1 can mushroom soup
1 onion, chopped

1-1/2 cups grated American
  cheese
4 cups Ritz crackers, crushed
1 tsp. salt
1 tsp. pepper

Simmer pheasant in water until tender and remove meat from bones. Blend together all above ingredients. Add chopped pheasant. Place mixture in a 13 x 9 inch baking dish. Bake for 1 hour and 15 minutes at 350°.

Note: This is my mother, Marge Brekke's, recipe. It always brings good memories of family pheasant hunt gatherings.

PHEASANT CRUNCH

Tom Dravland
Governor's Cabinet

2 pheasants (deboned & cubed)
2 cans cream of mushroom
  soup
1 can creamy onion soup
1 small jar pimentos

1 can water chestnuts
2 - 3 cups chopped celery
1 can cashews
cooked rice or egg noodles

Brown pheasant cubes, mix soups, pimentos, celery, and water chestnuts. Combine browned pheasant and soup mixture. Cook in crock pot until celery is soft. Serve over cooked rice or egg noodles. Sprinkle with cashews.

PHEASANT KIEV

Jerry Hofer
Governor's Cabinet

2 pheasant breasts, halved
1/4 cup butter
4 slices Swiss cheese
4 slices bacon
2 (14-oz.) cans chicken broth
1/2 cup dry rice

1/2 cup bread crumbs
2 tbls. Parmesan cheese
1/2 tsp. salt
1/2 tsp. basil
1/2 tsp. oregano
1/2 tsp. garlic powder

In a bowl, combine bread crumbs, Parmesan cheese, salt, basil, oregano, and garlic powder. Place dry rice on bottom of 2 quart dish or 8 x 8 inch pan. Pound meat flat and brush with butter. Roll meat in bread crumbs mixture, wrap with cheese and bacon then place on top of rice. Pour chicken broth on rice. Bake uncovered at 325° for 1-2 hours.

PHEASANT POT PIE

Steve Pirner
Governor's Cabinet

1 whole pheasant
1 onion
2-4 stalks celery
3-4 carrots
2 chicken bouillon cubes

1 tsp. parsley flakes
1 pkg. frozen peas
salt, pepper, and Mrs. Dash
cornstarch for thickening

Thaw and cut up pheasant; soak overnight in cold water; drain. Place in large pot and cover with water, add chopped onion and celery, boil for an hour, add sliced carrots and boil another 30 minutes until meat is tender. Take meat out and de-bone. Add bouillon cubes, parsley flakes, peas, and seasoning to broth; add water if necessary to cover, bring to a boil, and thicken by stirring in cornstarch paste. Pour into a large casserole or roasting pan and mix in meat.

Biscuits:

2 cups flour
3 tsp. baking powder
$1/2$ tsp. salt

$1/3$ cup shortening
$3/4$ cup milk

Combine flour, baking powder and salt; cut in shortening until crumbly; stir in milk; knead dough on floured surface and roll out to $1/2$ inch thick; cut or form into round biscuits; place on top of mixture in casserole with biscuits just touching each other. Bake uncovered at 450° for 20 minutes or until biscuits are browned.

PHEASANT TORTILLAS

Donna Morlock
Former Governor's Staff

12 flour tortillas
4 pheasant breasts
2 cans cream of chicken soup
1 16 oz. tub sour cream
$3/4$ lb. shredded cheddar cheese

$3/4$ lb. shredded Monterey jack cheese
$1/2$ cup green onion tops, chopped
2 cans green chilies

Cook pheasant breasts and cut up into bite size pieces. Combine soups, chilies, onion tops, sour cream and $2/3$ cup of the cheese. Set aside 2 cups of this mixture. Add pheasant to remaining mixture. Put 3 tbls. on top of tortilla and roll up. Place in buttered, shallow pan. Spread remaining 2 cups of sauce over the top and sprinkle with rest of the cheese. Bake at 350° for 45 minutes uncovered.

85104-07

PHEASANT WITH LEEK AND PECAN STUFFING

Mary Farrar Turner

2 young pheasants, about 4 lbs. each, thoroughly defrosted if frozen
1 tbls. olive oil
1/2 cup finely chopped yellow onion
1 large carrot, peeled and finely chopped
2 tbls. plus 1 tsp. dried marjoram
1/4 tsp. dried thyme
1 bay leaf
6 sprigs Italian parsley
3 cups chicken stock or canned chicken broth

salt and freshly ground black pepper, to taste
12 tbls. sweet butter (1-1/2 sticks)
10 medium leeks, white part only, well cleaned and thinly sliced
6 cups crumbs from good quality white bread
2 cups toasted pecans
1 cup finely chopped Italian parsley
4 slices pancetta, 1 oz. each
1/2 cup heavy cream

Rinse the pheasants thoroughly inside and out and pat dry with paper towels. Chop the neck, heart, and gizzard (save the liver for another use). Heat the olive oil in a small sauce pan. Brown neck and giblets well in the oil, turning frequently. Add the onion, carrot, and 1 tsp. of the marjoram. Reduce heat to low and cook, covered, until vegetables are tender, about 25 minutes. Uncover, add the thyme, bay leaf, parsley, and the stock, and season with a pinch of salt and freshly ground black pepper. (Canned broth and pancetta are both quite salty; do not salt the sauce again until just before serving). Bring to a boil, reduce heat and simmer, partially covered for 45 minutes. Strain the stock, discarding the solids, and reserve. Melt the butter in a skillet. Stir in the sliced leeks and cook, covered, over low heat for 30 minutes, or until leeks are very tender. Toss leeks, including their butter, with bread crumbs, pecans, chopped parsley, and remaining 2 tbls. of marjoram. Season lightly with salt and generously with pepper. Toss again; if the stuffing seems dry, moisten it with 1/4 cup or so of the reserved broth. Preheat oven to 375°. Stuff the pheasants loosely and drape the breasts with the pancetta. Tie it in place with kitchen twine and set the pheasants in a shallow roasting pan. Set roasting pan in the middle of the oven and bake for about 1 hour, basting the pheasants occasionally with the fat and juices that accumulate. Pheasants are done when the thighs, pricked with a fork at their thickest, dribble clear yellow juices. Remove the pheasants from the pan, cover with foil, and keep warm. Pour excess fat out of roasting pan. Pour reserved stock and the heavy cream into pan and set over medium heat. Bring to a boil, reduce heat and simmer, stirring and scraping up any browned bits, until sauce is reduced by

(continued)

about one third. Taste and correct seasonings. Carve the pheasants and arrange the meat on a platter. Mound the stuffing in the center and drizzle meat and stuffing with a few spoonfuls of the sauce. Serve immediately, passing remaining sauce in a gravy boat. Makes 6-8 portions.

Daughter of Governor Frank Farrar

Note: Pancetta is Italian bacon, cured but not smoked, and quite fatty, available in Italian markets. If you cannot find it, substitute American breakfast bacon, the flavor will be different, but good.

PIGS

Dick Beringson
Former Governor's Cabinet

2 lbs. hamburger
1 lb. sausage (pork)
1 head cabbage
salt and pepper

garlic powder
sauerkraut
1 cup rice

Mix hamburger, sausage, seasoning and rice. Peel cabbage leaves (steam to make soft.) Roll mixture in cabbage leaves. Layer in pot with sauerkraut. Fill with water - bring to boil - simmer 2 - 3 hours.

POPPY SEED HAM BUNS

Dottie Howe
Former Governor's Cabinet

4 dozen tea buns, sliced open
2 sticks margarine
1/2 medium onion, chopped fine

5 tbls. poppy seed
6 tbls. horseradish mustard

Mix together margarine, onion, poppy seed, and horseradish mustard. Spread generously on buns, top with slice of ham and Swiss cheese. Wrap each dozen in foil. Bake at 375° for 15 minutes. Serve warm.

144

PORK CHOP 'N' POTATO BAKE

Nicole Finke

6 center cut pork chops
vegetable oil
seasoned salt
1 can cream of celery soup
¹/₂ cup milk
¹/₂ cup sour cream

¹/₄ tsp. pepper
¹/₂ tsp. salt
4 oz. shredded cheddar cheese
1 (6-oz.) can French fried onions
1 (24-oz.) pkg. O'Brien or hash
brown potatoes (thawed)

Brown pork chops in lightly greased skillet, sprinkle with seasoned salt; set aside. Combine soup, milk, sour cream, pepper, and salt. Stir into potatoes, stir in ¹/₂ cup cheese and ¹/₂ can onions. Spoon into 9 x 13 inch greased pan. Arrange pork chops over potatoes. Bake 350° covered 40 minutes. Top with remaining cheese and onions - bake uncovered 5 minutes.

Granddaughter of Governor Joe Foss

QUICK CHICKEN CASSEROLE

First Lady Florence Gubbrud

1 (5-oz.) can boneless chicken
or ³/₄ cup diced cooked
chicken
1 cup sliced celery
2 tsp. finely chopped onion
¹/₂ cup chopped walnut meats
1-¹/₂ cups cooked rice
1 can cream of chicken soup

¹/₂ tsp. salt
¹/₄ tsp. pepper
1 tbls. lemon juice
³/₄ cup mayonnaise
¹/₄ cup water
3 hard-cooked eggs, sliced
2 cups crushed potato chips

In a large bowl, combine diced chicken, celery, onion, nutmeats, rice, chicken soup, salt, pepper, and lemon juice. Mix mayonnaise with water and add to chicken mixture. Gently stir in hard-cooked egg slices. Turn mixture into greased 9" square pan; top with crushed potato chips. Bake in a very hot oven (450°) for 15 minutes or until mixture is bubbly. If you wish, you may assemble this casserole in the morning and then refrigerate it. When you do this, you must add additional 5 to 10 minutes to the baking time.

RANDY'S MEAT LOAF

Deb Bowman
Governor's Cabinet

2 eggs
½ level tsp. chili powder
1 dash pepper
1 dash onion powder
3-½ tbls. Heinz Catsup

12 saltines, finely crushed
¼ tsp. Lawry's Seasoned Salt
3 lbs. lean ground chuck (90% or higher)
1 med. onion

Beat eggs and thoroughly mix in catsup and spices. Crush crackers finely and mix in with egg-catsup mixture. Let stand for 15 minutes so crackers soak up mixture. Finely dice onion, add to meat, mix onion and meat with egg-cracker mixture. (A dough hook in a heavy-duty mixer works well). Mix thoroughly and press into large bread pan. Bake at 350° for 75-90 minutes.

ROAST DUCK

Joseph 'Frank' Foss

Duck
Salt and pepper to taste
1 carrot
1 stalk celery
¼ onion

1 (14-oz.) can beef broth
½ cup cooking sherry
2 tbls. flour
1 cup liquid
2 tbls. cooking sherry

Be sure duck is cleaned inside and out. Put carrot, celery, and onion inside cavity. Place duck breast side down in small roaster. Pour beef broth and sherry over duck. Cover and bake at 300° for 2 hours. Skim off fat. Turn duck over and roast for another hour or until tender and brown. Baste frequently and add more water if needed. Remove duck to platter. Add flour to 1 cup liquid for gravy. Add tbls. of sherry to gravy. Serve gravy over sliced duck.

Son of Governor Joe Foss - recipe submitted by Mary Joe Foss Finke

85104-07

ROAST DUCK

First Lady June Foss

Clean duck thoroughly - cut off tail and skin like skin on joint of leg. Be certain all fuzz and pin feathers or wax is removed. Singe and wash good if necessary. Be sure inside is cleaned good. Salt and pepper inside and out. Put in side cavity - 1 carrot or ½ cup depending on size of duck, celery leaves, or celery, 1 quarter onion. Place breast side down in small roaster or 2 or 3 ducks in larger roaster. Pour over duck 1 can consomme or beef bullion and ½ can cooking sherry. Cover and bake at 300° for 2 hours. If fat duck or if it smells too fishy throw out the fat and bullion and add more. Most ducks you can just skim off fat if they smell good. If quite tender by now, turn over and leave off cover to roast for another hour or until tender and brown. Baste frequently and add more water if necessary. Remove duck to platter and add flour -water mixture 2 tbls. flour to 1 cup liquid for gravy - Add 2 tbls. sherry to gravy. Serve gravy over sliced duck.

Note: Recipe submitted by Mary Joe Foss Finke. June Foss, my mother, wrote this recipe out and it was passed down to her children. I condensed it somewhat but enjoy reading her instructions!

ROAST TURKEY

Jean Blow
Governor's Staff

8-10 lb. turkey
dressing (your own recipe)

½ to 1 stick butter
1 can Swanson's chicken broth

Make your own dressing recipe and stuff turkey. Roast turkey as you ordinarily do, including the dressing. When turkey is done (but not over-done), take dressing out, and transfer to a freezer proof dish, let turkey cool about 15 minutes and carve. In a 9 x 12 inch oblong pan that will fit into your freezer and oven, layer sliced white meat on one side of the pan, and dark meat on the other side, putting bits of butter between the layers. Use ½ to 1 stick of butter according to the size of your turkey, and your taste. One half stick is about right for a 10 lb. turkey. Poor one can of Swanson's Chicken Broth over the turkey, cover with foil, cool, and freeze. The day you are going to serve the turkey, put in the oven with foil on at 350° until hot, about an hour or more. Serves 10.

SALMON LOAF

*Recipe Box at the
Governors Residence*

1 14-16 oz. can salmon
½ cup diced celery
½ cup diced onion
¼ cup butter or margarine
¼ cup salmon liquid
½ cup soft bread cubes

¼-½ tsp. salt
¼ tsp. pepper
½ tsp. Accent
¼-½ tsp. dried dill weed
1 tbls. lemon juice
1 egg, slightly beaten

Drain salmon, reserve liquid, remove skin, flake. Fry celery and onions in butter until tender, but not brown. Add to salmon. Add remaining ingredients, mix well. Shape into loaf in a well greased loaf pan. Bake at 350° until slightly browned - about 1 hour.

Note: Serve with a rich, colorful sauce - we use shredded cheddar cheese. This is out of the world salmon loaf - it was used for Lincoln Day 1994.

SALMON PATTIES

Lt. Gov. Dennis Daugaard

2 (14-¾-oz.) cans pink salmon
1 cup uncooked oatmeal
2 eggs
1 egg white
1 tbls. mustard

½ cup minced onions
½ cup milk
½ cup minced celery
2 tbls. pickle relish

Drain salmon. Combine all ingredients. Makes 6 - 8 patties. Pan fry in olive oil, turning once, for 15 minutes at 350°.

SAUSAGE & PASTA STIR FRY

First Lady Jean Rounds

¼ cup chopped onion
¼ cup chopped green pepper
½ lb. mushrooms, sliced
2 cups fresh carrots and
  broccoli, chopped
2 tsp. garlic powder

3 tsp. oregano leaves
3 tbls. margarine
1 1 lb. pkg. Hillshire Farm
  Sausage
½ cup Parmesan cheese

Stir fry onion, green pepper, mushrooms, carrots, broccoli, garlic powder, and oregano leaves in 3 tbls. margarine until crisp-tender. Add the Hillshire Farm sausage (bite-sized pieces). Heat through. Stir in ½ cup Parmesan cheese. Serve over buttered pasta with additional Parmesan cheese. Makes 6-8 servings.

85104-07

SAUTÉED SAND CREEK TROUT

Governor Joe Foss

1 cup cornstarch
½ cup whole-wheat flour
½ cup yellow cornmeal

1 tsp. Spike
1 tsp. paprika
1 tsp. lemon pepper

After thoroughly cleaning trout, set in refrigerator 6 hours to firm. Filet, dry, and dip in mixture of above ingredients. Sauté in peanut oil until done.

SHRIMP BISQUE

Patti de Hueck Clodfelter
Former Governor's Cabinet

6 tbls. butter
4 tbls. finely chopped green
  pepper
4 tbls. chopped onion
1 scallion chopped
2 tbls. chopped fresh parsley
1½ cup sliced mushrooms
¼ cup finely chopped carrots
2 tbls. flour

1 cup milk
1 tsp. salt
⅛ tsp. white pepper
dash Tabasco sauce
1-½ cups half & half
1-½ cups cooked shrimp
½ cup chopped cooked bacon
3 tbls. dry sherry (optional)

Melt 4 tbls. butter in skillet. Add green pepper, onion, scallion, parsley, mushrooms, carrots and sauté until soft. In large saucepan, heat remaining 2 tbls. butter; stir in flour. Add milk, cook, stirring until thick and smooth. Stir in salt, pepper, and Tabasco. Add sautéed vegetables and half and half. Bring to boil, stirring, reduce heat, add shrimp and bacon; simmer uncovered 5 minutes. Just before serving add sherry.

SHRIMP CREOLE

Dottie Howe
Former Governor's Cabinet

**3 lbs. raw, shelled, deveined
  shrimp**

Cook, drain, and set aside.

Creole Sauce:

¼ **cup salad oil**
¾ **cup chopped onion**
½ **cup chopped celery**
½ **cup chopped carrots**
1 **clove garlic, crushed**
2 **cans (1 lb.) tomatoes**

2 **tsp. salt**
½ **tsp. curry powder**
½ **tsp. dried basil leaves**
¼ **tsp. pepper**
¼ **cup chopped parsley**

Stir onion, celery, carrots, and garlic in hot oil 10 min. Stir in tomatoes, salt, curry powder, basil, and pepper. Simmer 15 minutes.

Savory Rice:

2 **chicken bouillon cubes**
2 **tbls. salad oil**
2 **tsp. salt**

1 **tbls. minced onion**
2 **cups converted long grain
  white rice**

Bring to boil, reduce heat to low, cook covered until rice is tender and all liquid absorbed 25 - 30 minutes. Cut shrimp into bite size pieces, add Creole sauce to rice along with the shrimp. Mix well, place into large bowl. Serves 10 - 12.

SHRIMP CREOLE

*Recipe Box at the
Governors Residence*

½ **cup onion, chopped**
½ **cup celery, chopped**
1 **clove garlic, minced**
3 **tbls. shortening**
1 **(16-oz.) can tomatoes**
1 **(8-oz.) can tomato sauce**
1-½ **tsp. salt**
1 **tsp. sugar**

1 **tbls. Worcestershire sauce**
½-1 **tsp. chili powder**
1 **dash bottled hot pepper sauce**
2 **tsp. cornstarch**
1 **(12-oz.) pkg. frozen shelled
  shrimp, thawed**
½ **cup green pepper, chopped**

In skillet, cook onion, celery, and garlic in shortening until tender but not brown. Add tomatoes, tomato sauce, salt, sugar, Worcestershire sauce, chili powder and hot pepper sauce. Simmer uncovered 4 minutes. Mix cornstarch with 1 tbls. cold water, stir into sauce. Cook and stir till thickened and bubbly. Add shrimp and green pepper. Cover, simmer 5 minutes. Serve over rice. Serves 6. Double recipe, as it doesn't make much.

SHRIMP NEWBURG

Sandra Zinter
Governor's Cabinet

1 lb. frozen shrimp, thawed
2 tbls. butter, melted
1¾ tbls. flour
1 cup half & half

3 tbls. catsup
½ tbls. Worcestershire sauce
salt to taste

Stir flour into melted butter and add half and half to make a white sauce. Cook for 2 minutes or until the sauce has thickened. Then add the catsup, Worcestershire sauce, and salt. Do not boil. Add shrimp to the sauce and warm through. Serve over rice.

SLOPPY JOE'S

Susan Walker
Former Governor's Cabinet

2 lbs. ground beef
1 cup chopped onion
½ cup chopped green pepper
2 tbls. white vinegar
3 tsp. Worcestershire sauce

¼ tsp. black pepper
½ cup chopped celery
½ cup catsup
1 tbls. sugar
2 (10¾-oz.) cans tomato soup

In deep skillet, brown hamburger, onions, and green pepper over medium heat until done (or meat shows little or no pink). Drain excess fat. Add the vinegar, Worcestershire sauce, celery, catsup, sugar, pepper, and tomato soup. Stir and mix well. Reduce heat and simmer for 20 minutes. Salt to taste. Serve with warm hamburger buns.

Note: This easy and tasty recipe has been in my husband's family for many years and is a comfort food favorite of kids and adults alike! This is the double recipe and can be cut in half for 2-4 servings.

SOUPY CHOPPED MEAT

Otto Doll
Governor's Cabinet

1 lb. chopped meat
1 large onion
3 - 4 cups beef bouillon

1 large bag noodles, macaroni
or rice

Brown meat and drain off excess fat. Add chopped onions and brown. Add beef bouillon and simmer until flavors blend. Serve over cooked noodles, macaroni, or rice.

SOUR CREAM ENCHILADAS

Karl Adam

2 lb. hamburger
1 small chopped onion
1 small can green chilies
1 pkg. taco seasoning

small tortilla shells
grated cheese
(12-oz.) container sour cream
1 can cream of chicken soup

Brown hamburger, onions and green chilies. Drain and add taco seasoning mix. Mix sour cream and soup and warm together. Pour ¹/₂ of sour cream mixture on bottom of greased 9 x 13 inch baking pan. Fill shells with meat mixture and roll up. Lay filled shells on top of sour cream mixture in pan. Pour remaining sour cream mixture over top and cover with grated cheese. Bake at 350° for 20 minutes. Serve with salsa, lettuce and additional sour cream if desired.

Grandson of Governor George T. Mickelson and Nephew of Governor George S. Mickelson

ST. LOUIS EASY LASAGNA

Steve Wegman
Former Governor's Staff

1 lb. ground beef
3-¹/₂ cups (32 oz. jar) spaghetti sauce
1-¹/₂ cups water
2 cups (15 oz. container) ricotta or small curd cottage cheese
3 cups (12 oz.) shredded Mozzarella or Monterey Jack cheese

¹/₂ cup grated Parmesan cheese
2 eggs
¹/₄ cup chopped parsley
1 tsp. salt
¹/₄ tsp. pepper
1 (8-oz.) pkg. lasagna noodles, uncooked

Brown beef in 3-quart saucepan; drain off excess fat. Add sauce and water; simmer about 10 minutes. In a separate bowl, combine remaining ingredients, except lasagna noodles, for the filling. Pour about 1 cup sauce on bottom of 9 x 13 inch baking pan. Layer 3 pieces of uncooked lasagna over sauce. (Lasagna will expand to fill empty spaces). Cover with about 1-¹/₂ cups sauce. Spread ¹/₂ of cheese filling over sauce. Repeat layers of lasagna, sauce and cheese filling. Top with layer of lasagna and remaining sauce. Cover with aluminum foil and refrigerate overnight. Bake at 350° for 55-60 minutes. Remove foil; bake about 10 minutes longer. Allow to stand about 10 minutes before cutting for easier handling. Makes 8-10 servings.

85104-07

STUFFED CABBAGE ROLLS

Lt. Gov. James Abdnor

1 head cabbage (2 lbs.)
1 lb. meat (lamb or beef) cut
  into ½" or smaller cubes, or
  ground
1 cup rice
½ tsp. cinnamon

½ tsp. salt
pepper to taste
3 tbls. butter, melted
1 #2 can whole tomatoes
juice of ½ lemon

Core the center of the cabbage and insert the whole head in boiling water to wilt leaves. Drain and separate leaves. Mix meat and rice which has been soaked in cold water and drained. Add cinnamon, salt, pepper, and butter. Roll about 1 tbls. meat and rice mixture in half a leaf of cabbage. Line a saucepan with 2-3 leaves. Add cabbage rolls, arranging evenly. Add entire can of tomatoes and enough water to cover the rolls completely. Add the juice of lemon. Bring to a boil and lower heat to medium and cook for approximately 45 minutes or until rice is tender.

Note: This is my Mother's recipe, and a favorite dish for our family.

SWISS STEAK

Robert Duxbury
Former Governor's Cabinet

2-½ lbs. round steak
1 tsp. nutmeg
2 - 3 tbls. cooking oil
¾ cup flour

salt and pepper to taste
1 (10¾-oz.) can tomato soup
¼ cup brown sugar
1 large onion, sliced

Cut meat into 10 or 12 serving-size pieces. Pound meat to tenderize. Mix flour and nutmeg in a brown paper sack, add meat and shake. Heat oil in pan and brown meat. Season to taste. Spread about ⅓ of soup in bottom of 2 quart baking dish. Add sugar to remaining soup in can and mix. Layer meat, sliced onion, and sauce into dish. Cover and bake 1-½ hours at 350°.

TATOR TOT HOT DISH

Melanie Vedvei

2 lbs. hamburger
1 can cream of mushroom soup
1 can cream of chicken soup
1-½ cups milk

1 pkg. frozen mixed vegetables
  (thawed)
1 pkg. tator tots

Brown hamburger and season as desired. Put in bottom of a greased 9 x 13 inch pan. Next top with vegetables. Mix the soups and milk together and pour over top. Cover with tator tots. Bake 1 hour at 350°.

Niece of Governor M. Michael Rounds

THREE PEPPER BEEF KABOBS

*Recipe Box at the
Governors Residence*

1 boneless beef top sirloin
  steak, cut 1" thick
1 medium green, red or yellow
  bell pepper, cut into 1" pieces

8 large mushrooms

Cut beef steak into 1 inch pieces.

Marinade:

2 tbls. vegetable oil
1 tbls. fresh lemon juice
1 tbls. water
2 tsp. Dijon-style mustard

1 tsp. honey
½ tsp. dried oregano leaves
¼ tsp. pepper

In large bowl, whisk together marinade ingredients; add beef, bell pepper, and mushrooms, tossing to coat. Alternately thread pieces of beef, bell pepper, and mushrooms on each of four 12-inch metal skewers. Place kabobs on rack in broiler pan so surface of meat is 3-4 inches from heat. Broil 8-10 minutes for medium rare to medium doneness, turning occasionally. Season with salt if desired. Makes 4 servings.

TUNA IN THE BUN

*Dr. James Hansen
Former Governor's Cabinet*

1 can tuna
½ cup salad dressing (Miracle
  Whip)
3 hard-cooked eggs, diced

½ cup diced cheese (Velveeta)
3 tbls. diced celery
3 tbls. diced onion
3 tbls. diced green pepper

Mix together and put in buttered buns. Wrap each in foil. Warm in 275° oven for about 30 minutes. Filling for 8 large buns or 10 - 12 medium buns.

85104-07

VENISON ROAST

Steve Wegman
Former Governor's Staff

1 2-5 lb. venison roast
6 - 10 carrots, cleaned and cut in pieces
4 - 8 potatoes, peeled and cut in pieces
4 - 6 parsnips, cleaned and cut in pieces
2 large onions, peeled and quartered
salt and pepper
Lawry's seasoning

Brown roast on all sides, either under broiler or on stove top with small amount of oil in pan. Place browned roast in medium roaster and season well with salt, pepper and Lawry's seasoning. Add onions and carrots and 1 inch of water in pan. Cover and bake at 350° for 2-3 hours (depends on size of roast). About 45 minutes to 1 hour before roast is done, add potatoes and parsnips. Cover and bake at 350° until done.

WILD RICE HOT DISH

Dick Beringson
Former Governor's Cabinet

veal and pork steak
1 cup celery
¾ cup onions
mushrooms
2 cans chicken broth
2 cans mushroom soup
1 cup wild rice

Brown meat, celery, and onions - thin mushroom soup with chicken broth - add to meat- add mushrooms, well washed rice. Bake in covered casserole (buttered) for 1 hour. Remove cover, sprinkle with bread crumbs - dot with butter and brown.

YANKEE DOODLE CASSEROLE

Luz Naasz
Residence Staff

1-½ cup celery, chopped
½ cup green pepper, chopped
¾ cup onion, chopped
½ tsp. garlic
¼ cup oil
1 can olives, halved
2 tsp. salt
2 cups canned tomatoes
2 cups string beans
3 cups cooked macaroni or noodles
¾ cup Velveeta Cheese
1 can cream of mushroom soup

Simmer celery, green pepper, onion, garlic, and oil together until tender, then add salt, canned tomatoes, string beans, cooked macaroni or noodles, Velveeta Cheese, and cream of mushroom soup. Mix and put in greased casserole dish. Bake at 350° for 30 minutes.

Brunches & Breakfasts

BAKED EGGS

Dick Beringson
Governor's Cabinet

6 cups cubed bread
1 lb. cubed Velveeta cheese
1/2 green pepper, chopped
3/4 cup fresh mushrooms or one
   4 oz. can mushrooms
4 cups cubed ham
6 tbls. flour

1 1/2 tsp. dry mustard, optional
6 tbls. melted butter
6 cups milk
8 eggs, beaten
few drops Tabasco sauce,
   optional

Lightly grease a 9 x 13 inch pan. Layer 1/2 bread, cheese, green pepper, and ham. Combine flour and mustard; sprinkle on top. Drizzle with melted butter. Repeat layers. Beat milk, eggs, and Tabasco sauce together, pour over layers. Refrigerate overnight. Bake at 350° for 1 hour or until done. Serves 12 to 15 people.

BAKED FRENCH TOAST

Helen Vedvei

1 loaf French bread sliced
1 cup brown sugar
1/2 cup butter
2 tsp. corn syrup

6 eggs
2 cups milk
1-1/2 tsp. vanilla

Grease 9 x 13 inch pan. Cook sugar, syrup, and butter until syrupy. Pour into pan. Arrange bread in pan. Beat eggs, milk, and vanilla. Pour over bread, cover and refrigerate overnight. Bake uncovered at 325° for 30 to 40 minutes. To serve, flip with caramel sauce on top.

Mother of First Lady Jean Rounds

85104-07

BISCUITS AND CHOCOLATE GRAVY

DJ Holt

Chocolate Gravy:

1 cup sugar
3 tbls. cocoa
4 tbls. flour

1 tsp. salt
2 cups milk

Mix together all ingredients in sauce pan - add milk. Stir real well. Place on medium heat and stir until thickens. Serve on hot biscuits.

Biscuits:

4 cups flour
2 tbls. baking powder
1 tsp. salt

1 stick butter
2 cups milk

Mix flour, baking powder, and salt real good. Add butter using pastry knife or fork. It will look like little peas when mixed good. Add milk - little at a time until sticky. Knead it a few times and roll out and cut with glass or biscuit cutter. Place on ungreased cookie sheet and bake at 425° for 12 minutes or until golden brown.

Nephew of First Lady Jean Rounds

BREAKFAST BURRITO

Deb Hall
Former Governor's Staff

1 lb. bacon, chopped
½ bag frozen hash browns
1-½ dozen eggs, scrambled

1 can green chilies (optional)
1 lb. shredded cheese
1 - 2 pkgs. flour tortillas

Prepare all. Cool all. Mix bacon, hash browns, eggs, and green chilies in a large bowl. Place tortilla on flat surface. Drop ½ cup of mixture onto tortilla. Drop about 3 tbls. of cheese. Drop another ½ cup of mixture on top of cheese. (Put the cheese in the middle so it doesn't get overcooked when microwaved). You can make them larger or smaller depending on the size of the tortilla. Fold ends in and roll up. Place each burrito on a sheet of Saran Wrap and roll it up. Freeze on a flat surface (cookie sheet). You can make up you own way of preparing them, this is just what I found works best.

BREAKFAST CASSEROLE

Doreen Kayser
Former Governor's Staff

1 lb. spicy pork sausage, fried
  crisp
1 (12-14-oz.) pkg. frozen
  shredded hash browns, thawed
2 cups shredded cheddar
  cheese

8 eggs, beaten
2-1/2 cups milk
1 can cream of mushroom soup
1 cup sour cream
salt and pepper to taste

In a 9 x 13 inch pan, spread thawed hash browns on bottom; season
with salt and pepper; spread crumbled sausage over hash browns; mix
together eggs and milk, pour mixture over; sprinkle 1-1/2 cups of the
shredded cheese; mix together cream of mushroom soup and sour
cream, spread mixture on top; season with salt and pepper; sprinkle
remaining cheese on top. Bake for 1 hour at 350°.

Note: May make the night before and refrigerate. Bake 1-1/2 hours at
350°. I have made this in the crock pot and cooked on low all night for
an early morning breakfast.

BREAKFAST EGG CASSEROLE

First Lady Jean Rounds

6 cups French bread, cubed
6 cups cooked ham, cubed
1 lb. grated cheddar cheese
6 tbls. flour

2 tbls. dry mustard
6 cups milk
8 eggs

In 9 x 13 inch pan, layer 1/2 bread, ham, cheese. Combine flour and
mustard, sprinkle 1/2 over layer; drizzle with 2 tbls. melted butter. Repeat
layer, beat eggs and milk. Pour over layers in pan. Cover, refrigerate
overnight. Bake uncovered at 350° for 1 hour.

BREAKFAST EGG CASSEROLE

Dr. James Hansen
Former Governor's Cabinet

6 cups shredded hash browns
  (1 bag)
2 cups shredded cheese
2 cups diced ham (or bacon)

8 eggs
2 cans evaporated milk
salt and pepper to taste

Grease 9 x 13 inch baking dish. Arrange potatoes evenly in the bottom
of the dish. Sprinkle with cheese and ham. Combine the eggs, milk,
salt, and pepper and then pour over top of casserole. (The dish can be
covered and refrigerated at this point.) Bake uncovered at 350° for
40-45 minutes (or 55-60 minutes if made ahead and chilled) OR until
center appears set. Let stand for 5 minutes before serving.

85104-07

BREAKFAST PIZZA

Harla Jessop
Former Governor's Staff

1 lb. sausage or bacon,
  browned
1 pkg. crescent rolls
1 cup frozen hash browns,
  thawed
1 cup shredded cheddar cheese

5 eggs, slightly beaten
$1/4$ cup milk
$1/4$ tsp. pepper
$1/2$ tsp. salt
2 tbls. Parmesan cheese

Separate crescent rolls into 8 triangles and press into ungreased 12 inch round pizza pan. You can double recipe and place in larger pan. Spoon on sausage or bacon and hash browns. Top with cheese. Mix together eggs, milk, salt and pepper. Pour over crust. Sprinkle with Parmesan cheese. Bake at 375° for 30 minutes.

BRUNCH CASSEROLE

Karon Schaack
Former Governor's Cabinet

3 cups frozen shredded hash
  brown potatoes
$3/4$ cup (3 oz.) shredded
  Monterey Jack cheese with
  jalapeño peppers (or shredded
  cheddar cheese)
1 cup diced fully cooked ham or
  Canadian bacon

$1/4$ cup sliced green onions
4 beaten eggs (or 1 cup frozen
  egg substitute)
1 (12-oz.) can (1-$1/2$ cup)
  evaporated milk (or evaporated
  skim milk)
$1/4$ tsp. pepper
$1/8$ tsp. salt

Grease a 2-qt square casserole. Arrange potatoes evenly in the bottom of the dish. Sprinkle with cheese, ham, and green onion. In a medium mixing bowl, combine eggs, milk, pepper, and salt. Pour egg mixture evenly over potato mixture in casserole. The dish may be covered and refrigerated at this point for several hours or overnight. Bake, uncovered, in a 350° oven for 55-60 minutes (if you made it ahead and chilled it), until center appears set. Remove from oven and let stand 5 minutes before serving. Makes 6 servings max. I like to add more cheese on top during the last 5-10 minutes of baking.

BRUNCH DISH

Recipe Box at the
Governors Residence

1 stick margarine
1 (32-oz.) bag frozen shredded
  hash browns
2 cups shredded cheddar
  cheese

2 cups chopped ham
1 dozen eggs
1 cup milk
salt and pepper to taste

Melt the margarine in 9 x 13 inch prepared pan. Layer the hash browns, cheese, and ham - start and end with the hash browns. Beat the eggs, milk, salt, and pepper; pour over the layered ingredients in pan and refrigerate over night. Bake at 350° for 1 hour; keep checking, dish could cook faster. Serves 12 or more.

CHERRY COFFEE CAKE BARS

Deb Hall
Former Governor's Staff

1 cup butter
1-1/2 cups sugar
4 eggs, beaten
1-1/2 tsp. baking powder

1 tsp. vanilla
1/2 tsp. salt
3 cups flour
1 can pie filling

Cream butter and sugar. Add eggs one at a time and mix in. Blend in the rest of the ingredients. Pour 2/3 of the batter in a 10 x 15 inch pan. Spread pie filling on top of batter. Spread remaining batter on top of filling (plop by spoonful). Bake 25-30 minutes at 350°.

Note: I have made this with apple, blueberry, cherry, and peach pie filling.

EASY BREAKFAST ROLLS

Bonnie Untereiner Bjork
Former Governor's Cabinet

3 pkgs. buttermilk biscuits
cinnamon
sugar
1/2 cup butter or margarine, soft
  or melted

1/2 cup brown sugar
1/2 cup melted vanilla ice cream

Dip biscuits in cinnamon and sugar, and line up in Bundt pan so it makes a round ring. Combine butter or margarine, brown sugar and ice cream. Cover the biscuits with this mixture. Bake 25 minutes at 350°. Turn onto waxed paper as soon as you remove from oven.

85104-07

EGG AND BACON BREAKFAST CASSEROLE

Craig Burma

1 lb. bacon, cooked and crumbled or 1 pkg. Hormel cooked bacon bits
1/2 cup melted butter
4 cups unseasoned croutons
8 eggs

2 cups sharp grated cheddar cheese
1/2 tsp. dry mustard
1 tsp. salt
2 tbls. onion flakes
3 cups milk

Preheat oven to 325°. Melt butter in bottom of 9 x 13 inch pan in oven. Mix croutons into butter and spread evenly over bottom of pan. Sprinkle with cheese. Mix eggs, milk, mustard, salt and onion flakes and pour over croutons. Sprinkle with bacon. Bake one hour. Let stand for 10 minutes before cutting.

Grandson of Governor Walter Dale Miller

EGGS MORNAY

First Lady Patricia Miller

1 lb. bacon

Cook bacon over low heat until grease is rendered; do not brown. Drain and chop coarsely. Set aside.

Mornay Sauce:

$\frac{1}{2}$ **cup butter**
1 cup all-purpose flour
6 cups milk, scalded

1-$\frac{1}{2}$ cups fresh Parmesan cheese, grated
$\frac{1}{2}$ **cup Swiss cheese, grated**

Melt butter, whisk in flour. Cook over low heat until smooth and bubbly, stirring constantly. Remove from heat and add half of milk, whisking until smooth. Return to medium heat and add remaining milk. Cook and whisk constantly until smooth and thick. Add cheeses and stir until melted. Set aside.

Eggs:

24 eggs
1 cup whipping cream
2 tsp. salt
$\frac{1}{2}$ **tsp. freshly ground pepper**
1 tsp. Herbs De Provence, crumbled

$\frac{3}{4}$ **cup butter (reserve $\frac{1}{4}$ cup)**
8 - 10 green onions, chopped
1 lb. fresh mushrooms, sliced

Combine eggs, cream, salt, pepper and herbs. Beat until smooth. Set aside. Melt $\frac{1}{2}$ cup butter in large skillet, add onions and mushrooms. Sauté slowly until all moisture is evaporated, about 5 minutes. Remove from skillet. Add remaining $\frac{1}{4}$ cup butter to skillet and melt. Stir in egg mixture. Cook over moderate heat stirring until soft mass forms. Do not overcook. Add mushroom mixture and stir gently. Remove from heat. Brush 10 x 14 or 11 x 15 inch casserole dish with melted butter and layer ingredients as follows: $\frac{1}{3}$ Mornay sauce; $\frac{1}{2}$ egg mixture; $\frac{1}{2}$ bacon; $\frac{1}{3}$ Mornay sauce; $\frac{1}{2}$ egg mixture; $\frac{1}{2}$ bacon; $\frac{1}{3}$ Mornay sauce. Cover and refrigerate overnight. Bring casserole to room temperature. Preheat oven to 300°. Bake, uncovered, 1 hour or until thoroughly heated. Sprinkle with Parmesan cheese, chives and parsley.

85104-07

FANCY EGGS

Helen Vedvei

1-¹/₂-2 lbs. sausage, browned
12 eggs
1 (8-oz.) pkg. grated cheddar
cheese

¹/₂ pt. whipping cream

Butter sides and bottom of a 9 x 13 inch pan. Add sausage and pour beaten eggs over sausage. Add salt and pepper to taste. Sprinkle half of cheese over eggs. Pour cream over the cheese, and then add the remaining cheese. Cover and refrigerate 10 hours or more. Bake uncovered 30 to 40 minutes at 350°.

Mother of First Lady Jean Rounds

HAM AND EGG SOUFFLÉ

Darrell Butterwick
Former Governor's Cabinet

8 slices white bread, de-crusted
1 lb. Velveeta Cheese, sliced
¹/₂ lb. sliced turkey or ham

6 eggs, beaten
3 cups milk

In a greased 9 x 13 inch casserole, place de-crusted bread slices lying flat, butter bread slices on top, cover with cheese slices, then with choice of meat slices; top with more cheese slices. Set aside. In mixing bowl mix the 6 beaten eggs and milk, stir well and pour carefully over bread and cheese casserole. Cover and refrigerate overnight. Bake at 325° for 1 hour.

HOLIDAY MORNING FRENCH TOAST

Linda Fridley
Governor's Staff

1 cup brown sugar
¹/₂ cup dried cranberries
¹/₂ cup butter, melted
1 loaf French bread, 1" slices
3 tsp. ground cinnamon, divided

3 tart apples (granny smith)
1-¹/₂ cups milk
6 large eggs
1 tbls. vanilla

Combine brown sugar, butter, and 1 tsp. cinnamon in 13 x 9 inch dish. Add apples and cranberries; toss to coat well. Spread apple mixture evenly over bottom of dish. Arrange slices of bread on top. Mix eggs, milk, vanilla, and remaining 2 tsp. cinnamon until well blended. Pour mixture over bread, soaking bread completely. Cover and refrigerate 4-24 hours. Bake covered with foil, in preheated 375° oven for 40 minutes. Uncover and bake for 15 minutes. Remove from oven and let stand 5 minutes. Serve warm.

MAKE-AHEAD EGG BRUNCH DISH

Patricia Van Gerpen
Former Governor's Cabinet

6 slices of white bread
8 oz. mushrooms, washed and
  sliced
1/2 cup sliced pimento-stuffed
  olives
3/4 lb. Swiss and Cheddar
  cheese, grated

4 eggs, beaten
2 cup milk
1/2 tsp. dry mustard
1/4 tsp. salt

Break the bread into pieces about the size of a quarter. Place half the bread in a buttered 3-qt casserole. Over this, top in layers: mushrooms, olives and the grated cheese. Spread the remaining bread pieces over the top. Beat the eggs, add milk and seasonings. Pour the egg mixture over the top of the bread mixture. Refrigerate overnight. Bake uncovered for one hour at 350°. Let stand about 10 minutes before serving.

MAKE-AHEAD EGGS BENEDICT

Lavon Mickelson Meyers

8 eggs
8 thin slices of Canadian bacon

4 English muffins, split and
  toasted

Poach eggs about 3 minutes each, and place on English muffin with bacon. Place in 13" x 9" baking dish.

Sauce:

1/4 cup butter
1/4 cup flour
1 tsp. paprika
1/8 tsp. nutmeg

2 cups milk
2 cups shredded Swiss cheese
1/2 cup dry white wine

Melt butter in sauce pan, stir in flour, paprika, and nutmeg. Slowly stir in milk, stirring and cooking until thick and bubbly. Stir in cheese until melted. Gradually stir in wine. Spoon over eggs; cover and refrigerate. To serve, bake uncovered 20 - 25 minutes until heated through.

Daughter of Governor George T. Mickelson and Sister of Governor George S. Mickelson

85104-07

MONICA'S GOOD BISCUITS

Recipe Box at the
Governors Residence

1 can Hungry Jack Biscuits
1 cup grated Swiss cheese
1/4 cup mayonnaise

4-6 slices bacon, fried crisp and
  crumbled

Put biscuits in muffin tin, push down in the middle of biscuit to make a hole in the center. Combine cheese, mayonnaise, and bacon and spoon into hole in the center of biscuits. Bake at 400° for 10 minutes.

NANCY'S BREAKFAST CASSEROLE

R. Van Johnson
Former Governor's Cabinet

2 lbs. frozen hash browns
1 lb. shredded cheddar cheese
2 lb. sausage - links or ground
  (you may use bacon or ham)
5 eggs
3-1/4 cups milk, divided

3/4 tsp. dry mustard
2 cans mushrooms
1/4-1/2 cup chopped onion
salt and pepper
cream of mushroom soup

Grease a 9 x 13 inch pan. Spread hash browns on bottom of pan. Cover hash browns with cheese. Then layer with browned sausage, or any meat. Beat eggs with fork. Mix with eggs: 2-1/2 cups milk, mustard, mushrooms, onions, salt and pepper. Pour egg mixture over meat. Cover and refrigerate overnight. Mix soup and 3/4 cup milk and pour over the top of casserole. Bake covered for 1 hour at 350°. Uncover and bake 1/2 hour more.

PANCAKES

Patti Edman
Former Governor's Staff

1 cup flour
2 tsp. sugar
1/2 tsp. salt
1/4 tsp. baking soda
1/2 tsp. baking powder

3/4 cup buttermilk
1/4 cup milk (plus 1 tbls. if batter
  is too thick)
1 large egg
2 tbls. butter, melted

Mix dry ingredients in medium bowl. Pour buttermilk and milk into 2-cup glass measuring cup. Whisk in egg, then stir in melted butter. Dump wet ingredients into dry ingredients all at one; whisk until just mixed. Cook on a hot griddle that has been brushed with butter or oil. When pancake bottoms are brown and top surface starts to bubble, flip cakes and cook until the remaining side is brown.

RANDY'S BUTTERMILK PANCAKES

Deb Bowman
Governor's Cabinet

2 eggs
¼ cup oil
2 tbls. sugar
1 tsp. soda

2 cups buttermilk
1-¾ cups all-purpose flour
2 tsp. baking powder
1 tsp. salt

Heat griddle or skillet to medium-high heat. In large bowl, mix eggs, stir in buttermilk and oil. Add remaining ingredients, beat just until large lumps disappear. Lightly grease heated griddle. Pour batter, about ¼ cup at a time onto hot griddle. Bake until bubbles form and edges start to dry, turn and bake other side.

Hint: To test to see if griddle or skillet is the right temperature, drop a few sprinkles of water on the griddle or skillet and if the drops sizzle and bounce the heat is just right.

STUFFED EGGS AU GRATIN

Patti de Hueck Clodfelter
Former Governor's Cabinet

6 hard-cooked eggs
½ tsp. dry mustard
1 tbls. vinegar

2 tbls. melted butter
½ tsp. salt
½ cup finely chopped ham

Cut eggs in half lengthwise; remove and mash yolks. Add remaining ingredients, mix well. Fill whites with yolk mixture. Place in a buttered shallow casserole dish.

Au Gratin Sauce:

3 tbls. melted margarine
3 tbls. flour
1 tsp. salt

½ tsp. basil
2 cups milk
½ cup grated cheddar cheese

In a small pan, melt butter; blend with flour, salt, and basil. Gradually add milk. Cook over low heat until thickened, stirring constantly. Pour over eggs, sprinkle with cheese. Bake uncovered at 350° for 25 minutes.

THIN BUTTERMILK PANCAKES

Governor Nils A. Boe

2 eggs
1 cup flour
2 cups buttermilk

2 tsp. sugar
1 tsp. soda
¼ tsp. salt

Beat eggs thoroughly; add buttermilk. Sift together the dry ingredients and add to liquid mixture. Stir batter until well mixed. Cook small-size cakes on heavy griddle. Servings depend on appetites!

YUMMY COFFEE CAKE

Rosemary Rounds

1 loaf frozen bread dough
¼ cup soft butter
¼ cup brown sugar
¼ cup white sugar

¼ cup flour
½ tsp. cinnamon
½ tsp. vanilla

Put bread dough in greased 9" or 10" pie plate. Also spray dough on both sides. Cover with wax paper. Let rise overnight. Punch down in the morning, and make holes in the dough with your fingers. Mix together butter, brown sugar, white sugar, flour, vanilla, and cinnamon. Sprinkle over dough and press into the holes in the dough (I wet my fingers so the mixture doesn't stick to them). Bake at 350° for 20-30 minutes. Garnish each piece with ½ maraschino cherry after taking out of the oven. Yield: 6 or 8 servings.

Frosting:

½ cup powdered sugar, sifted
½ tsp. vanilla
1 tbls. butter, melted

water (enough to thin for drizzling over cake)

Mix powdered sugar, vanilla, butter, and water. Drizzle over coffeecake about 5-10 minutes after taking it out of the oven.

Stepmother of Governor M. Michael Rounds

Recipe Favorites

Recipe Favorites

BREADS & ROLLS

(Photo courtesy of the South Dakota State Historical Society Archives)

LOCKE HOTEL

The Locke Hotel was the Governors Residence in Pierre from 1895 to 1901. Governor Charles H. Sheldon and Governor Andrew E. Lee and their families lived there.

W.P. Locke of Waterville, NY, built the Locke Hotel in 90 days in 1890 at a cost of $80,000. It was located at the corner of Dakota Avenue and Fort Street. It had an electric alarm, electric light plant, steam heat, and hot and cold water for each of the 100 sleeping rooms. The elevator of the four-story hotel was operated by water-power and there was a 250-seat dining room on the fourth floor.

On the first floor was a large lobby, rooms and business suites. On the second floor there was a large 40x70 foot long parlor surrounded by rooms. The parlor was open to the fourth floor ceiling.

Up to that point, the Wells House had been the center of political and social events. In 1892, the Locke Hotel built a 62x25 foot wide addition containing a plunge bath from artesian wells. The plunge bath was ten feet deep at one end and one could swim as well as bathe.

The Locke Hotel continued to be the main hotel in Pierre until 1911 when the St. Charles opened. It continued as a hotel and as an apartment hotel until it was razed in 1980.

TIDBITS

Lavinia Curtis Robinson Crawford was the second wife of Governor Coe Crawford. She married her sister's husband. Her sister died while she was attending college and Mr. Crawford asked Lavinia for help in raising her sister's three children. After two years, Coe and Lavinia were married.

———◆———

During World War I, Lavinia Curtis Robinson Crawford devoted many hours in the cutting room making pajamas for American troops.

———◆———

Florence Albert Vessey married her childhood friend, Robert Vessey.

———◆———

Emilie Beaver Byrne was a Christian Scientist and wrote a novel with a religious theme, *The Song Beneath the Keys* and she also wrote poetry sharing her innermost thoughts.

———◆———

Harriet Russell McMaster helped entertain President and Mrs. Coolidge in a log cabin in the Black Hills.

———◆———

Harriet Russell McMaster was partial to outdoor sports. She was an expert tennis player, liked to boat, and participated in skating and coasting in the winter.

BREADS & ROLLS

BANANA BREAD

Governor Harvey Wollman

1 cup white sugar
1 egg
¼ cup shortening
1 banana, or more

1-½ cups flour
1 tsp. soda
1 pinch salt
½ cup sour milk

Mix in order given. Makes one loaf or two small loaves. Add nuts if desired. Bake at 350° for 35-45 minutes.

BANANA BREAD

Brian & Kerry Rounds

1 cup sugar
½ cup butter
3 eggs
3 bananas

1 tbls. cold water
1 tsp. baking soda
1 tsp. baking powder
2-½ cups flour

Preheat oven to 350°. Cream sugar and butter together. Add 3 eggs, beaten, and 3 bananas, mashed fine. Add 1 tbls. cold water and mix together. Put in 1 tsp. baking soda, 1 tsp. baking powder and 2-½ cups flour. After mixing, pour into greased (Pam) loaf pan. Bake about 1 hour. Test by inserting toothpick. If it comes out clean, it's done.

Son and Daughter-in-Law of Governor M. Michael Rounds and First Lady Jean Rounds

BANANA BREAD

Gretchen Lord Anderson
Former Governor's Staff

1 cup canola or sunflower oil
2 cups sugar
4 eggs
1 cup nuts
4 large bananas, cut up

4 cups flour
½ tsp. salt
2 tbls. lemon juice
2 tsp. baking soda

Cream oil and sugar. Add eggs and bananas. Add flour, salt, and nuts. Add lemon juice. Add soda last. Bake for 1 hour at 350°.

BANANA CHOCOLATE CHIP MUFFINS

Deonne Bloomberg
Former Governor's Staff

2 ripe mashed bananas
2 eggs
1 cup brown sugar
1/2 cup melted butter
1 tsp. vanilla
2 1/4 cup flour

2 tsp. baking powder
1/2 tsp. cinnamon
1/2 tsp. salt
1 cup chocolate chips (mini)
1/2 cup chopped walnuts

Beat bananas, eggs, brown sugar, butter, and vanilla until well blended. Add flour, baking powder, cinnamon, salt, chocolate chips, and walnuts. Grease muffin tins and bake at 350° for 25 - 30 minutes.

BANANA-NUT BREAD

Mardell Davis
Governor's Staff

1 cup sugar
1/2 cup shortening
2 eggs, well beaten
3 large ripe bananas
2 cups flour

1 tsp. soda
1 tsp. salt
1 tsp. vanilla
1 cup walnuts, chopped

Cream sugar and shortening. Add beaten eggs. Mix soda with mashed bananas; add to first mixture. Blend in remaining ingredients: flour, soda, salt, vanilla, and walnuts. Bake in greased loaf pan at 350° for 1 hour. Yield: 15 servings.

BEER BREAD

Corrie Holt

1 (12-oz.) can beer at room
  temperature
3 cups self-rising flour

1/3 cup sugar
1 tbls. oil

Mix all ingredients by hand. Put in a greased bread loaf pan. Let rise on counter for 5 minutes. Bake at 350° for 50 minutes.

Niece of First Lady Jean Rounds

85104-07

BUTTER HORN DINNER ROLLS

Mary Miller

3 eggs
1 cup warm water
1 pkg. yeast
1 tbls. sugar

½ cup sugar
½ cup shortening (Crisco)
½ tsp. salt
5 cups flour

Beat eggs and water together, then add yeast and 1 tbls. sugar and let stand 15 minutes. Then add the ½ cup sugar, shortening, salt and flour. Knead well. Let stand covered in refrigerator overnight, divide into 2 parts and roll out in 12 inch circle, cut into 16 wedges and roll up starting with the wide end. Let rise 3-4 hours. Bake at 400° for 15 minutes. Brush with butter.

Daughter-in-Law of Governor Walter Dale Miller

CINNAMON ROLLS

Recipe Box at the
Governors Residence

2 loaves frozen bread, thawed
1 stick butter
1 cup brown sugar

1 cup vanilla ice cream
cinnamon
sugar

Break bread loaves into chunks and roll in cinnamon and sugar. Put in a greased 9 x 13 inch pan. Let rise. Melt together butter, brown sugar and ice cream. Heat until it begins to boil. Pour mixture over dough. Bake at 350° for approximately 20 minutes.

DOUGHNUTS

First Lady Florence Vessey

1 cup sour cream (not too thick)
1 cup sweet milk
1 cup sugar

1 scant tsp. soda
1 scant tsp. baking powder
nutmeg

Mix soft. Fry in hot oil until golden brown.

Note: This recipe submitted by Arlein Fransen, Dunham Historical Society of Wessington Springs, SD.

ENGLISH RAISIN BUNS

Deb Vedvei

1 egg
1 cup brown sugar
1/4 cup vegetable oil
1/2 tsp. salt
2 cups warm water
2 pkg. of active dry yeast
5 - 5 1/2 cups all-purpose flour

1 tsp. cinnamon
1 tsp. ginger
1 tsp. cloves
1 tsp. nutmeg
1 tsp. allspice
1 cup raisins

In a large mixing bowl, combine egg, sugar, oil, and salt. Beat until smooth. Dissolve yeast in warm water and add to egg mixture. Let stand 5 minutes. Add 3 - 4 cups flour or enough to make a thick batter. Beat at high speed for 2 minutes. Mix together cinnamon, ginger, cloves, nutmeg, allspice, and add to dough. Add raisins and mix. Stir in 1 or 2 cups more of flour to make a soft dough. Dough might be sticky. Knead on a floured board. Put back in bowl and let rise until double. Punch down and shape into buns. When double in size, bake until golden brown at 350° about 20 minutes.

Sister-in-Law of Governor M. Michael Rounds

FROZEN BREAD CARAMEL ROLLS

Rob Skjonsberg
Governor's Staff

2 loaves frozen bread dough
1/2 cup butter
1 cup brown sugar
2 small pkgs. of vanilla pudding
 (NOT instant pudding)

2 tbls. milk
1/2 tsp. cinnamon

Thaw the two bread loaves, BUT DO NOT LET THEM RISE! Grease a 9 x 13 inch pan. Cut loaf #1 into small pieces and place in pan. Melt the butter and add rest of the ingredients and mix until smooth. Pour over the small pieces of bread dough in the pan. Cut loaf #2 into small pieces and place on top. Let this rise. Preheat oven to 350°F. Bake for 30 minutes. Let stand 10 minutes then turn out onto wax paper or cookie sheet.

Note: Don't make the pudding. Use dry ingredients of the boxes to mix with milk, cinnamon, brown sugar, and melted butter.

85104-07

FROZEN DOUGH CINNAMON ROLLS

Kris Ingram
Governor's Staff

2 frozen bread loaves
½ cup butter
1 cup brown sugar
½ tsp. cinnamon

1 pkg. vanilla cook and serve
   pudding mix
2 tbls. milk

Grease 9 x 13 inch pan (make sure it has lid). Break up or tear apart one unthawed bread loaf and put in pan. Let rise about 20 minutes. In saucepan combine ½ cup butter, 1 cup brown sugar, ½ tsp. cinnamon, 1 pkg. Cook & Serve Vanilla Pudding mix and 2 tbls. milk. Pour this mixture over dough in pan. Tear up another loaf and put on top of mixture. Let rise again, then bake at 325° for 30 minutes. When finished baking, put cover on pan and flip over.

GARLIC BUBBLE BREAD

Donna Morlock
Former Governor's Staff

1 loaf frozen bread dough
¼ cup butter, melted
1 egg, beaten

1 tsp. dried parsley
½ tsp. garlic powder
¼ tsp. salt

Thaw dough. Mix butter, egg, parsley, garlic powder, and salt. Cut off pieces of dough (size of walnut). Dip into mixture and place bits of dough into well greased loaf pan. Cover and let rise to top of pan. Bake at 350° for 30-35 minutes.

GERMAN KUCHEN BREAD

Dottie Howe
Former Governor's Cabinet

1-½ pkg. dry yeast
2 cups warm water
¾ cup dry milk
¼ cup sugar
¾ tsp. salt

2 eggs
¾ tsp. vanilla
½ cup shortening
6 cups flour

Soften yeast in half of the warm water. Combine rest of water, dry milk, sugar, shortening, salt, eggs, and vanilla with 2 cups of the flour. Beat well, then beat in softened yeast. Gradually add remaining flour to form a soft dough. Place in greased bowl, cover, let rise. Push down and let rise again. Cut dough into six pieces, dust each with flour, twist and pull into 14 inch lengths. Put three together on cookie sheet, braid together. Repeat on additional cookie sheet. Be sure to pinch ends of braid together. Let rise in warm oven. Bake at 350° until lightly browned. These braids can be decorated with frosting and pieces of maraschino cherries. Very good bread!!

KATHY'S BANANA BREAD

R. Van Johnson
Former Governor's Cabinet

½ cup shortening (I use butter)
1 cup sugar
2 eggs - room temperature
¾ cup mashed ripe bananas

1-¼ cup flour
¾ tsp. soda
½ tsp. salt

Cream shortening and sugar until fluffy. Add eggs, one at a time, beating well after each. Stir in banana. Sift together dry ingredients, add to banana mixture; mix well. Pour into greased bread pan, 9 x 5½ x 2½". Bake at 350° for 1 hour.

LEFSE

Helen Vedvei

Peel potatoes and boil. Do not put in salt. Five lbs. of potatoes make about 2 dozen lefse. Drain potatoes when done and put through a potato ricer. Measure 3 cups of warm riced potatoes and put in a bowl. Add 3 tbls. melted butter. Mix well and shape into a ball. Cover with wax paper or dish towel. Put in a cool place overnight but do not refrigerate.

Next morning: Mix 1 cup flour into 1 ball. Add 2 teaspoons sugar and ½ teaspoon salt, knead well. Measure ⅓ cup mixture and roll on floured board. The thinner you roll the lefse the better. (A lefse rolling pin or regular rolling pin covered with a rolling pin cover makes it easier to get them thin.) Fry on lefse frying pan until little tan spots appear on bottom. Turn once. When cool wrap in plastic. Freeze well.

Mother of First Lady Jean Rounds

LEMON BREAD

Doug Loen
Former Governor's Staff

1 cup water
½ cup oil
4 eggs

1 lemon cake mix
1 lemon instant pudding

Mix all together and bake at 325° for about 45 minutes. Makes 5 small loaves or 2 large loaves.

85104-07

LEMON POPPY SEED BREAD

Linda Fridley
Governor's Staff

1 lemon cake mix
1 pkg. instant lemon pudding
1 cup water

½ cup oil
4 eggs
¼ cup poppy seeds

Mix all ingredients well. Pour batter into 2 greased and floured loaf pans. Bake at 350° for 30-40 minutes. Remove from pans after 10 minutes.

MONKEY BREAD

Rick Melmer
Governor's Cabinet

4 (12-oz.) tubes buttermilk
  biscuits
½ cup sugar

2 tsp. cinnamon
1 stick margarine
1 cup brown sugar

Spray Bundt pan. Cut up biscuits in small pieces. Dip biscuits in cinnamon/sugar. Put in Bundt pan. Heat margarine and brown sugar until melted, pour over biscuits. Cook at 350° for 25 to 30 minutes.

MUFFINS

Lori Shangreaux
Governor's Staff

1 cup flour
¼ cup sugar
3 tsp. baking powder
½ tsp. salt

1 cup oatmeal
1 egg
1 cup milk
3 tbls. oil

Mix all together. Spoon into lined or well greased muffin tin (makes 12 muffins). Bake 425° for 15 minutes.

OVERNITE ROLLS

Larry Gabriel
Former Governor's Cabinet

4 cups warm water
1 pkg. yeast
3 eggs, beaten
1 cup salad oil

1-½ cups sugar
3 tsp. baking powder
1 tbls. salt
12 - 13 cups flour

Mix around 5 p.m. Cover. Put on cookie sheets around 9 p.m. and press dough real flat. Cover with dish towels. Bake in morning at 350° for 15-20 minutes. Makes 48-52 buns.

PECAN CARAMEL ROLLS

Sheila Bonrud
Governor's Staff

2 pkgs. yeast
3-1/2 cup warm water
2/3 cup sugar
1/2 cup shortening

2 eggs
1 tbls. salt
8 - 9 cups flour

Sprinkle yeast on warm water and let bubble about 15 minutes. Add remaining ingredients with 4 cups flour and beat on medium speed of electric mixer for 5-7 minutes, add 2 cups of flour and beat. Put onto floured board and add enough flour to knead into a smooth and elastic dough. You will need most of the 9 cups of flour. Let rise until double. Punch down, let stand 10 minutes. Divide dough into half, roll 1/2 inch thick. Spread with oleo, brown sugar, and cinnamon to cover well. Roll up and slice 1 inch thick. Put in prepared pans - 12 to a pan which has been covered with caramel. At this point you may freeze or bake. Oven is not preheated for frozen rolls. Bake these at 300° for 45 minutes or until done. Before I freeze them I let them rise some. Bake at 350° for 1/2 hour if you are not freezing them. Check for doneness by tapping rolls to see if they sound hollow.

Caramel:

2 cups brown sugar
1 cup oleo

1/2 cup white Karo syrup
pecans

Mix in a saucepan and heat until dissolved and smooth. Put into 2 - 9 x 13 inch prepared pans. Sprinkle pecans on bottom of pan.

PUMPKIN BREAD

Donna Morlock
Former Governor's Staff

2 cups pumpkin
4 eggs
1-1/2 tsp. cinnamon
2 cups sugar
3 tsp. baking soda
1 cup vegetable oil or
   margarine, melted

2/3 cup water
1 tsp. nutmeg
1/2 tsp. cloves
1-1/2 tsp. salt
3-1/2 cups flour

Mix together. Put into greased and floured loaf tins and bake 1 hour at 350°.

85104-07

PUMPKIN BREAD OR BARS

Doreen Kayser
Former Governor's Staff

4 eggs
1 cup vegetable oil
2 cups sugar
1 (16-oz.) can pumpkin
½ tsp. salt

1 tsp. cinnamon
1 tsp. nutmeg
1 tsp. soda
2 cups flour

Mix all ingredients together. For bread - bake at 350° for 40-45 minutes (makes 2 large or 5 small loaves). For bars - spread into an 11 x 17" pan, bake at 350° - frost with cream cheese frosting.

QUICK CINNAMON BREAD

Nila Novotny
Governor's Staff

¼ cup vegetable oil
1 cup sugar
1 egg
1 cup buttermilk
1 tsp. baking soda

2 cups flour
½ tsp. salt
1 tbls. cinnamon
½ cup sugar

Combine all ingredients and mix thoroughly with spoon. Pour ½ of batter in greased bread pan. Mix 1 tbls. of cinnamon and ½ cup of sugar and sprinkle one half of mixture over first layer of batter. Layer with the rest of the batter and sprinkle other half of sugar/cinnamon mixture on top. Run knife through batter to swirl gently but thoroughly. Bake 60 minutes at 375°.

QUICK ORANGE ROLLS

Susan Bushfield Beckman

1 tbls. orange juice
2-3 tsp. grated orange rind
½ cup honey or light corn
  syrup

2 tbls. butter

Combine orange juice, honey, and butter; boil 3 minutes. Remove from heat and add orange rind. Pour into 12 well greased muffin cups.

Dough:

2 cups flour
1 tsp. salt
3 tsp. baking powder
¼ cup sugar

1 cup sugar
1 cup milk
4 tbls. butter

Combine flour, salt, baking powder and sugar; mix well. Cut in butter with a pastry blender, then pour in milk. Mix only until combined then pour into muffin cups on top of syrup. Bake 15 minutes at 400°. Turn out onto greased paper so syrup runs down over rolls.

Granddaughter of Governor Harlan Bushfield

SISSEL'S DUMPLINGS

Mrs. Sissel Boe

2 cups flour
4 tsp. baking powder
1-½ tsp. salt

2 tbls. cold butter
¾ cup cold milk

Sift together the flour, baking powder, and salt. Work the cold butter into the flour mixture with your fingertips. (A pastry blender also works). Add milk 1 tbls. at a time until all the milk is dissolved in the dough. Turn the dough out on a floured pastry board and roll out with floured rolling pin until it is about ¾ of an inch thick. Cut circles out with wet glass, tin can, or cookie cutter. Put on buttered plate. Place plate over kettle of boiling water and cover tightly with a lid and steam for 12 minutes. (Don't peek even once). Dough cutouts may be placed directly on vegetables or meat in a Dutch oven and steamed there. For drop dumplings, increase milk until dough is sticky. Drop by heaping tbls. on meat or vegetables and steam in the same manner.

Mother of Governor Nils Boe

Note: Recipe submitted by Carol Mashek, Minnehaha County Historical Society

85104-07

SOUR CREAM BUNS

Esther Curry
Former Governor's Staff

1 pkg. active dry yeast.
¼ cup warm water (105°-115°)
1 (8-oz.) carton dairy sour cream
3 tbls. granulated sugar
2 tbls. shortening
1 tsp. salt
⅛ tsp. baking soda

1 egg (room temperature)
3 - 3-¼ cups all-purpose flour
2 tbls. soft butter
⅓ packed cup brown sugar
1 tsp. cinnamon
¾ cup sifted powdered sugar
2 - 4 tsp. water

Dissolve yeast in warm water. In small saucepan, combine sour cream, granulated sugar, shortening and salt. Heat and stir over medium heat until warm (120°) and shortening is almost melted. Stir in baking soda. Stir sour cream mixture and egg into yeast. Stir in as much flour as you can. Turn dough onto lightly floured surface; knead in enough of remaining flour to make moderately soft dough (3 to 5 min. total). Cover and rest for 5 minutes. Grease twelve 2-½ inch muffin tins. On lightly floured surface, roll dough into 18 x 12" rectangle; spread on softened butter. Combine brown sugar and cinnamon, sprinkle over dough, roll up, slice into 1-½" pieces. Place buns in muffin pan. Cover and let rise in warm place until ½" above top of pan (above 45 minutes). Bake at 400° about 15 minutes or until golden brown. Combine powdered sugar and enough water to make icing to drizzle over rolls. Serve warm.

Note: Recipe submitted by Kit Curry for Esther Curry. Mother Curry didn't use recipes, but breads and pies were her specialties.

THREE HOUR BUNS

Shirley Jenssen
Former Governor's Staff

3 tsp. yeast
2 cups warm water
⅓ cup sugar
1 tsp. salt

⅓ cup oil
1 egg, beaten
5-¾ cup flour

Dissolve yeast in warm water. Add sugar, salt, oil, beaten egg, and flour. Knead for 5 minutes. Let rise until double in bulk. Shape into buns. Let rise until light. Bake 375° for 20 minutes.

WHITE SPONGE BREAD

Borghild Boe

Sponge:

1 cake baker's yeast
2 pt. lukewarm water

1 qt. flour (1 lb.)

In the evening, break and soak cake of yeast 20 minutes in 1 pint of lukewarm water. Mix with 1 quart (1 lb.) flour to medium sponge. Cover. Let the sponge set in a warm place overnight. Potato water may be used in this sponge if desired.

Dough:

4 tbls. lard or Crisco
2 qts. flour (2 lbs.),
   approximately

4 tsp. salt
4 tbls. sugar

Early in the morning, mix the sponge with remaining 1 pint of lukewarm water, salt, sugar, and lard. Add the 2 quarts (2 lbs.) flour and mix to medium dough. Knead on floured board about 15 minutes. Let rise 2-1/2 - 3 hours. Should double in bulk. Knead down again and let rise 1 hour. Mold dough into 5 loaves and place in buttered bread pans. Let rise until doubled in bulk, and bake 45 minutes - 1 hour until bread sounds hollow when knocked, and top is golden brown and crisp. Butter while loaves are hot so that crusts are soft. Dinner rolls may be made when the bread is ready to shape into loaves. Shape pieces of dough into desired shapes - Parker House - bake in muffin pans; Cloverleaf - three small balls in muffin pans; Corkscrew - rolling dough in long snakes and wrapping around buttered clothespins. Let rise and bake 30-35 minutes. All bread is baked in a 375° oven.

Note: Recipe submitted by Carol Mashek, Minnehaha County Historical Society

ZUCCHINI BREAD

Mary Bisson
Former Governor's Staff

1 egg
1 cup cooking oil
1 tsp. baking soda
2-1/4 cups flour
1 tsp. salt
1 cup chopped nuts

1 cup sugar
1 tsp. vanilla
1/2 tsp. baking powder
2 cups shredded zucchini
2 tsp. cinnamon

Beat eggs well, add sugar and cooking oil. Beat in flour, salt, baking powder, soda, chopped zucchini, vanilla, cinnamon and then fold in nuts. Grease 3 large loaf pans or 6 small loaf pans and flour well. Bake 1 hour 10 minutes at 325° or until knife inserted in middle comes out clean. Yield: 3 large or 6 small loaves.

180

ZUCCHINI LEMON BREAD

Governor William Janklow

2 cups oil
6 eggs
4 cups sugar
4 cups zucchini (grated with no
  peels)
1 tsp. vanilla

1 tsp. lemon extract
6 cups flour
$\frac{1}{2}$ tsp. baking powder
2 tsp. salt
2 tsp. baking soda
2 lemons

Put 2 whole lemons (cut off ends and take seeds out, but leave skin on) in food processor. Add enough zucchini to make 4 cups. Beat in eggs, oil, vanilla and lemon extract. Mix well. Add dry ingredients. Grease and flour 5 big loaf pans. Bake for 60 minutes at 350°. When loaves are cool, drizzle with glaze.

Glaze:

1 cup powdered sugar
1 tbls. butter, melted

lemon juice (just enough to
  dissolve sugar)

Mix powdered sugar with lemon juice. Then add melted butter. Drizzle over cooled loaves.

Recipe Favorites

Recipe Favorites

85104-07

DESSERTS

NORBECK HOUSE

This Georgian revival house at 106 E. Wynoka was home to Governor Peter Norbeck and his family from 1917 to 1921.

The house, which is on the National Register of Historic Places, was built in 1904 for Colonel E. P. Farr and his wife, Dr. Mary Noyes-Farr. The architect was E. J. Donahue of St. Paul, MN.

This style became popular in the first years of the twentieth century and was inspired by the Georgian houses of New England. The house was one of the only houses of this style built in Pierre and is distinguished by the quality of workmanship throughout. The interior had oak woodwork and a three-foot high, hand-painted mural by Y. Edward Soderberg which formed a frieze in the dining room. The living room contained a fireplace fronted with rose quartz glass tile. In the dining room is an oak mantel with a bevel-edged plated glass mirror over the mantel and a built-in china cabinet of oak with leaded bevel-edged glass in the doors.

The building serves both as a private residence and a Bed and Breakfast.

TIDBITS

Madge Ellen Turner Mickelson was an accomplished athlete at Aberdeen Normal, now Northern State University. She lettered in five sports. She also won the National Javelin Throwing Championship.

Madge Ellen Turner Mickelson is the only woman to be a wife of a governor and a mother of a governor.

Kristen Anderson, daughter of Governor Sigrud and First Lady Vivian Anderson was the second child born to a sitting governor. Kristen became the only child of the Anderson's in 1954.

June Shakstad Foss had a child, Cheryl, who had disabilities. June was instrumental in planning the Children's Care Hospital in Sioux Falls.

June Shakstad Foss had a bomb shelter installed in the Governors Residence.

Lorna Buntrock Herseth is the only First Lady elected to a statewide office. She served as Secretary of State from 1972-1978.

Lorna Buntrock Herseth was the South Dakota "Mother of the Year" in 1979.

Governor and First Lady George T. Mickelson acquired the first china, linen, and silver coffee service for use in the state dining room. They also added the grand piano in the state reception room.

Governor and First Lady Ralph Herseth added an electric organ in the reception room. The family liked to gather around the organ for informal singing.

DESSERTS

ALABAMA PEACH COBBLER

Michael Gorman
Former Governor's Cabinet

1 stick butter
1 cup self-rising flour
1 cup buttermilk

1 cup sugar
1 (16-oz.) pkg. frozen peaches

Preheat oven to 375°. In an 8 x 12 inch cake pan, melt butter in heated oven. While butter is melting, mix flour, buttermilk, and sugar until just blended. Pour mixture into cake pan and spread to cover bottom of pan. Arrange frozen peaches on top of the batter and bake at 375° for 30 minutes or until golden brown. Let cool slightly on a rack, then cut and serve. This is great with vanilla ice cream.

APPLE - CRANBERRY CRISP

Recipe Box at the
Governors Residence

Filling:

3 lbs. Granny Smith apples (7-8)
1 bag fresh - or frozen
  cranberries
1 cup sugar

5 tbls. flour
$\frac{3}{4}$ cup cranberry juice (little less
  than $\frac{3}{4}$ cup)

Peel and slice apples. Put all the ingredients into large pot and cook until berries pop. Pour into baking dish (8 x 10 x 2 inch). Cover with crumbles. Bake 30 - 45 minutes at 350°. Top should be brown.

Crumbles:

$\frac{1}{2}$ cup sugar
$\frac{1}{4}$ cup brown sugar
$\frac{3}{4}$ cup flour

1-$\frac{1}{2}$ cup nut pieces
4-$\frac{1}{2}$ oz. butter (cold) and cut
  into little pieces

Mix everything together with hands. It's easiest to mush butter in your palm and then press other ingredients into butter. The result is coarse large chunks.

APPLE CAKE

*Recipe Box at the
Governors Residence*

3 eggs
1-$\frac{1}{2}$ cups vegetable oil
2 cups sugar
1 tsp. salt
1 tsp. baking soda

2 tsp. cinnamon
2 tsp. vanilla
3 cups flour
3 cups chopped apples
1-$\frac{1}{2}$ cups chopped nuts

Mix together the eggs, vegetable oil, and sugar. Add salt, soda, cinnamon, vanilla, and flour - batter will be stiff. Add and mix by hand the apples and nuts. Pour into greased and floured 9 x 13 inch pan and bake at 350° for 1 hour. Serve either warm or cold with the following caramel sauce.

Caramel Sauce:

1 cup sugar
1 packed cup brown sugar
1 cup butter (not margarine)

1 cup whipping cream (or small carton)

Bring to a boil, but do not boil. Place on top of piece of cake. This makes plenty, so don't be stingy.

APPLE CRISP

Charlie Vedvei

4 cups apples
1 cups sugar

1 tsp. cinnamon

Place apples in 9 x 9 inch sprayed pan and sprinkle with sugar and cinnamon.

Topping:

1 cup flour
1 cup brown sugar

$\frac{1}{2}$ cup melted butter

Mix butter, sugar, and flour and crumble over apples. Bake for 1 hour at 350°.

Brother of First Lady Jean Rounds

85104-07

APPLE CRUNCH

Governor Sigurd Anderson

1 can apple pie mix
1 box small white cake mix
cinnamon

nutmeg
½ stick margarine
Cool Whip or cream, if desired

Grease 8" x 8" baking pan or dish. Pour in one can of apple pie mix, add a dash of cinnamon and nutmeg. Blend a small package of white cake mix with ½ stick margarine, sprinkle over apple pie mix. Bake at 350° until crunch is lightly browned and apple mixture is heated through. Serve with Cool Whip or cream. Serves 6.

Note: Recipe submitted by daughter Kristen K. Anderson

APPLE GOODIE CRISP

Rosemary Rounds

6 cups sliced apples
½ cup sugar

1-¼ tsp. cinnamon

Spread apples in 8 x 8 inch or 9 x 9 inch pan which has been sprayed with cooking spray. Mix sugar and cinnamon and sprinkle over apples

Topping:

½ cup butter, softened
1 cup brown sugar

1 cup flour

Mix butter, brown sugar, and flour together. Drop on top of apples Bake at 325° for 1 hour or until apples are tender. Yield: 9 servings. If you wish to make a double batch place in a sprayed 9 x 13 inch pan.

Stepmother of Governor M. Michael Rounds

APPLE TORTE

Lisa Albers-Koppmann

1 cup sugar
1/4 cup butter
1 egg
1 cup flour
1 tsp. baking soda

1/2 tsp. nutmeg
1/2 tsp. cinnamon
1 pinch salt
2-1/2 cups diced apples
3/4 cup chopped nuts

Cream sugar and butter, add egg - mix well. Add flour, soda, spices and salt - mix well. Add apples and nuts. Pour into greased 8 or 9 inch pan. Bake at 350° for 30-40 minutes. Serve with warm vanilla sauce.

Vanilla Sauce:

1 cup sugar
1 tbls. cornstarch
1/2 cup butter

1/2 cup evaporated milk
1 tsp. vanilla

Boil until thick and serve over apple torte.

Granddaughter of Governor Walter Dale Miller

ATOMIC CAKE

Alan Vedvei

3 cups flour
2 cups sugar
3/4 cup oil
6 tbls. cocoa

1 tsp. salt
2 tsp. soda
2 tbls. vinegar
2 cup cold water

Mix all cake ingredients and pour into a greased 9 x 13 inch pan. Bake 35 minutes at 350°. Top immediately with marshmallows.

Frosting:

1/2 cup white sugar
1/2 cup brown sugar
1/4 cup milk

1 tbls. butter
1/2 cup chocolate chips
3 - 4 cups mini marshmallows

Heat sugars and milk and boil 1 minute. Add butter and chips. Spread over cake and marshmallows while cake is still warm.

Brother of First Lady Jean Rounds

85104-07

BANANA SPLIT DESSERT

Catherine Sulzle
Former Governor's Staff

2 cups graham cracker crumbs
½ cup butter, melted
1 lb. powdered sugar (approx. 3-½ cups)
2 (8-oz.) pkg. cream cheese, softened
1 tsp. vanilla
5 bananas, sliced

1 med. size can crushed pineapple, drained
1 (12-oz.) container Cool Whip
6-8 maraschino cherries, quartered
⅓ cup walnuts, chopped
chocolate syrup

Mix graham cracker crumbs and melted butter, pat into bottom of greased 9 x 13 inch pan. Beat powdered sugar, cream cheese, and vanilla until fluffy and put on top of crust. Then layer in order the bananas, crushed pineapple, Cool Whip, maraschino cherries, and chopped walnuts. Drizzle with chocolate syrup. Keep refrigerated until ready to serve.

BEST CHOCOLATE CAKE

First Lady Mary Dean Janklow

2 cups flour
¾ cup Hershey's cocoa
2 cups sugar
1 tsp. soda
¾ tsp. salt
½ tsp. baking powder

¾ cup water
¾ cup buttermilk
¾ cup shortening
2 eggs
1 tsp. vanilla

Grease and flour 3-8" or 2- 9" layer pans or one 13 x 9-½" pan. Measure all ingredients in a large mixer bowl. Blend ½ minute on low speed, scraping bowl. Mix 3 minutes on high speed, scraping bowl occasionally. Pour into pans. Bake at 350° for 30-35 minutes. (35-40 minutes for larger pan). Cool and frost with favorite frosting.

BREAD PUDDING WITH VANILLA CREAM SAUCE

First Lady Patricia Miller

¾ cup sugar
1 tsp. ground cinnamon
3 medium eggs
1 cup heavy cream

1 tsp. pure vanilla extract
5 heaping cups cinnamon swirl
   bread, cut into 1 inch cubes

Preheat oven to 350°. Grease an 8 inch square baking pan. Combine sugar, cinnamon, and nutmeg in a large bowl. Beat in the eggs until smooth, work in the heavy cream. Add the vanilla and bread crumbs. Allow the bread to soak up the custard. Pour into baking dish and bake for 25-30 minutes or until the pudding has a golden color and is firm to the touch. It should be moist, not runny or dry. Cool to room temperature.

Vanilla Cream Sauce:

1 cup white sugar
½ cup butter

½ cup heavy cream
1 tsp. pure vanilla extract

Combine sugar, butter, cream, and vanilla in large saucepan. While stirring, bring to a boil. Reduce heat to low and stir 3 minutes more. Spoon over bread pudding.

BROWNIES

Cindy Louder
Former Governor's Staff

1 square unsweetened
   chocolate (8 T. - 4 oz.)
⅔ cup shortening
2 cups sugar
4 eggs

1-½ cups flour
1 tsp. baking powder
1 tsp. salt
1 cup chopped nuts

Grease baking pan 13 x 9 inch. Heat oven to 350°. Melt chocolate and shortening over low heat. Beat in sugar and eggs. Measure flour by dipping method or by sifting. Blend flour, baking powder and salt. Stir in nuts (optional). Spread in pan. Bake 25 to 30 minutes or until toothpick stuck in center comes out clean. Cut in bars. Frost if desired.

85104-07

BUSTER BARS

Governor George S. Mickelson

1 lb. crushed Oreo cookies
½ cup melted margarine
½ gallon vanilla ice cream
1-½ cups Spanish peanuts
1-½ cups evaporated milk

⅔ cup chocolate chips
2 cups powdered sugar
½ cup butter
1 tsp. vanilla

Mix the Oreo cookies and melted margarine. Pat this crust mixture into a 9 x 13 inch pan. Place the ice cream on the crust. Sprinkle the peanuts over the ice cream. Mix the evaporated milk, chocolate chips, powdered sugar, and butter in a pan. Boil for 8 minutes, stirring constantly. Add the vanilla. Cool this sauce. Pour the sauce over the peanuts and freeze. Serves 18-24.

BUTTERCREAM FROSTING

Sheila Bonrud
Governor's Staff

8 cups powdered sugar
1 cup butter (softened)
1 cup shortening

⅓ cup milk
2 tsp. vanilla or almond extract

Mix sugar, butter and shortening on low speed until creamy. Add extract and beat in powdered sugar 2 cups at a time. Beat until smooth. This recipe is large one. You can freeze this or put into fridge for up to 2 weeks. If you freeze or refrigerate whip up after it is warm to add air. This recipe is great to decorate cakes and cookies.

BUTTERMILK BROWNIES

Janice Mickelson Carmody

2 cups sugar
1/4 tsp. salt
2 cups flour
2 sticks margarine
4 tbls. cocoa
1 cup water

1/2 cup buttermilk
2 eggs, beaten
1 tsp. vanilla
1 tsp. soda
1/4 tsp. salt

Mix sugar, salt, and flour together, set aside. Bring to a rapid boil the margarine, cocoa and water; pour over flour/sugar mixture and beat for 2 minutes. Add buttermilk, eggs, vanilla, soda and salt to this mixture and mix again. Pour into greased and floured jelly roll pan. Bake at 350° for 20 minutes.

Frosting:

1-1/2 cups sugar
6 tbls. oleo
6 tbls. milk

1-1/2 cups chocolate chips
1 tsp. vanilla

Boil for 2 minutes. Add chocolate chips and vanilla - beat until thick enough to spread.

Daughter of Governor George T. Mickelson and Sister of Governor George S. Mickelson

CARAMEL DUMPLINGS

Mardell Davis
Governor's Staff

Dumplings:

1 cup flour
1/4 cup sugar
2 tsp. baking powder
1/2 tsp. salt

3 tbls. shortening
1/2 cup milk
1/2 cup chopped nuts
1/2 tsp. vanilla

Combine dumpling ingredients in bowl.

Syrup:

3 cups water
1 cup brown sugar

2 tbls. butter
1 tsp. vanilla

Combine syrup ingredients in skillet. Bring to boil and boil 5 minutes. Add dumpling batter 1 teaspoon at a time. Cover and simmer over low heat 15-20 minutes without removing lid. Serve warm with whipped cream or with vanilla ice cream. Yield: 4-6 servings.

85104-07

CARAMEL PECAN DREAM BARS

Jim Soyer
Governor's Staff

1 yellow cake mix (moist or with
  pudding)

½ cup oleo or butter
1 egg

Heat oven to 350°. Grease a 9 x 13 inch pan. In large bowl, combine cake mix, oleo and egg. Mix at highest speed until crumbly. Press into prepared pan.

Filling:

1 (14-oz.) can sweetened
  condensed milk
1 egg

1 bag Heath Bit O'Brickle chips
1 tsp. vanilla
1 cup chopped pecans

In small bowl, beat milk, egg, and vanilla until blended. Stir in pecans and Bit O'Brickle chips. Pour over base in pan. Spread to cover (might take whole bag of chips). Bake 25-35 minutes. Center may appear loose, but it will set when cool.

CARROT BARS

Janice Mickelson Carmody

2 cups sugar
2 cups self-rising flour
1 tsp. salt
1-½ cups vegetable oil

4 eggs, beaten
3 cups grated carrots
2 tsp. cinnamon
2 tsp. baking soda

Combine all - beat until blended, pour into greased jelly roll pan. Bake at 350° for 30-35 minutes. Cool completely, ice with cream cheese frosting and top with chopped pecans.

Cream Cheese Frosting:

1 stick butter or margarine
  (softened)
1 (8-oz.) pkg. cream cheese
  (softened)

1 tsp. vanilla
1 lb. powdered sugar

Mix butter and cream cheese until smooth; add vanilla and powdered sugar. Spread on cooled bars and sprinkle with 1 cup of chopped pecans (or any nut).

Daughter of Governor George T. Mickelson and Sister of Governor George S. Mickelson

CARROT CAKE

Jackie Rounds

2 cups sugar
2 tsp. cinnamon
2 tsp. baking soda
1 tsp. nutmeg
2 cups flour
2-1/4 tsp. salt

1/2 cup salad oil
4 eggs
4 cup grated carrots
1/2 cup chopped nuts
1/2 to 1 cup crushed pineapple
(optional)

Makes 1-8 x 11" sheet and 2-8 1/2" layers. Preheat oven to 350°, grease and flour pans. Mix sugar and oil together until creamy; add 1 egg at a time. In small bowl combine cinnamon, nutmeg, baking soda, flour, and salt and sift into creamed mixture. Add carrots, nuts and pineapple, mix thoroughly and pour into floured pans. Bake at 350° for 30-35 minutes.

Frosting:

1 (8-oz.) pkg. cream cheese
1/2 cup butter
1 (12-oz.) pkg. flaked coconut

1 lb. powdered sugar
2 tsp. vanilla
1/2 cup nuts

In medium bowl, mix butter and cream cheese until creamy. Sift in powdered sugar; when well blended, add coconut, vanilla and nuts.

Sister-in-Law of Governor M. Michael Rounds

CHANTAL'S NEW YORK CHEESECAKE

*Recipe Box at the
Governors Residence*

15 graham crackers, crushed
2 tbls. butter, melted
4 (8-oz.) pkgs. cream cheese
1-1/2 cups sugar
3/4 cup milk

4 eggs
1 cup sour cream
1 tbls. vanilla extract
1/4 cup all-purpose flour

Preheat oven to 350°. Grease a 9 inch springform pan. In a medium bowl, mix graham cracker crumbs with melted butter. Press onto bottom of springform pan. In a large bowl, mix cream cheese with sugar until smooth. Blend in milk, and then mix in the eggs one at a time, mixing just enough to incorporate. Mix in sour cream, vanilla and flour until smooth. Pour filling into prepared crust. Bake in preheated over for 1 hour. Turn the oven off, and let cake cool in oven with the door closed for 5-6 hours; this prevents cracking. Chill in refrigerator until serving.

85104-07

CHEESECAKE

*Recipe Box at the
Governors Residence*

1 pkg. Pecan Sandies Cookies	2 eggs
2 (8-oz.) pkg. cream cheese	1 tsp. vanilla
1/2 cup sugar	

Beat ingredients together. Put foil liners into cupcake pan. Fill each liner with 1 Pecan Sandie cookie, then put 1 large dollop of cream cheese mixture on top. Bake at 350° for 10 minutes or until they dimple.

CHEESECAKE (KNOWN AS THE BEST ONE)

*Recipe Box at the
Governors Residence*

2 cups graham cracker crumbs	5 tbls. unsalted butter, melted
1/4 cup brown sugar, packed	2 tsp. fresh lemon juice

Make crust, freeze 15 minutes. Bake 10 minutes at 350°.

Filling:

4 (8-oz.) pkgs. cream cheese (room temp.)	1/4 cup whipping cream
1-3/4 cups sugar	1/3 cup fresh lemon juice
1 cup sour cream	2 tsp. vanilla extract
	4 large eggs (room temp.)

Mix cream cheese and sugar until fluffy. Add sour cream, whipping cream, lemon juice, and vanilla - add eggs one at a time. Pour filling into crust. Bake 55 minutes. Cool cake 5 minutes.

Topping:

1-1/2 cups sour cream	1 tsp. vanilla
1/4 cup sugar	

Mix sour cream, sugar, and vanilla in medium bowl. Spoon over hot cake. Bake 10 minutes. Cool 10 minutes. Place hot cheesecake directly in refrigerator. Chill uncovered overnight.

CHERRY ANGEL DESSERT

Dr. James Hansen
Former Governor's Cabinet

8 cups ½ inch cubes angel food cake

1 can (2-½ cups) cherry pie filling

1 pkg. instant vanilla pudding
1-½ cups milk
1 cup sour cream

Place ½ of cake pieces in 9 x 9 x 2 inch pan. (Reserve ⅓ cup cherry filling). Spoon cherry filling over cake. Top with remaining cake. Combine pudding, milk and sour cream; beat until smooth. Spoon mixture over cake layer. Chill 5 hours in refrigerator. Cut in squares. Garnish with ⅓ cup filling (about 1 teaspoon on each square). Other fruit filling can be used.

CHERRY CREAM CHEESE TARTS

Carrie Rounds Larson

2 (8-oz.) pkgs. cream cheese, softened (I use fat-free)
1 cup sugar (½ cup Splenda and ½ cup sugar works just as well)

1 tsp. vanilla extract
2 eggs
12 vanilla wafers
1 (21-oz.) can cherry pie filling, or other pie filling

Preheat oven to 350°. Place a paper cupcake liner in each cup of a muffin pan. Beat cream cheese with a handheld electric mixer until fluffy. Add sugar and vanilla, beating well. Add eggs, 1 at a time, beating well after each addition. Place a vanilla wafer, flat side down, in each muffin cup. Spoon cream cheese mixture over wafers. Bake for 20 minutes. Allow tarts to cool completely. Serve with cherry filling on top, or pie filling of your choice.

Daughter of Governor M. Michael Rounds and First Lady Jean Rounds

85104-07

CHILLED RASPBERRY TARTS

Kristin Rounds

1 (3-oz.) pkg. Raspberry Jell-O
1 (8-oz.) pkg. cream cheese
  (softened)
12 individual graham cracker
  crusts

24 fresh raspberries for garnish
1/8 cup honey
1 (12-oz.) container Cool Whip
  (thawed)
1/2 cup raspberries

Whip cream cheese and honey together with electric mixer until smooth. Sprinkle in the raspberry Jello and blend until smooth. Fold in the Cool Whip and stir until well mixed. Add 1/2 cup raspberries and stir until evenly mixed. Spoon into graham cracker crusts. Garnish with 2 fresh raspberries per crust. Chill at least 2 hours before serving. Make 12 individual crusts.

Sister-in-Law of Governor M. Michael Rounds

CHOCOLATE CHERRY CAKE

First Lady Mary Dean Janklow

Cake:

1 box chocolate cake mix
2 eggs

1 can cherry pie filling
1-1/2 tsp. almond extract

Mix cake ingredients in large mixing bowl. Pour batter into greased 9 x 13 inch pan. Bake for 25 - 35 minutes at 350°. Let cake cool completely before frosting.

Frosting:

1 cup brown sugar
4 tbls. milk

4 tbls. butter or margarine
1 heaping cup chocolate chips

To prepare frosting, melt brown sugar, milk, and butter over medium heat, stirring constantly. Bring to a boil and boil mixture for 1 to 1-1/2 minutes. Remove from heat and add chocolate chips. Stir until melted. Spread on cooled cake. If frosting gets too thick, add a little milk and stir.

CHOCOLATE CHIP BUNDT CAKE

First Lady Nancy Kneip Paprocki

1 pkg. yellow cake mix
1 small instant chocolate
 pudding mix
1/2 cup sugar
3/4 cup oil

3/4 cup water
4 eggs
1 (8-oz.) container sour cream
1 (12-oz.) pkg. chocolate chips

Grease and flour Bundt pan. Mix all ingredients well. Bake at 350° for 1 hour. After completely cool, sprinkle with powdered sugar or make a thin powdered sugar frosting and drizzle over top. Use a plastic knife to go around the cake inside the pan so it will come out easily.

CHOCOLATE CREAM PIE

Bart Miller

1 cup white sugar
1/3 cup flour
6 tbls. cocoa
1 dash salt
2 cups milk

3 egg yolks, beaten
2 tsp. butter
1 tsp. vanilla
1 baked pie shell

Combine sugar, flour, cocoa, salt, and milk; bring to boil, and boil for 3 minutes. Temper the egg yolks by combining a few tbls. of hot mixture to the beaten egg yolks; combine with cooked mixture and cook for another 3 minutes. Add the butter and vanilla; pour into baked pie shell. Top with whipped cream or meringue.

Grandson of Governor Walter Dale Miller

CHOCOLATE PIE

First Lady Mary E. Elrod

4 tbls. grated chocolate
2 tbls. cornstarch
6 tbls. sugar

yolks of 2 eggs
1 pint water

Boil until thick and flavor with 1 teaspoon vanilla. Bake the crust; pour in the filling; cover with white of egg, beaten with 2 tbls. powdered sugar, and brown in oven.

Note: Submitted by Ailene Luckhurst - Clark County Historical Society.

85104-07

CHOCOLATE PIE

Elaine Smith

1 baked pie crust
1/3 cup flour
2 cups milk
1 cup sugar
1/4 tsp. salt

2 egg yolks
1 tsp. vanilla
2 squares Baker's Chocolate
meringue

Scald milk in double boiler; mix sugar, flour, and salt with a little milk and mix smooth. Then stir into scalded milk and cook until thick and smooth. Beat egg yolks and add to custard, stirring well. Take from fire and add graded chocolate and stir until dissolved. Add 1 tbls. butter (improves flavor). Cool and add vanilla. Pour into baked pie shell and cover with meringue. Brown in oven. Serves 6-8.

CHOCOLATE REVEL BARS

Anne Farrar

3 cups quick cooking oats
1-1/2 cups all-purpose flour
1 tsp. baking soda
1 tsp. salt
1 cup butter, softened
2 cups packed brown sugar
2 eggs
4 tsp. vanilla extract

1 (14-oz.) can sweetened
   condensed milk
2 tbls. butter
1/2 tsp. salt
1/2 cup walnuts
1-1/2 cups semi-sweet chocolate
   chips

Preheat oven to 350°. Lightly grease a 9 x 13 inch baking pan. In a large bowl, beat together 1 cup butter and brown sugar until fluffy. Mix in eggs and 2 tbls. vanilla. In another bowl, combine oats, flour, baking soda and 1 tsp. salt. Stir into butter mixture. Set aside. In a medium sauce pan, heat sweetened condensed milk, chocolate chips, 2 tbls. butter, 1/2 tsp. salt over low heat, stirring until smooth. Remove from heat, stir in walnuts (optional) and 2 tsp. vanilla. Pat 2/3 of the oat mixture into the prepared pan. Spread chocolate mixture evenly over the top. Dot remaining oat mixture on top of chocolate mixture. Bake for 30-35 minutes in preheated oven. Let cool on wire rack. Cut into bars.

Daughter of Governor Frank Farrar

CHOCOLATE SHEET CAKE

Gretchen Lord Anderson
Former Governor's Staff

2 cups flour
2 cups sugar
1 cup margarine
1 cup water
4 tbls. cocoa

1/2 cup buttermilk
1 tsp. soda
2 eggs
1 tsp. vanilla

Combine flour and sugar and set aside. Bring margarine, water, and cocoa to a boil. Add to flour. Add buttermilk, soda, eggs, and vanilla. Beat well. Pour into a 11 x 16 x 1" pan. Bake at 400° for 20 minutes.

Icing:

1/2 cup margarine
4 tbls. cocoa
6 tbls. milk

1 1 lb. pkg. powdered sugar
1 tsp. vanilla
nuts

Bring to a boil the margarine, cocoa, and milk. Add remaining ingredients and beat. When slightly cooled, put on hot cake.

CHOCOLATE-TOPPED DATE CAKE

First Lady Anne Wollman

1 cup finely sliced dates
1-1/4 cup boiling water
1 tsp. soda
3/4 cup shortening
1 cup sugar
2 eggs

1-1/2 cups flour
1/4 tsp. salt
1/3 cup chocolate chips
1 tbls. sugar
1/2 cup chopped nuts

Place dates in bowl. Dissolve soda in boiling water and pour over dates. Let stand until cold. Cream shortening and sugar until fluffy. Beat in eggs. Sift flour, measure, and sift again with salt. Mix well into creamed mixture. Stir in date mixture. Spread in greased 8 x 12 inch pan. Sprinkle the top with chocolate chips, nuts and 1 tablespoon sugar. Bake at 350° about 45 minutes.

85104-07

COOKIE AND ICE CREAM DESSERT

Jason Dilges
Governor's Staff

⅔ cup margarine
2 cups powdered sugar
3 egg yolks, beaten
3 egg whites, beaten

2 squares semi-sweet chocolate
1 pkg. chocolate sandwich
 cookies
2 qts. vanilla ice cream

Cream margarine, powdered sugar, egg yolks, and melted semi-sweet chocolate together. Add 3 stiffly-beaten egg whites to creamed mixture. Crush package of cookies. Put ½ of cookies on bottom of 9 x 13 inch pan, layer ½ of creamed mixture on top of cookies. Add ice cream. Place remaining ½ of creamed mixture on top of ice cream. Top with remaining cookie crumbs. Freeze at least 4 hours. Serve.

CREAM OF RHUBARB PIE

Mrs. Sissel Boe

1 good pie crust, unbaked, 9"
1 cup skinned and finely
 chopped fresh rhubarb
1 cup sugar
rind of one orange or lemon

3 egg yolks
1 tbls. cornstarch
1 tbls. cold water
1 cup boiling water

Add sugar to the rhubarb, mix, and let sit 1 hour. Add graded citrus rind. Mix again. Put the tbls. of cold water in a cup. Add the tbls. of cornstarch and mix until there are no lumps. Add more water if needed to make a thin paste. Add the boiling water to fill the cup to the top. Cool. Add to the 3 beaten egg yolks a bit at a time, beating between each addition. Add the egg and water mixture to the sweetened rhubarb. Stir gently. Pour into 9" pie dish in which the pie dough has been placed. DO NOT ADD A TOP CRUST! Bake in center of oven at 325° for 45 minutes - 1 hour until a silver knife comes out of the middle clean. Cool completely and then add meringue and bake again.

Meringue:

3 egg whites
½ tsp. cream of tartar

1 cup powdered sugar
1 drop vanilla

Beat the egg whites with the cream of tartar until stiff but not dry. Sprinkle powdered sugar a tbls. at a time into the egg whites, beating after each addition. Add vanilla. Pile on top of cooled pie and bake at 400° until golden brown.

Mother of Governor Nils Boe

Note: Recipe submitted by Carol Mashek, Minnehaha County Historical Society

CREPES WITH CARAMELIZED APPLES AND RUM SAUCE

Marcia Donnan Mitchell
Former Governor's Cabinet

3 large eggs
1 cup whole milk
2 tbls. dark rum
2 tbls. butter, melted
1 tbls. sugar

½ tsp. salt
½ tsp. ground cinnamon
1 cup all-purpose flour
additional melted butter

Place all ingredients in a blender and whir until smooth. Cover, let stand for 30 minutes. Heat a 5" or 7" skillet until moderately hot. Very lightly brush with melted butter. Fill a quarter-cup measuring cup about ⅔ - ¾ full, swirl batter into pan, tilt to make almost paper-thin pancake. Turn when bottom is lightly browned and edges pull away from skillet. Stack between sheets of aluminum foil.

Apples:

5 tbls. butter
3 lbs. golden delicious apples, peeled, quartered, cored, each cut into 3 wedges
¾ packed cup golden brown sugar

½ cup apple juice
2 tbls. lemon juice
1 tsp. grated lemon peel
1 tsp. ground cinnamon
3 tbls. dark rum
vanilla ice cream

Melt butter in large skillet over high heat. Add apples, sauté until deep golden and tender, tossing often, about 15 minutes. Add sugar, apple juice, lemon juice, peel, cinnamon. Simmer until juices thicken and apples are very tender, turning with spatula, about 3 minutes. Remove from heat. Butter a large ovenproof rimmed platter. Fill crepes, leaving juice in the skillet. Arrange on platter with seam side down. Stir rum into sauce in skillet, bring to boil, stirring. Preheat over to 350°. Spoon sauce over crepes. Bake until warm, about 10 minutes. Serve with ice cream.

85104-07

DAD'S LEMON DESSERT

Karey Albers

1 stick butter
graham crackers
2 pkgs. Lemon Jell-O
3 cups hot water
1 cup evaporated milk, cold

1 cup cream
juice of 2 lemons
1 tsp. vanilla
½ cup sugar

Melt butter and mix enough graham crackers to cover bottom of 9 x 13 inch pan. Dissolve lemon Jell-O in hot water; let stand until it starts to set. Beat cold evaporated milk and cream, lemon juice, vanilla, and sugar. Add this to the lemon Jell-O, and whip. Pour on top of graham cracker crumbs. Top with a few crumbs and let set for at least 4 hours.

Daughter of Governor Walter Dale Miller

DAVE'S FAVORITE PUMPKIN BARS

David Mickelson

2 cups flour
2 tsp. baking powder
2 tsp. salt
1 tsp. cinnamon
1 tsp. baking soda
4 eggs

2 cups sugar
2 cups pumpkin
1 cup oil
1 tsp. vanilla
1 cup walnuts (optional)

Mix flour, baking powder, salt, cinnamon, and baking soda together. In a large bowl, beat eggs. Then add sugar, pumpkin, oil, and vanilla, mixing well. Add the flour mixture slowly, mixing well. Stir in walnuts if desired. Pour in greased 9 x 13 inch pan and bake at 350° for 30 minutes or until set in the middle. Cool, then frost with cream cheese frosting.

Frosting:

1 (8-oz.) pkg. cream cheese
1 stick margarine

1 1 lb. pkg. powdered sugar
2 tsp. vanilla

Blend until smooth. Frost cooled bars.

Son of Governor George S. Mickelson and Grandson of Governor George T. Mickelson

DEVIL'S FOOD CAKE

Borghild Boe

1 cup sugar
1 heaping tbls. butter
3 egg yolks (save the whites for frosting)
4 squares unsweetened chocolate, broken into pieces

½ cup milk
1 cup plus 2 level tsp. flour (sifted)
½ tsp. salt
½ tsp. baking soda
½ tsp. baking powder

Preheat oven to 350°. In a large bowl, blend butter and sugar. Add egg yolks and beat in one at a time until the mixture is a creamy yellow. Melt chocolate in the milk in a double boiler or in a pan over boiling water. Do not boil chocolate! Cool slightly. Mix a bit of the batter into the chocolate a tbls. at a time so the eggs don't cook. Sift flour, salt, baking soda, and baking powder together. Add slowly to wet mixture. Bake in an 8 x 11 inch pan which has been buttered and floured, for 30 minutes or until toothpick or broom straw comes out of the middle clean. Cool before frosting with divinity frosting.

Divinity Frosting:

3 egg whites
⅛ tsp. salt
1-½ cups sugar

½ cup cold water
1 tbls. light corn syrup
1-½ tsp. vanilla extract

Heat water in bottom of double boiler to boiling. In top of pan, mix together the 3 egg whites, salt, sugar, and cold water. Add corn syrup. Heat mixture, beating constantly until frosting holds its shape when dropped from a spoon. Turn mixture into bowl. Add the vanilla and beat until the frosting can be spread on the cooled cake.

Sister of Governor Nils Boe

Note: Recipe submitted by Carol Mashek, Minnehaha County Historical Society

DUMP BARS

Bonnie Untereiner Bjork
Former Governor's Cabinet

2 cups sugar
1-¾ cups flour
5 eggs
1 tsp. salt

1 cup oil
1 tsp. vanilla
½ cup cocoa
1 cup chocolate chips

Dump all ingredients except chocolate chips together in a bowl. Mix with spoon until all ingredients are moistened. Spread in greased 9 x 13 inch pan. Sprinkle chocolate chips on top (I use nuts, too). Bake at 350° for 35-40 minutes, or until a toothpick inserted comes out clean. Cool. This is great to make when you need to bring a treat on short notice because it uses ingredients most people have on hand.

85104-07

EASY PATRIOTIC FLAG DESSERT

Julie Johnson
Former Governor's Cabinet

3 cups boiling water, divided
2 pkgs. Jell-O Brand berry blue
  flavor gelatin
2 cups ice cubes, divided
2 (8-oz.) pkgs. Philadelphia
  Cream Cheese, softened
¼ cup sugar

1 (8-oz.) tub Cool Whip whipped
  topping, thawed, divided
2 pkgs. Jell-O Brand strawberry
  flavor gelatin, or any red flavor
2 cups halved strawberries
½ cup blueberries

Stir 1-½ cups of the boiling water into dry blue gelatin in medium bowl at least 2 minutes until completely dissolved. Add 1 cup of the ice cubes; stir until ice is completely melted. Pour into 13 x 9 inch dish. Refrigerate 20 minutes or until gelatin is set but not firm. Place cream cheese, sugar and half of the whipped topping in large bowl; beat until well blended. Spoon over blue gelatin layer in dish; spread carefully to evenly cover gelatin layer. Stir remaining 1-½ cups boiling water into strawberry gelatin in separate bowl at least 2 minutes until completely dissolved. Add remaining 1 cup ice cubes; stir until ice is completely melted. Let stand at room temperature 5 minutes or until slightly thickened. Spoon over cream cheese layer in dish. Refrigerate 3 hours or until set. Spread remaining whipped topping over dessert just before serving. Decorate with strawberries and blueberries to resemble a flag. Store leftover dessert in refrigerator.

ELEGANT DESSERT

Susan Stoneback
Former Governor's Staff

6 egg whites
$\frac{1}{2}$ tsp. cream of tartar
$\frac{1}{4}$ tsp. salt
1 tsp. vanilla
1-$\frac{3}{4}$ cups white sugar
2 small pkgs. slivered almonds
2 (3-oz.) pkgs. cream cheese
1 cup sugar
1 tsp. vanilla

2 envelopes Dream Whip
  (already prepared according to
  package directions)
2 cups miniature marshmallows
1 can cherry pie filling
1 (10-oz.) pkg. frozen
  raspberries or sliced
  strawberries, thawed

Beat the 6 egg whites until stiff. Then add cream of tartar, salt, vanilla, and white sugar; beat again until stiff and glossy. Then add the almonds. Spread this mixture in a buttered 9 x 13 inch pan. Place in a 400° oven. Let the oven temperature come back to 400° if it cooled a little when the door was opened. TURN OFF THE OVEN AND LEAVE THE PAN IN FOR 8 HOURS OR OVERNIGHT. Cream the cream cheese, sugar, and vanilla. Fold in the Dream Whip and marshmallows. Spread this mixture over the meringue and refrigerate overnight. Combine the cherry pie filling and berries to make a topping. To serve: cut in squares and serve with the cherry pie filling and berry topping.

EXTRAORDINARY PUDDING CAKE

John Rounds

1 pkg. cake mix (2 layer size),
  any flavor
2 pkgs. Jell-O Brand instant
  pudding (4 serving size), any
  flavor

4 cups cold milk
1 cup sugar

Prepare cake mix as directed on package, baking in 13 x 9 inch pan. Remove from oven. Poke holes at once down through the cake to the pan with the round handle of a wooden spoon. Holes should be 1 inch apart. Only after poking holes, combine pudding mix with sugar in large bowl. Gradually stir in milk. Then beat at low speed of electric mixer for not more than 1 minute (do not overbeat). Quickly, before the pudding thickens, pour one half of the thin pudding evenly over warm cake and into holes to make the stripes. Allow remaining pudding to thicken slightly, then spoon over the top, swirling it to "frost" the cake. Chill at least 1 hour. Store cake in refrigerator.

Son of Governor M. Michael Rounds and First Lady Jean Rounds

85104-07

FLAG CAKE

Julie Johnson
Former Governor's Cabinet

2 pints strawberries
1 (12-oz.) pkg. frozen pound
  cake, thawed, cut into 14 slices

1-1/3 cups blueberries, divided
1 (12-oz.) tub Cool Whip
  Whipped Topping, thawed

Slice 1 cup of the strawberries; set aside. Halve remaining strawberries; set aside. Line bottom of 9 x 13 inch baking dish with cake slices. Top with sliced strawberries and 1 cup of the blueberries. Spread whipped topping evenly over berries. Place strawberry halves and remaining 1/3 cup blueberries on whipped topping to create a flag design. Refrigerate until ready to serve.

FORGOTTEN DESSERT

Susan Bushfield Beckman

5 egg whites
1/2 tsp. cream of tartar
1-1/2 cups sugar

1 tsp. vanilla
berries
whipping cream or ice cream

Beat egg whites until fluffy, then add cream of tartar and mix. Add sugar slowly while continuing to beat egg whites. Beat mixture 15 minutes on high. Pour into a well greased 10 inch pie tin. Place in a 450° oven and turn off the heat. Leave it in the oven overnight. Fill shell with berries and whipped cream or ice cream. Chill.

Granddaughter of Governor Harlan Bushfield

FRESH PEACH PIE

Lauren Albers

4 cups sliced fresh peaches
1/2 cup white sugar
3 tbls. flour

1/4 tsp. salt
1 tbls. lemon juice
1 unbaked pie crust

Toss all above lightly and pour into unbaked pie crust.

Topping:

1/2 cup brown sugar
1/4 cup flour

1/2 tsp. cinnamon
2 tbls. butter

Combine and put on top of peaches. Bake at 400-425° about 45 minutes.

Great-granddaughter of Governor Walter Dale Miller

FROZEN STRAWBERRY DESSERT

Linda Fridley
Governor's Staff

1 cup flour
½ cup oleo, melted
¼ cup brown sugar, packed
½ cup chopped nuts
1 (10-oz.) pkg. frozen
  strawberries, thawed

2 egg whites
1 cup sugar
1 tsp. lemon juice
1 tsp. vanilla
1 half pint whipping cream or 4
  oz. Cool Whip

Mix flour, oleo, brown sugar, and nuts. Put in 9 x 13 inch greased pan, and bake at 350° about 15 minutes, stirring a few times. Cool about 10 minutes. Press in pan when cool. Reserve a little of this to sprinkle on top of dessert. Combine strawberries with juice, egg whites, sugar, lemon juice, and vanilla in large mixing bowl. Beat at high speed for about 20 minutes. Fold in whipping cream that has already been whipped (or Cool Whip). Put this mixture on top of baked crust (this mixture will be really fluffy), and add crumb mixture to top. Freeze. This keeps well. Serves 12.

FROZEN STRAWBERRY DESSERT

Reagan Rebecca Caldwell

2 egg whites
⅔ cup white sugar
1 (16-oz.) pkg. semi-frozen
  strawberries

3-½ cups Cool Whip

Beat egg whites to stiff peaks, then add sugar and berries and mix well. Fold in the Cool Whip, and pour on top of crust.

Crust:

1 cup flour
½ cup butter

¼ cup brown sugar
½ cup finely chopped walnuts

Put in 9 x 13 inch greased pan. Bake at 350° for 20 minutes, crumble up and leave ¾ of this mixture in pan for bottom of crust; reserve the remaining crumbs for the top. Pat down, add finished filling, and top with the remaining crust crumbs. Freeze and cut in squares to serve.

Granddaughter of Governor Walter Dale Miller

85104-07

FRUIT SPECTACULAR PLATTER PIZZA

Luz Naasz
Residence Staff

1 (18-oz.) pkg. refrigerated sugar
"slice and bake" cookies
1 (8-oz.) pkg. cream cheese,
softened
1 (8-oz.) tub frozen whipped
topping, thawed

1 pint fresh strawberries, halved
2-3 fresh bananas, sliced
1 1 lb. can sliced cling peaches,
drained
1 (8-oz.) can pineapple chunks,
drained or several kiwi, sliced

Cut cookie dough into ⅛ inch thick slices. Arrange cookie slices on lightly greased baking pan, beginning ¼ inch from groove of pan. Continue to arrange in circular pattern, slightly overlapping. Press lightly together to seal. Place pan in oven and bake 10-12 minutes at 350°. Crust is done when edges just begin to brown; top of crust will not be browned. Blend cream cheese with whipped topping. Spread evenly over cooled crust. Arrange strawberry halves around edge of cookie crust. Place banana slices in a circle next to strawberries, overlapping slightly. Place peaches in a circle next to bananas. Mound pineapple chunks in center. Place several strawberry halves in center of pineapple. Spoon orange sauce over fruits. Cut pie in wedges and serve with remaining sauce.

Orange Sauce:

½ cup sugar
1 tbls. lemon juice
1 dash salt

2 tbls. cornstarch
½ tsp. grated orange peel
2 cups orange juice

Stir together sugar, salt, and cornstarch in small saucepan. Gradually stir in orange juice, lemon juice, and water. Cook over medium heat, stirring constantly until mixture thickens and boils. Boil and stir 1 minute. Remove from heat. Stir in grated orange peel. Cool.

GERMAN CHOCOLATE CAKE

*Richard Benda
Governor's Cabinet*

1 (4-oz.) pkg. Baker's Sweetened
  Chocolate
1/2 cup boiling water
1 cup butter or margarine
2 cups sugar
4 egg yolks

4 egg whites
1 tsp. vanilla
2-1/2 cups sifted cake flour
1 tsp. baking soda
1/2 tsp. salt
1 cup buttermilk

Mix the package of chocolate with the boiling water until melted; set aside. Preheat oven to 350°. Mix butter or margarine with sugar using electric mixer until fluffy and rich. Slowly add egg yolks while beating, and beat until mixed well. Add melted chocolate and vanilla and beat until mixed well. Sift flour, then add baking soda and salt. Add the milk and the flour mixture alternating between the two - don't stop mixing. Beat until mixture is smooth. Beat egg whites until they peak - about 5 minutes. Fold the egg whites into the chocolate mixture SLOWLY - DO NOT BEAT THEM IN! Coat the inside of 3 round cake pans with shortening, then flour. Then put waxed paper in the bottom. Pour equal amount of batter into each pan. Bake cakes for 30-40 minutes. Do not open the oven until the cake is done, as it will fall. Remove from oven and cool for 15 minutes, then remove from pans by running a knife or spatula around the edge of the pan, then flip if over and remove the wax paper from the bottom. Frost with Coconut Pecan Frosting.

Coconut Pecan Frosting:

1 cup evaporated milk
1 cup sugar
3 beaten egg yolks
1/2 cup butter

1 tsp. vanilla
1-1/3 cups Baker's Angel Flake
  Coconut
1 cup chopped pecans, roasted

In medium saucepan, mix evaporated milk, sugar, egg yolks, butter, and vanilla with whisk over medium heat for 12 minutes. Add the coconut and roasted pecans and mix well. Cool frosting until it is firm and easy to spread. Divide frosting into separate, but equal parts. Frost top of one layer, add second layer, frost, then top with third layer and frost. Then frost sides - it may be difficult, but just slap it on and make it stick. Refrigerate to set frosting.

GRAMMA REINARTZ'S NEVER FAIL CHOCOLATE CAKE

Sophie Reinartz (1908 - 1976)

2 cups sugar
¹/₂ cup cocoa
2-¹/₂ cups flour
¹/₂ tsp. salt
2 tsp. soda

2 eggs
1 cup milk
1 cup shortening
1 tsp. vanilla
1 cup boiling water

Preheat oven to 350°. Grease and flour two 9 inch round baking pans or one 13 x 9 inch pan. In large bowl combine dry ingredients. Add eggs, milk, shortening, and vanilla. Beat on medium speed 2 minutes. Stir in boiling water. Pour into prepared pan(s). Bake 30 - 35 minutes for round pans or 35 - 40 minutes for rectangular pan.

Frosting:

6 tbls. butter
6 tbls. milk
1-¹/₂ cups sugar

1 (12-oz.) pkg. semi-sweet
chocolate chips

Combine butter, milk, and sugar in medium saucepan. Heat slowly, and boil for one minute. Add chocolate chips and stir until melted. Spread on cooled cake.

Grandmother of Governor M. Michael Rounds

GRANDMA GOODALE'S CHOCOLATE CAKE

Kris Ingram
Governor's Staff

½ scant cup cocoa
1 cup cold water
2 cups sugar
½ cup butter
1 tsp. vanilla
3 eggs, beaten

½ cup cake flour
1 cup plain flour
1 cup buttermilk
1 tsp. soda
¼ tsp. salt
1 tsp. red food coloring

In a saucepan boil cocoa and cold water until thick, then let cool. Cream together sugar, butter, and vanilla, then add well-beaten eggs. To this mixture add the cooled cocoa mix. Add the flour alternately with buttermilk, beating well after each addition, ending with flour. Then add the soda and salt and mix well again. Lastly, fold in the red food coloring. Bake at 350° for 45 minutes.

Chocolate Frosting:

1 cup sugar
2 rounded tbls. cocoa
3 tbls. corn syrup

⅓ cup butter
¼ cup milk
1 tsp. vanilla

Combine in saucepan: sugar, cocoa, corn syrup, butter, and milk. Cook over medium heat. When mixture comes to a full boil, cook for 1 minute. Remove from heat and add vanilla. Stir until frosting consistency is smooth and dull in color. Spread on chocolate cake.

GRANDMA'S APPLE CRUMB PIE

R. Van Johnson
Former Governor's Cabinet

4 large tart apples
1 cup sugar, divided
1 tsp. cinnamon

¾ cup flour
⅓ cup butter
2 pie crusts

Cut up apples in a 9" pastry-lined pie pan. Sprinkle with ½ cup sugar mixed with cinnamon. Sift remaining ½ cup sugar with the flour; cut in butter until crumbly. Sprinkle over apples. Put top crust on pie; flute edges and cut slots in it. Bake in hot oven (450°) 10 minutes. Then bake in moderate oven (350°) about 40 minutes, or until apples are tender.

85104-07

HOT FRUIT

Pam Janklow Derheim

3 cans lite fruit cocktail
1 tall can pineapple tidbits
1 tall can mandarin oranges

1 can cherry pie filling
½ cup white wine

Drain all fruit overnight. Put drained fruit in 9 x 13 inch glass pan. Spread pie filling over the top. Pour ½ cup white wine over the top. Bake for 1 hour at 350°. Remove from oven and sprinkle topping over the top. Bake for another 15 minutes.

Topping:

¼ cup brown sugar
2 tbls. flour
2 tbls. butter

1 tsp. cinnamon
½ cup chopped nuts

Daughter of Governor William J. Janklow

ICE CREAM CAKE

First Lady Nancy Kneip Paprocki

1 box ice cream sandwiches (12 large) cut them to fit tightly in pan
1 (16-oz.) bottle hot fudge sauce - Hershey is good

1 container Cool Whip (medium size)

Spray 9 x 13 inch pan with Pam. Then layer the ice cream sandwiches, hot fudge sauce and Cool Whip. Drizzle caramel sauce over top. Sprinkle with toffee bits and chopped peanuts. Freeze and cut into squares.

IRISH BREAD PUDDING WITH CARAMEL-WHISKEY SAUCE

Karon Schaack
Former Governor's Cabinet

¼ cup butter, melted
1 (10-oz.) French bread baguette, cut into 1"-thick slices
½ cup raisins
¼ cup Irish whiskey
1-¾ cups 2% milk

1 cup white sugar
1 tbls. vanilla
1 (12-oz.) can evaporated milk
2 large eggs, lightly beaten
cooking spray
1 tbls. sugar
1 tsp. cinnamon

Preheat oven to 350°. Brush melted butter on one side of French bread slices, and place bread, butter side up, on a baking sheet. Bake bread at 350° for 10 minutes, or until lightly toasted. Cut bread slices into ½-inch cubes and set aside. Combine raisins and whiskey in small bowl; cover and let stand 10 minutes or until raisins are soft. Do NOT drain! In large mixing bowl, combine 2% milk and next four ingredients (sugar, vanilla, evaporated milk, and beaten eggs). Stir well with a whisk. Add bread cubes and raisin mixture, pressing gently to moisten. Let stand 15 minutes. Spoon bread mixture into a 9 x 13 inch baking dish coated with cooking spray. Combine 1 tbls. sugar and cinnamon, sprinkle over bread mixture. Bake at 350° for 35 minutes until set. Serve warm with Caramel Whiskey Sauce. Yield: 12 servings (3-inch squares).

Note: ¼ cup apple juice may be substituted for Irish whiskey, if desired.

Caramel-Whiskey Sauce:

1-½ cups white sugar
⅔ cup water
¼ cup butter
2 oz. low-fat (NOT fat-free) cream cheese (about ½ cup)

¼ cup Irish whiskey
¼ cup 2% milk

Combine sugar and water in a small heavy saucepan over medium-high heat; cook until sugar dissolves, stirring constantly. Stop stirring and cook an additional 15 minutes or until golden (do not stir during this phase). Remove from heat. Carefully add butter and cream cheese, stirring constantly with a whisk. Mixture will be hot and will bubble vigorously. Cool lightly, and stir in whiskey and milk. Yield: 1-½ cups.

85104-07

ITALIAN CREAM CAKE

Dean Anderson
Former Governor's Cabinet

2 cups sugar
1/2 cup shortening
1/2 cup margarine
5 eggs, separated
1 cup buttermilk
2 cups flour

1 tsp. baking soda
1 tsp. vanilla
1 cup chopped pecans, or nuts
1 cup angel flake coconut
1 cup maraschino cherries, cut
up (optional)

Cream sugar, shortening, and margarine. Separate eggs, adding yolks one at a time. Beat well. Alternately add buttermilk with flour and soda, beating well. Fold in pecans, coconut, and cherries (optional). Beat egg whites until stiff and fold in. Grease and line with waxed paper 3 - 8" or 9" layer pans. Divide dough evenly and bake at 325° for 30 minutes. Or, pour into a 9 x 13" pan and bake at 350° for 40 minutes.

Icing:

1 (8-oz.) pkg. cream cheese,
softened
1/2 cup margarine
1/2 cup chopped pecans, or nuts

1 1 lb. pkg. powdered sugar
1 tsp. vanilla
1/2 cup angel flake coconut

Beat ingredients together. Spread between layers and over cake. Can be made 1 day ahead and refrigerated. Also freezes well.

KUCHEN BARS

Jean Blow
Governor's Staff

1/2 cup Crisco
1/2 cup margarine
2 cups flour
1 cup sugar

2 eggs
1 tsp. vanilla
fruit

Beat above ingredients together and spread in a lightly greased and floured 9 x 13 inch pan. Lay pieces of drained, canned fruit on crust (peaches, pears, apples, or whatever fruit you like).

Filling:

2 cups milk
1 cup sugar
3 eggs

3 tbls. cornstarch
fruit (canned)
sugar and cinnamon

Scald the milk and then add the rest of the ingredients, cooking it on low heat until it thickens. Cool filling and spread it over the fruit on the crust. Sprinkle with sugar and cinnamon and bake at 375° for 20-25 minutes.

KUCHEN BARS

Donna Morlock
Former Governor's Staff

1 cup butter, melted
1 tsp. vanilla
2 eggs

2 cups flour
1 cup sugar

Mix to thick batter and spread into 10 x 16 inch pan. Arrange fruit over batter. I like peaches, apricots, cooked prunes, rhubarb, or blueberries.

Custard:

1-3/4 cup (1 pt.) whipping cream
4 eggs, beaten

1 tbls. flour
1/2 cup sugar

Mix above ingredients well so flour blends. Pour custard over fruit and sprinkle with cinnamon. Bake at 350° until custard is set, for about 45-50 minutes.

LAYERED DESSERT

Governor Walter Dale Miller

2 cups flour
2 sticks margarine or butter
1 cup chopped nuts
1 (8-oz.) pkg. cream cheese
1 cup powdered sugar

1 (8-oz.) tub Cool Whip
2 (3-1/2-oz.) pkgs. chocolate or
  butterscotch instant pudding
1 tsp. vanilla
3 cups milk

First layer: Mix flour, butter, and nuts, mix well. Place in 9 x 13 inch pan. Bake 10 minutes at 350°. Let cool. Second layer: Mix until smooth cream cheese, powdered sugar and 1 cup Cool Whip. Pour over first layer. Third layer: Mix pudding and milk, add vanilla. Mix and let stand in refrigerator until set. Pour over second layer. Top with remaining Cool Whip and nuts. Refrigerate.

LEMON BUNDT CAKE

Mrs. Robert Pritchard

1 pkg. lemon cake mix
1 pkg. instant lemon pudding
4 eggs
$\frac{1}{2}$ cup oil

1 cup water
1-$\frac{1}{3}$ cups powdered sugar
5 tbls. lemon juice
$\frac{1}{3}$ cup coconut

Heat oven to 350°. Grease and flour Bundt pan or tube angel food pan. Mix all ingredients except last three together. Pour into pan. Bake 45-50 minutes until it tests done to the touch. Cool 5 minutes before turning out on large plate and pouring over it the glaze made by blending powdered sugar, juice, and adding coconut. Spoon over warm cake, covering all of it. Serves 10. Cake will keep moist several days.

Topping:

1 pt. commercial sour cream
$\frac{1}{3}$ cup brown sugar

$\frac{1}{2}$ cup halved seedless grapes
$\frac{1}{2}$ cup fresh blueberries

If you do not have the fruit, the topping is delicious without it, but the fruit adds the finishing touch! It always brings raves when it is served. Freezes well.

LEMON CHEESE BARS

Bonnie Untereiner Bjork
Former Governor's Cabinet

1 pkg. yellow cake mix with
  pudding

1 egg
$\frac{1}{3}$ cup vegetable oil

Mix together until crumbly. Reserve 1 cup of mix. Put remainder in ungreased 9 x 13 pan and bake at 350° for 15 minutes.

Filling:

1 (8-oz.) pkg. cream cheese,
  softened
$\frac{1}{3}$ cup sugar

1 tsp. lemon juice
1 egg

Beat these together until light and smooth. Spread over baked layer. Sprinkle with remaining crumb mixture and bake 15 minutes longer.

LEMON PIE

Eston Blake Miller

1-$\frac{1}{2}$ cups white sugar
$\frac{1}{3}$ cup cornstarch
1-$\frac{1}{2}$ cups water
$\frac{1}{2}$ cup lemon juice

2 tsp. grated lemon peel
2 - 3 drops yellow food coloring
3 egg yolks, beaten
1 baked pie crust

Bring sugar, cornstarch, and water to a boil and cook for 1 minute. Remove from stove and add lemon juice, lemon peel, and food coloring. Temper egg yolks by combining a few tbls. of hot mixture to the beaten egg yolks, combine with cooked mixture and cook for another 1 minute. Pour into baked pie crust. Top with meringue and brown meringue.

Meringue:

1 tbls. cornstarch
$\frac{1}{2}$ cup water
2 tbls. white sugar

3 egg whites
6 tbls. white sugar

Combine cornstarch, water, and 2 tbls. white sugar and cook until thickened; set aside to cool. Beat egg whites until stiff; add sugar 1 tbls. at a time, then add the cooled cornstarch mixture and beat until soft peaks form. Spread over pie mixture and bake in oven at 375° until meringue is golden brown.

Grandson of Governor Walter Dale Miller

LIGHT CHOCOLATE CAKE

Bonnie Untereiner Bjork
Former Governor's Cabinet

2 egg whites
1 can Diet Coke

1 box chocolate cake mix

Mix ingredients together and bake at temperature and length as instructed on box. (Also can use spice cake).

85104-07

LOW-FAT FLAG CAKE

Julie Johnson
Former Governor's Cabinet

2 pints strawberries
1 (13.6-oz.) pkg. fat-free pound cake, cut into 12 slices

1-1/3 cups blueberries, divided
1 (12-oz.) tub Cool Whip Fat-Free whipped topping, divided

Slice 1 cup of the strawberries; set aside. Halve remaining strawberries; set aside. Line bottom of 13 x 9 inch baking dish with cake slices. Top with sliced strawberries and 1 cup of the blueberries. Spread whipped topping evenly over berries. Place strawberry halves and remaining 1/3 cup blueberries on whipped topping to create a flag design. Refrigerate until ready to serve.

MANDARIN ORANGE CAKE

Cleo Shroyer
Governor's Staff

2 eggs
2 cups flour
2 cups sugar
2 cans mandarin oranges, drained

1 tsp. soda
1 tsp. salt
1 tsp. vanilla

Mix altogether and bake in greased 9 x 13 inch pan at 350° for 30 - 40 minutes.

Topping:

1-1/2 cups brown sugar
6 tbls. butter

6 tbls. milk

Bring to boil, cook until sugar is dissolved. Make holes in hot cake with a fork and pour mixture over cake. Serve with ice cream or whipped cream. (Cool Whip works, but I like the real stuff).

MISS ETHEL'S COCONUT CREAM PIE

Dr. Howell W. Todd
Former Governor's Cabinet

½ cup sugar
2 heaping tbls. flour
3 large egg yolks, beaten
½ stick butter

1 cup flaked coconut
2-½ cups milk
1 tsp. vanilla
1 unbaked 9" pie crust

Mix flour and sugar well in heavy saucepan. Add remaining ingredients and cook slowly, stirring constantly with a spatula, until thickened. May be cooked in a double boiler, also. Pour into unbaked pie crust and cook at 350° until pie crust is brown. Immediately add meringue while hot and bake at 375° until meringue is to desired brownness.

NOTE: This makes a big pie, so use an appropriately sized pie crust.

Meringue:

2 tbls. sugar
1 tbls. cornstarch
½ cup water

5 egg whites
3 tbls. sugar

Mix 2 tbls. sugar, cornstarch, and water in small saucepan. Heat until mixture boils slightly and becomes clear. Set aside. Beat egg whites until slightly stiff and add 3 tbls. sugar and the sugar/cornstarch mixture. Continue beating until desired degree of stiffness. Spread on pie, top with a little coconut, and brown in 375° oven.

85104-07

MOCHA CAKE

Jeff Vonk
Governor's Cabinet

1 cup sugar
1 cup flour
½ cup cocoa
1 tsp. salt
1 egg, beaten

1 tsp. vanilla
½ cup melted shortening
1 tsp. baking soda
1 cup hot coffee

Mix sugar, flour, cocoa, and salt together. Add egg, vanilla, melted shortening and hot coffee (with baking soda dissolved in it) to dry ingredients. Mix with electric mixer until smooth. Bake at 350° approximately 35 minutes in greased 9 x 9" pan. While cake bakes, prepare icing.

Icing:

3-¾ tbls. flour
¾ cup milk
¾ cup sugar

¾ cup shortening
¼ tsp. salt
1 tsp. vanilla

Combine flour and milk in saucepan with whisk. Cook over low heat, stirring constantly until thickened. Cool in refrigerator until cold. Cream sugar, shortening, and salt in electric mixer bowl. Add vanilla and cold flour-milk mixture. Beat until creamy like whipped cream (and sugar crystals have dissolved). Frost cooled cake.

MRS. RISTY'S CAKE

Mrs. Sissel Boe

¼ cup hot water
1 tsp. baking soda
2 eggs
1 cup brown sugar
1 cup sour cream

2 cups flour, sifted
½ tsp. allspice
½ tsp. cinnamon
3 tbls. melted butter
¼ cup powdered sugar

Dissolve baking soda in hot water. Beat eggs until lemon colored. Add the brown sugar. Add the sour cream. Add cooled hot water and baking soda mixture. Beat after each addition. Sift flour with allspice and cinnamon. Beat in melted butter. Pour into buttered 8 x 11 inch pan and bake at 350° for 45 minutes - 1 hour. Test with toothpick to see if done. Dust with powdered sugar. Serve warm. (Good with coffee).

Mother of Governor Nils Boe

Note: Recipe submitted by Carol Mashek, Minnehaha County Historical Society

NAPA VALLEY CHEESECAKE

Betty Oldenkamp
Former Governor's Cabinet

1 box cake mix-chocolate,
  yellow, or white
1 egg
1 stick butter - softened

2 cups powdered sugar
1 (8-oz.) pkg. cream cheese,
  softened
2 eggs

Mix box cake, 1 egg and butter till moist and press into 9 x 13 inch cake pan. Mix powdered sugar, cream cheese, and 2 eggs; spread over cake mix. Bake at 350° for 25 minutes.

NUTTY CRACKER DELIGHT

Bonnie Untereiner Bjork
Former Governor's Cabinet

½ cup butter
½ cup sugar
1 tsp. vanilla

1 cup slivered almonds
42 club crackers

Line 15 x 10 inch pan with heavy aluminum foil. Lay 42 club crackers (with holes on top) in pan. Melt butter on medium heat, when butter is melted, add sugar until boiling - stirring constantly for 2 minutes. Take off burner and stir in vanilla. Pour mixture over crackers and spread evenly with knife until crackers are covered. Put slivered almonds on top. Bake at 350° for 10 minutes. Remove crackers immediately from pan and put on wire rack until cooled. Keep in airtight container. May freeze.

OATMEAL CHOCOLATE CHIP CAKE

Nila Novotny
Governor's Staff

1-¾ cups boiling water
1 cup oatmeal
1 cup brown sugar
1 cup white sugar
½ cup margarine
2 large eggs

1-¾ cups flour
1 tsp. baking soda
½ tbls. salt
1 tbls. cocoa
1 (12-oz.) pkg. chocolate chips
¾ cup walnuts

Pour boiling water over oatmeal in bowl and let stand 10 minutes. Add brown sugar, white sugar, margarine, and stir until margarine melts. Add eggs and mix well. Sift together flour, baking soda, salt, and cocoa and add to oatmeal mixture. Add ½ of chocolate chips and pour into greased and floured 9 x 13 inch pan. Sprinkle nuts and other half of chocolate chips on top and bake 40 minutes at 350°.

ORANGE DESSERT

Deb Hall
Former Governor's Staff

2 (3-oz.) pkgs. Orange Jell-O or
  1 large pkg.
2-1/2 cups hot water
1 pint orange sherbet

1/2 large carton Cool Whip
2 small cans mandarin oranges,
  or 1 large can, drained

Dissolve Jell-O in hot water, cool until it thickens slightly. (While this is setting up, take sherbet and Cool Whip out to thaw a little). Whip in sherbet and Cool Whip. Add to oranges and refrigerate. May also be frozen.

ORANGE SUMMER DESSERT

First Lady Jean Rounds

1/2 lb. Ritz crackers, crushed
1/4 cup sugar
1/4 cup margarine
1 can sweetened condensed
  milk

1 (6-oz.) can frozen orange juice
2 cans mandarin oranges,
  drained
1 (8-oz.) container Cool Whip

Mix crackers, sugar, and margarine. Press into 9 x 13 inch pan. Combine milk and orange juice. Add mandarin oranges and fold in whipped topping. Pour onto crumb crust and sprinkle a few reserved crumbs on top. Refrigerate.

PATRIOTIC LOG CAKE

First Lady June Foss

3 eggs, separated
$^2/_3$ cup sifted cake flour
$^3/_4$ cup sugar
1 tsp. baking powder
$^1/_2$ tsp. salt

4 tsp. cold water
$^1/_4$ tsp. vanilla extract
few drops almond extract
$^3/_4$ to $1^1/_2$ cups heavy cream
   (whipped)

Beat the egg yolks until thick and light. Sift flour with the sugar, baking powder, and salt. Add gradually to the egg yolks, beating well after each addition. Add the water and flavorings. Beat egg whites until stiff and fold into cake batter. Grease a 9 x 12 inch pan and line with waxed paper. Pour batter into pan and spread evenly. Bake in moderate oven (375°) 12 to 15 minutes. Turn out on a towel sprinkled with powdered sugar, trim away the crusty edges and roll from the 12-inch side into a tight roll. Cool; unroll; spread with jelly or whipped cream and roll again. Sprinkle the outside thickly with instant cocoa. Place on a platter and press on warmed but not melted chocolate pieces. Push pieces of whole cinnamon into the sides at an angle to give the illusion of broken branches. Decorate with flags and maraschino cherries.

Served at Pierre for Legislative Wives Tea in February 1958. It was very good.

Note: Recipe submitted by Daughter Mary Joe Foss Finke

PATRIOTIC TRIFLE

*Recipe Box at the
Governors Residence*

whipped topping
instant vanilla pudding mix
1 pound cake
1 pkg. frozen blueberries,
   thawed

1 pkg. frozen strawberries,
   thawed

Combine whipped topping and instant vanilla pudding mix. Cut off all brown crust on pound cake and cut into slices to fit into glass baking dish. Combine blueberries with a touch of sugar in bowl (1 part sugar to 4 parts berries). Combine strawberries with a touch of sugar in a separate bowl (1 part sugar to 4 parts berries). To assemble cake: put a small amount, about 1-2 tbls. of filling (whipped topping & pudding mix) in bottom of glass baking dish and top with pound cake slice, add approximately 1-$^1/_2$ oz. blueberries, top with approximately 2-3 oz. of filling. Layer in another slice or two of pound cake. Ladle in 2-3 oz. strawberries and juice. Pipe filling over the top, using a pastry bag with a star tip. Garnish with a fresh strawberry and chocolate hazelnut pirouette (made by Pepperidge Farms). Chill & serve.

PEACH PIE

Otto Doll
Governor's Cabinet

sliced peaches
unbaked pie crust

cinnamon

Topping:

1 cup sugar
1 cup butter
1/3 cup flour

1 egg
1/4 tsp. vanilla

Slice peaches into unbaked pie crust. Sprinkle with cinnamon. Make topping by mixing sugar and butter, then add rest of ingredients. Spread topping on pie. Bake 1 hour at 300° or until brown. (Can also be frozen before baking).

PEACH PIE

Robert Duxbury
Former Governor's Cabinet

4 cups fresh peaches, sliced
1/2 cup granulated sugar

2 tbls. tapioca

Combine fresh peaches, sugar, and tapioca in bowl and let stand 15 minutes.

Topping:

1/2 cup flour
1/4 cup butter or oleo

1/2 cup brown sugar
1/2 cup chopped nuts (optional)

Blend all ingredients, sprinkle 1/3 of the mixture on the bottom of an unbaked 8" pie shell. Pour in peaches. Add rest of the topping mixture. Bake at 450° for 10 minutes, then 350° for 25 to 30 minutes.

PEACH-HONEY DUMPLINGS

Dean Anderson
Former Governor's Cabinet

peaches, peeled and pitted
pie crust
1 cup powdered sugar

1/2 cup butter
3 tbls. cream
2 tbls. honey

Put a whole, peeled, and unpitted peach into a square of pie crust. Pull four corners up and around the peach. (Make 8 squares from one double crust pie recipe). Bake in moderate (350°) oven for 1 hour. Cream together the powdered sugar and butter. Add cream and honey. Cook in a double boiler until clear. Serve hot over peaches.

223

PECAN BARS

Amy Mickelson Brecht

Crust:

1-⅓ cups flour   ½ cup butter
1 cup brown sugar

Mix until crumbly. Press into 9 x 13 inch greased pan and bake at 350°
for 15 minutes.

Filling:

2 eggs, beaten   1 tsp. vanilla
½ cup dark corn syrup   ½ tsp. salt
1 cup brown sugar   ½ cup chopped pecans
2 tbls. flour

Mix all filling ingredients, except nuts. Pour over baked crust and sprinkle
pecans over top. Bake at 350° for 25 minutes or until topping is set.
While bars are hot, sprinkle one bag milk chocolate chips over top.
When melted, spread thin.

Daughter of Governor George S. Mickelson and Granddaughter of Governor George T. Mickelson

PINA COLADA CAKE

First Lady Mary Dean Janklow

1 pkg. yellow cake mix   2 tsp. rum flavoring
1 (8-oz.) can crushed pineapple, 1 (8-oz.) container whipped
  drained   topping
½ cup shredded coconut   ½ cup toasted coconut

Mix cake according to package ingredients and instructions except substitute pineapple for water. Stir in coconut and rum flavoring. Pour batter
into two 9 inch round greased baking pans. Bake as directed. Cool 10
minutes and then remove cake from pans. Once completely cool, frost
first layer with whipped topping. Place second layer on top and continue
frosting top and sides with remaining whipped topping. Sprinkle with
toasted coconut. Refrigerate well before serving.

85104-07

PINEAPPLE UPSIDE-DOWN CAKE

*Recipe Box at the
Governors Residence*

1/2 packed cup brown sugar
2 tbls. margarine or butter,
  melted
1/2 fresh pineapple, cleaned,
  cored and sliced 1/2 inch thick

maraschino cherries, halved
1 (18.25-oz.) pkg. yellow cake
  mix

Prepare cake mix batter according to package directions. Mix sugar and margarine or butter in small bowl. Evenly crumble on bottom of lightly greased 13 x 9 x 2 inch baking pan. Arrange pineapple slices over sugar mixture. Place a cherry half in each pineapple ring; set aside. Pour cake mix batter over pineapple slices. Bake at 350° for 40-45 minutes or until toothpick inserted in center of cake comes out clean. Cool in pan on wire rack 5 minutes. Invert cake onto serving platter. Cool cake 10 more minutes and serve warm or cool completely before serving. Makes 12 servings.

POPPY SEED CAKE

Amy Mickelson Brecht

1 yellow cake mix
1 vanilla instant pudding
4 eggs
1/2 cup oil

1 cup sour cream
1/2 cup water
1/2 cup poppy seeds
vanilla

Mix ingredients well. Bake in a greased Bundt pan at 350° for 50 minutes. Top with orange glaze when cake is cool. Glaze: Orange juice & powdered sugar.

Daughter of Governor George S. Mickelson and Granddaughter of Governor George T. Mickelson

PUMPKIN BARS

Recipe Box at the Governors Residence

2 cups flour
2 cups sugar
2 tsp. baking soda
2 tsp. cinnamon
$1/2$ tsp. cloves
$1/2$ tsp. nutmeg

$1/2$ tsp. ginger
$1/2$ tsp. allspice
1 cup vegetable oil
4 eggs
1 small can pumpkin

Combine dry ingredients in large bowl. In small bowl, beat together vegetable oil and eggs; add pumpkin and blend together. Add to dry mixture and mix well. Pour into greased and floured 9 x 13 inch pan. Bake at 350° for 45 minutes - 1 hour. Frost with cream cheese frosting.

Frosting:

1 (8-oz.) pkg. cream cheese
$1/2$ cup margarine
3-$1/2$ cups powdered sugar

1 tbls. milk
1 tsp. vanilla

Combine ingredients and beat until creamy. Frost cooled bars.

85104-07

PUMPKIN CHEESECAKE

Mary Bisson
Former Governor's Staff

1-¼ cups gingersnap cookie crumbs (about 20 2" cookies)
¼ cup margarine or butter, melted
3 (8-oz.) pkgs. cream cheese, softened
1 cup sugar
1 tsp. ground ginger

1 tsp. ground cinnamon
½ tsp. ground cloves
1 (16-oz.) can pumpkin
3 eggs
2 tbls. sugar
12 walnut halves
¾ cup chilled whipping cream

Heat oven to 350°. Mix cookie crumbs and margarine. Press evenly on bottom of springform pan, 9 x 3 inches. Bake 10 minutes; cool. Reduce oven temperature to 300°. Beat cream cheese, 1 cup sugar, the cinnamon, ginger, and cloves in 4-quart bowl on medium speed until smooth and fluffy. Add pumpkin. Beat in eggs, one at a time on low speed. Pour over crumb mixture. Bake until center is firm, about 1-¼ hours. Cool to room temperature. Cover and refrigerate at least 3 hours but no longer than 48 hours. Cook and stir 2 tbls. sugar and the walnuts over medium heat until sugar is melted and nuts are coated. Immediately spread on a dinner plate or aluminum foil; cool. Carefully break nuts apart to separate if necessary. Cover tightly and store at room temperature up to 3 days. Loosen cheesecake from side of pan; remove side of pan. Beat whipping cream in chilled 1-½ quart bowl until stiff. Pipe whipped cream around edge of cheesecake; arrange walnuts on top. Refrigerate any remaining cheesecake immediately. Makes 12 servings.

PUMPKIN JELLYROLL

First Lady Jean Rounds

3 eggs
1 cup sugar
1 cup pumpkin
1 tsp. vanilla
3/4 cup flour
2 tsp. cinnamon

1 tsp. baking powder
1 tsp. ginger
1/2 tsp. nutmeg
1/2 tsp. salt
1 cup nuts, chopped finely

Beat eggs for 5 minutes. Gradually beat in sugar, pumpkin, and vanilla. Mix flour, cinnamon, baking powder, ginger, nutmeg, and salt. Fold into pumpkin and egg mixture. Spread in greased and floured 15 x 10 x 1 inch jellyroll pan. Top with chopped nuts. Bake at 375° for 15 minutes - no longer. Turn out on a towel sprinkled with powdered sugar. Roll as for jellyroll - cool - unroll and fill with the filling.

Filling:

1 cup powdered sugar
1 8 oz. pkg. cream cheese

4 tbls. butter
1/2 tsp. vanilla

Spread on cake, re-roll and chill.

85104-07

RASPBERRY TRIFLE

Pam Janklow Derheim

1 (10¾-oz.) loaf frozen pound
  cake
1-½ cups whipping cream
¾ cup sugar (divided)
2 (8-oz.) pkgs. cream cheese,
  softened

2 tsp. lemon juice
1½ tsp. vanilla extract
2 (10-oz.) pkgs. frozen
  raspberries
2 tbls. baking cocoa

Trim the darker crust from the pound cake and slice into 18 - 20 slices about ½ inch thick, set aside. Place the raspberries in a colander with about ¼ cup of sugar on them (optional) so they can thaw and drain (be sure to reserve the juice). In a mixing bowl, beat whipping cream with ¼ cup of the sugar until soft peaks have formed. In another mixing bowl, beat the softened cream cheese, lemon juice, vanilla, and remaining ½ cup sugar. Fold 2 cups of the whipping cream into the cream cheese mixture. Set aside remaining whipped creamed for topping. Line the bottom of a 3-quart glass bowl or trifle bowl with ⅓ of the cake slices. Drizzle some of the raspberry juice on the cake. Next, spread ¼ of the cream cheese mixture over the cake. Sift ¼ of the cocoa over the top. Sprinkle with ⅓ of the berries. Repeat this layer combination twice. End with the cream cheese mixture, then top with the set aside whipping cream and a little sprinkle of cocoa. Cover and refrigerate for at least 4 hours or overnight. When ready to serve, garnish with raspberries, if desired.

Daughter of Governor William J. Janklow

RAW APPLE CAKE

Linda Fridley
Governor's Staff

2 cups apples, diced
1 cup sugar
1 egg
¼ cup oil
½ tsp. salt

1 cup raisins
1 cup walnuts
1 cup flour
1 tsp. baking soda
1 tsp. cinnamon

Mix egg, sugar, oil, cinnamon, salt, and soda. Stir in flour and apples. Add raisins and nuts. Bake in prepared glass baking pan 1 hour at 350°. Serve with whipped cream. A good holiday cake.

RED, WHITE, AND BLUE SALAD

Aaron Miller
Governor's Staff

1 pkg. nonfat vanilla instant
  pudding (4 servings size)
1 (12-oz.) container Fat-Free
  Cool Whip
1-½ cups milk

1 (10-oz.) angel food cake -
  cubed
1 pint strawberries - cut up
1 bag frozen blueberries

In a medium size bowl, whip the pudding mix, milk, and Cool Whip. In another bowl, place one layer of the cubed cake, then place a layer of the pudding mixture and a layer of strawberries and blueberries.

Note: If you use a 6-½ oz. vanilla pudding mix, use an additional ½ cup of milk.

RHUBARB CAKE

Donna Morlock
Former Governor's Staff

1-½ packed cups brown sugar
½ cup shortening
2 eggs
¼ tsp. salt
1 tsp. soda

1 cup sour milk or buttermilk
2 cups flour
3 cups rhubarb, diced
1 tsp. vanilla

Mix in order given. Bake in greased and floured 9 x 13 inch pan. Sprinkle top with a mixture of ½ cup sugar, 1 teaspoon cinnamon. Bake at 350° for 35-40 minutes.

RHUBARB CHEESECAKE PIE

Lori Shangreaux
Governor's Staff

1 9" unbaked pastry shell
½ cup sugar

2-½ cups chopped rhubarb
1 tbls. flour

Stir sugar and flour together, mix with rhubarb, put into crust. Bake at 425° for 15 minutes. Remove from oven. Lower temperature to 350°.

1 (8-oz.) pkg. cream cheese
½ cup sugar

2 eggs

Beat cream cheese. Add eggs, one at a time, then add sugar. Mix well and pour over hot rhubarb layer. Bake 30 minutes.

¾ cup sour cream
1 tsp. vanilla

2 tbls. sugar

Mix well and spread on hot pie. Cool 3 hours in refrigerator.

RHUBARB DELIGHT

Patti de Hueck Clodfelter
Former Governor's Staff

Crust:

1 cup flour
2 tbls. sugar

½ cup butter

Combine flour, sugar, and butter into a crumbly mixture and press into a 9 x 9 inch pan. Bake at 350° for 20-25 minutes. Cool. Make filling by combining ingredients. Cook in saucepan, stirring until thickened. Make meringue and place over top of filling. Bake at 375° until meringue is set and slightly brown.

Filling:

1-¼ cup sugar
3 egg yolks, beaten thick
2-¼ cup chopped rhubarb

⅓ cup cream
2 tbls. flour

Meringue:

3 egg whites

½ cup sugar

RHUBARB DESSERT

Luz Naasz
Residence Staff

1 cup flour
2 tbls. brown sugar
1 stick butter
2 cups rhubarb, chopped

1-½ cups sugar
⅓ cup cream cheese
3 eggs, yolks and whites
  separated

Mix flour, brown sugar, and butter together. Press out on a greased cookie sheet. Then mix the rhubarb, sugar, and cream cheese and egg yolks - pour over mixture. Beat egg whites and 2 tablespoons of sugar and pour over top. Bake at 350° until good and brown.

RHUBARB SURPRISE

Luz Naasz
Residence Staff

1 cup flour
½ packed cup brown sugar
⅓ tsp. salt

½ cup walnuts, chopped
¼ cup margarine or butter
1 tsp. vanilla

Blend with the margarine or butter. Press in an ungreased 9 x 13 inch pan. Bake at 375° for 10-15 minutes or until golden brown.

Filling:

2 (8-oz.) pkgs. cream cheese, softened
¾ cup sugar

1 tsp. vanilla
3 eggs

Beat cream cheese until light and fluffy. Mix in sugar and vanilla. Add eggs, one at a time, mixing well after each. Pour cheese mixture on baked crust and bake at 375° for 15-20 minutes or until set and edges are light brown.

Topping:

3 cups fresh rhubarb, chopped
¾-1 cup sugar
¼ tsp. cinnamon

¼ cup water
1 tbls. cornstarch

In large sauce pan, combine chopped rhubarb, sugar, cinnamon, water, and cornstarch. Cook, stirring constantly until thickened and rhubarb is tender. Cool. Pour over cheese filling, then chill. Serve with whipped cream if desired.

85104-07

RHUBARB TORTE

Susan Stoneback
Former Governor's Staff

1-½ cups flour
1-½ cups oatmeal
1 cup brown sugar
1 cup shortening

½ cup chopped nuts (optional, may be sprinkled on top before baking)

Place ¾ of the crust mixture in a 9 x 13 inch pan, patting down to form a bottom crust. Bake 8 - 10 minutes at 350°.

Dessert filling:

3 cups rhubarb
2 tbls. cornstarch
1-½ cups sugar

¼ cup water
1 (3-oz.) pkg. Strawberry Jell-O
1 tsp. vanilla

Cook the rhubarb, cornstarch, sugar, and water until they thicken. Then add, and stir well the strawberry Jell-O and vanilla. Pour the rhubarb mixture on the bottom crust. Add the remaining crust mixture as the top. Optional: You can sprinkle the top with the chopped nuts. Bake at 350° for 30 minutes. Serve as is or with ice cream or Cool Whip.

RUBY RASPBERRY PIE

Mrs. Delores Raeder

Crust:

2 cups flaked coconut
2 tbls. sugar

1 tbls. flour
2 tbls. butter, melted

Combine coconut, sugar, and flour with melted butter. Press into a 9" pie pan. Bake at 350° for 10 minutes. Cool.

Filling:

4 cups miniature marshmallows
1 (10-oz.) pkg. frozen raspberries, thawed and drained

½ cup reserved raspberry syrup
few drops of red food coloring
1 cup heavy cream

Melt miniature marshmallows with ½ cup raspberry syrup in top of double boiler, stirring and cooking until smooth. Add red food coloring; mix well. Chill until thickened. Stir until well blended; fold in drained raspberries and whipped cream. Pour into crust; chill until firm.

SALAD DRESSING CAKE

Scott Burma

1 cup white sugar
2 cups flour
2 tsp. baking soda

3 tbls. cocoa
1 cup water
1 cup mayonnaise

Sift together the sugar, flour, baking soda, and cocoa. Add the water and mayonnaise. Mix thoroughly and bake at 350° for 30-45 minutes.

Great-grandson of Governor Walter Dale Miller

SOUR CREAM POUND CAKE

John Cooper
Former Governor's Cabinet

1/2 lb. butter
3 cups sugar
6 eggs
3 cup plain flour

1/2 tsp. salt
1/2 tsp. soda
2 tsp. vanilla
1/2 pint sour cream

The secret lies in putting cake in a cold oven. Sift together flour, salt, and soda. Cream butter and sugar. Add 2 eggs and beat. Add 1 cup flour. Continue to alternate 2 eggs and flour - beat after each addition. Add vanilla and mix. Fold in sour cream. Put in Bundt or tube pan - pre greased with butter. Place in COLD oven and turn temperature to 325°. DO NOT OPEN OVEN FOR 1 HOUR. Cook 1-1/2 hours. Cool and remove from pan.

SOUR CREAM RAISIN BARS

Shirley Jenssen
Former Governor's Staff

1-3/4 cups flour
1 cup margarine
1 cup brown sugar
1 tsp. soda
1-3/4 cups oatmeal

4 egg yolks
3 tbls. cornstarch
2 cups sour cream
1-1/2 cups brown sugar
2 cups raisins

Mix flour, margarine, brown sugar, soda, and oatmeal like pie crust. Remove 1-1/2 cups of mixture. Press remaining mixture into a 9 x 13 inch pan. Bake at 350° for 15 minutes. Combine egg yolks (beaten), cornstarch, sour cream, brown sugar, and raisins. Cook until thick. Pour over crust, sprinkle with remaining crumbs - and return to oven for 20 minutes.

Note: Instead of sour cream, use a 13 oz. can of carnation milk, add plain milk to make 2 cups then add 1-1/2 tbls. lemon juice or vinegar to milk.

85104-07

SOUR MILK GINGERBREAD

First Lady Madge Turner Mickelson

¼ cup shortening
½ cup sugar
1 egg
½ cup molasses
1-¼ cups flour

1 tsp. soda
1 tsp. cinnamon
1 tsp. ginger
¼ tsp. salt
½ cup sour milk

Cream shortening and add sugar gradually. Add well beaten egg and molasses. Sift flour before measuring. Sift flour, soda, cinnamon, ginger, and salt together. Add dry ingredients alternately with sour milk, mixing well after each addition. Pour into well-greased and floured 9" square pan. Bake in 350° oven for 30 minutes.

Wife of Governor George T. Mickelson and Mother of Governor George S. Mickelson

Note: Submitted by Lavon Mickelson Meyers from recipe box of Madge Turner Mickelson, deceased.

SOUTH DAKOTA SHEET CAKE

Doneen Hollingsworth
Governor's Cabinet

2 cups flour
2 cups sugar
1 tsp. baking soda
1 tsp. cinnamon
1 cup water

4 tbls. cocoa
1 cup margarine
1 tsp. vanilla
½ cup buttermilk
2 eggs, beaten

Mix flour, sugar, baking soda, and cinnamon in a large bowl. In a saucepan, melt margarine. Add cocoa and water and bring to a boil. Pour over dry ingredients, stir well. Mix together vanilla, buttermilk, and eggs. Add into above mixture. Pour into a well-greased, large sheet cake pan and bake at 400° for 15-20 minutes.

Frosting:

½ cup margarine
6 tbls. milk
1 tsp. vanilla

4 tbls. cocoa
1 lb. powdered sugar

Melt margarine in saucepan. Stir in cocoa and milk and bring to a boil. Remove from heat and add powdered sugar. Mix until smooth. Add vanilla. Spread warm frosting over warm cake.

SOUTHERN COCONUT CAKE

Dr. Howell W. Todd
Former Governor's Cabinet

1 cup Crisco
2 cups sugar
3 cups plain flour
½ tsp. salt

1 cup milk
2 tsp. vanilla
3 tsp. baking powder
8 egg whites, stiffly beaten

Cream sugar and Crisco until light and fluffy. Sift flour and salt, and add alternately with milk, beginning and ending with flour mixture. Do not overbeat. Add vanilla and baking powder. Fold in egg whites and mix only enough to properly integrate the egg whites into the batter. Bake in three 9" layers at 325° until inserted toothpick comes out clean. You can also use four 8" layers.

Icing:

2 fresh coconuts
1 cup water
⅔ cup white Karo syrup
3 cups sugar

4 egg whites, stiffly beaten
1 tsp. vanilla
4 tbls. confectioners sugar

Pierce coconuts and drain milk. Extract coconut and shred in a food processor. Strain coconut milk and set aside. Combine water, sugar, and Karo syrup in a saucepan and boil until the mixture spins a thread. Gradually add the sugar mixture to the beaten egg whites. Continue beating and after 2-3 minutes, add the confectioners sugar and vanilla. Beat until icing holds a stiff peak. It will take several minutes! While icing is beating, add coconut milk to the saucepan where sugar mixture was prepared. Bring to a slight boil allowing leftover sugar mixture in the saucepan to mix with coconut milk. As the cake is assembled, soak the layers with the coconut milk (don't overdo it!), spread icing on the layer, and sprinkle with shredded coconut until cake is assembled. Once the icing is complete, generously sprinkle coconut on top and sides of cake.

STRAWBERRY AND RHUBARB PIE

Catherine Sulzle
Former Governor's Staff

1-½ cups sugar
3 tbls. quick-cooking tapioca
¼ tsp. salt
¼ tsp. nutmeg
1 lb. rhubarb, cut in ½" pieces
  (3 cups)

1 cup sliced strawberries
1 pastry for 9" lattice-top pie
1 tbls. butter or margarine

Combine sugar, tapioca, salt, and nutmeg. Add rhubarb and strawberries; mix to coat fruit. Let stand about 20 min. Turn into pastry-lined 9" pie place. Dot with butter. Adjust lattice top; seal. Bake at 400° for 35-40 minutes.

STRAWBERRY CAKE

Pam Roberts
Governor's Cabinet

1 (18-oz.) box white cake mix
  (sifted)
¾ cup frozen sweetened
  strawberries (drained &
  puréed)

1 (3-oz.) box strawberry Jell-O
1½ tsp. vanilla
4 eggs (beaten)
½ cup water
¾ cup vegetable oil

Add all ingredients together in a large bowl and mix well. Pour into a 9 x 13 inch pan and bake in a pre-heated 350° oven for 30 - 35 minutes, or until a small knife inserted into the center of the cake comes out clean; or grease and flour two 9" round cake pans. Divide batter evenly between prepared pans and bake 25-30 minutes. Cool over a wire rack for 10 minutes, then tap out to cool completely.)

Strawberry Icing:

1 stick butter
1 box (3 cups) powdered sugar
½ cup frozen sweetened
  strawberries (drained and
  puréed)

In a bowl, cream together butter, powdered sugar, and strawberries. Frost the cake and keep refrigerated.

STRAWBERRY DESSERT

Michele Rounds Brich

1 can sweetened condensed
  milk
1 (8-oz.) pkg. cream cheese,
  softened

1 (8-oz.) pkg. Cool Whip
1 angel food cake, torn into
  small pieces
1 qt. fresh strawberries

Fold sweetened condensed milk into cream cheese. Fold Cool Whip into mixture. In bowl or cake pan, layer ingredients in the following order: angel food cake pieces, cream cheese mixture, strawberries. Repeat layering, ending with strawberries. Chill before serving.

Sister of Governor M. Michael Rounds

TEA TIME TASSIES

Governor Archie Gubbrud

1 (3-oz.) pkg. cream cheese
½ cup butter or margarine

1 cup sifted enriched flour

CHEESE PASTRY: Let cream cheese and butter soften at room temperature; blend. Stir in flour. Chill slightly, about 1 hour. Shape in 2 dozen 1 inch balls. Place in tiny ungreased 1-¾" muffin cups. Press dough on bottom and sides of cups.

1 egg
¾ cup brown sugar
1 tbls. soft butter or margarine

1 tsp. vanilla
dash salt
⅔ cup pecans, coarsely broken

PECAN FILLING: Beat together egg, sugar, butter, vanilla, and salt just until smooth. Divide half the pecans among pastry-lined cups; add egg mixture and top with remaining pecans. Bake in slow oven (325°) 25 minutes or until filling is set. Cool and remove from pan.

85104-07

TIRAMISU

Lynne DeLano
Former Governor's Cabinet

20 lady fingers (approximately)
1 lb. mascarpone cheese
5 tbls. sugar
5 egg whites
2 tbls. rum

5 egg yolks
2 cups espresso coffee
2 tbls. powdered cocoa
   (bittersweet)

Make the espresso coffee and let cool. Beat egg whites until stiff. In another bowl, beat egg yolks with sugar for 2-3 minutes. Add the mascarpone and mix again. Fold in the egg whites. Add the rum to the cooled coffee and dip the ladyfingers into the coffee/rum mix. Do not over soak. Place a layer of the soaked ladyfingers in a 9 x 13 inch dish. Cover the ladyfingers with half the egg and cheese mixture. Sift some cocoa on top. Place another layer of soaked ladyfingers on top of this mixture and cover with the remaining egg/cheese mixture. Sift more cocoa. Cover with plastic wrap and refrigerate at least 8 hours.

Note: Be sure to alert guests this dish contains raw eggs. It's a recipe from DaGino's in Gais, Italy.

239

TIRAMISU

Jamie Rounds

1-½ cups egg substitute (about 6 eggs worth)
2-½ - 3 cups sugar
2 - 3 tbls. vanilla
2 glugs rum, Marsala, or other liqueur (more or less)
1 (16-oz.) pkg. mascarpone cheese, softened

2 pints heavy whipping cream
2 pkgs. savoiardi (lady fingers)
2 - 3 cups espresso or very, very strong coffee (cooled)
cocoa powder (for dusting)
grated/shaved chocolate for garnish

Brew coffee, add 1-2 tbls. of vanilla and a glug of liqueur. Set aside to cool (add an ice cube if necessary). Mix sugar into eggs until the batter pulls away from the side of the bowl. Add 1-2 tbls. of vanilla and a glug of liqueur. Set aside. Whip the heavy whipping cream until stiff peaks appear. While whipping, add 1 tbls. of sugar. (It can take about 5 minutes to get stiff peaks). Set aside. In another large bowl, beat the cheese until softened. Fold the whipped topping into the cheese. (Folding the topping into the softened cheese creates a smoother texture). Fold the egg and sugar mixture into the cheese and whipped topping mixture. Dip the lady fingers (or pound cake strips) into the coffee (the longer they are dipped, the soupier the tiramisu). Layer the bottom of a large bowl with the lady fingers. Spoon the cheese mixture over the lady fingers. Dust with cocoa powder (dusting is easier if you pour some cocoa into a sieve or strainer and tap the strainer over the tiramisu). Repeat the layering until the bowl is full. Dust with cocoa one last time and garnish with chocolate shavings. Refrigerate overnight if possible. This recipe is intended to be spooned from a bowl. To make it like a cake, add more cheese and whipped cream.

Brother of Governor M. Michael Rounds

Note: Substitutions: For egg substitute: 9-12 raw yolks, at your own risk; for mascarpone cheese, 16 oz. cream cheese with 2-4 tbls. of heavy whipping cream or sour cream blended in; for heavy whipping cream, 32 oz. of whipped topping; for lady fingers, 2 pound cakes, cut into strips about ½-1" square and 3" long or so.

85104-07

TURTLE CHEESECAKE

Deonne Bloomberg
Former Governor's Cabinet

2 cups vanilla wafer crumbs
6 tbls. melted butter
1/2 cup sugar
2 eggs
1/2 cup semi-sweet chocolate chips melted

1 tsp. vanilla
1 (14-oz.) bag caramels
(5-oz.) can evaporated milk
1 cup chopped pecans
2 (8-oz.) pkg. softened cream cheese

Mix crumbs and butter press onto bottom and sides of 9 inch springform pan. Bake for 10 minutes at 350°. Melt caramels and milk until smooth. Pour over crust and top with pecans. Beat cream cheese, sugar and eggs. Blend in chocolate and vanilla and pour over pecans. Place pan on cookie sheet and bake 45 minutes longer. Loosen cake from rim of pan, cool before removing rim. Refrigerate and age 1 day. Garnish with whipped cream and finely chopped pecans if desired.

TWINKIE CAKE

Governor William J. Janklow

1 box chocolate cake mix
2 eggs
2 cups milk

1 pkg. instant chocolate pudding

Mix cake mix, eggs, milk, and pudding together and bake cake according to package time and temperature. Allow cake to cool, then split in half.

Filling:

1 cup milk
5 tbls. flour
1 cup sugar
1/2 tsp. salt

1/2 cup Crisco shortening
1/2 cup butter
1 tsp. vanilla

Mix milk and flour together in saucepan. Boil until mixture is thick. Cool. Next beat this mixture with a mixer until fluffy. Add remaining ingredients one at a time, beating well after each addition. Spread filling between cake layers. Frost cake with entire can of Dark Fudge ready-to-spread frosting. You can add a pinch of baking powder to frosting before spreading. Let cake stand at least 6 hours to develop flavor.

VIKING (CARROT) CAKE

Rosemary Rounds

4 eggs
2 cup sugar
1-$\frac{1}{2}$ tbls. corn oil
2 tsp. vanilla
2-$\frac{1}{2}$ cups flour
2 tsp. cinnamon
$\frac{1}{2}$ tsp. salt

1 tsp. baking soda
3 cups (about $\frac{3}{4}$#) raw carrots, finely grated
1 cup crushed pineapple, undrained
$\frac{1}{2}$ cup chopped walnuts if desired

Beat eggs, sugar, corn oil, and vanilla until smooth. Sift together flour, cinnamon, salt and baking soda. Add to creamed mixture. Add carrots, crushed pineapple, and nuts. Mix thoroughly. Bake at 350° for 50-60 minutes. Yield: 18 servings.

Frosting:

6 oz. cream cheese
2 tbls. butter, melted
1 tsp. vanilla

pinch salt
2-$\frac{3}{4}$ cups powdered sugar

Mix thoroughly and spread on cool cake.

Stepmother of Governor M. Michael Rounds

WAVE YOUR FLAG CAKE

Julie Johnson
Former Governor's Cabinet

1 qt. strawberries (about 4 cups), divided
1-$\frac{1}{2}$ cups boiling water
1 pkg. Jell-O, any red flavor (or 2 pkgs. 4-serving size)
ice cubes

1 (12-oz.) pkg. pound cake, cut into 10 slices
1-$\frac{1}{3}$ cups blueberries, divided
1 (8-oz.) tub Cool Whip Whipped Topping, thawed

Slice 1 cup of the strawberries; set aside. Halve remaining strawberries; set aside. Stir boiling water into dry gelatin, mix in large bowl 2 minutes until completely dissolved. Add enough ice to cold water to measure 2 cups. Add to gelatin; stir until ice is melted. Refrigerate 5 minutes or until slightly thickened (consistency of unbeaten egg whites). Meanwhile, line bottom of 13 x 9 inch dish with cake slices. Add sliced strawberries and 1 cup of the blueberries to thickened gelatin; stir gently. Spoon over cake slices. Refrigerate 4 hours or until firm. Spread whipped topping over gelatin. Arrange strawberry halves on whipped topping for "stripes" of "flag." Arrange remaining $\frac{1}{3}$ cup blueberries on whipped topping for "stars." Store leftover cake in refrigerator.

85104-07

WAVE YOUR FLAG CHEESECAKE

Julie Johnson
Former Governor's Cabinet

1 qt. strawberries, divided
1-½ cups boiling water
2 pkgs. Jell-O Brand strawberry flavored gelatin (4 serving size each)
ice cubes
1 cup cold water
1 (10.75 -oz.) pkg. pound cake, cut into 10 slices

1-⅓ cups blueberries, divided
2 (8-oz.) pkg. Philadelphia Cream Cheese, softened
¼ cup sugar
1 (8-oz.) tub Cool Whip whipped topping, thawed

Slice 1 cup of the strawberries; set aside. Halve the remaining 3 cups strawberries; set aside. Stir boiling water into dry gelatin mixes in large bowl at least 2 min. until completely dissolved. Add enough ice to cold water to measure 2 cups. Add to gelatin; stir until ice is completely melted. Refrigerate 5 minutes or until gelatin is slightly thickened (consistency of unbeaten egg whites). Meanwhile, line bottom of 13 x 9 inch dish with cake slices. Add sliced strawberries and 1 cup of the blueberries to thickened gelatin; stir gently. Spoon over cake slices. Refrigerate 4 hours or until set. Beat cream cheese and sugar in large bowl with wire whisk or electric mixer until well blended; gently stir in whipped topping. Spread over gelatin. Arrange strawberry halves on cream cheese mixture to resemble the stripes of a flag. Arrange remaining ⅓ cup blueberries on cream cheese mixture for the stars. Store any leftover dessert in refrigerator.

WELCOME TO THE NEIGHBORHOOD CHOCOLATE CHIP CAKE

David Mickelson

1 box yellow cake mix
1 small box instant chocolate pudding
½ cup sugar
¾ cup vegetable oil

¾ cup water
4 eggs
1 (8-oz.) container sour cream
1 (6-oz.) bag chocolate chips

Blend cake mix, instant pudding, sugar, oil, water, eggs, and sour cream with a mixer. Add chocolate chips and stir by hand. Place in greased Bundt pan and bake at 350° for 1 hour or until cake is set.

Son of Governor George S. Mickelson and Grandson of Governor George T. Mickelson

WHOOPIE PIES

Mary Farrar Turner

2 cups all-purpose flour
²/₃ cup Dutch-process cocoa
  powder
1-¼ tsp. baking soda
1 tsp. salt

1 cup well-shaken buttermilk
1 tsp. vanilla
1 stick unsalted butter, softened
1 packed cup brown sugar
1 large egg

Preheat oven to 350°. Whisk together flour, cocoa, baking soda, and salt in a bowl until combined. Stir together buttermilk and vanilla in a small bowl. Beat together butter and brown sugar in a large bowl with an electric mixer at medium-high speed until pale and fluffy, about 3 minutes in a standing mixer or 5 minutes with a handheld mixer, then add egg, beating until combined well. Reduce speed to low and alternately mix in flour mixture and buttermilk in batches, beginning and ending with flour, scraping down side of bowl occasionally, and mixing until smooth. Spoon ¼ cup mounds of batter about 2 inches apart onto 2 buttered large baking sheets. Bake in upper and lower thirds of oven, switching position of sheets halfway through baking, until tops are puffed and cakes spring back when touched, 11-13 minutes. Transfer with a metal spatula to a rack to cool completely.

Filling:

1 stick unsalted butter, softened
1-¼ cups confectioners sugar
2 cups marshmallow creme
  such as Marshmallow Fluff

1 tsp. vanilla

Beat together butter, confectioners sugar, marshmallow creme, and vanilla in a bowl with electric mixer at medium speed until smooth, about 3 minutes. Spread a rounded tablespoon filling on flat sides of half of cakes and top with remaining cakes.

Daughter of Governor Frank Farrar

Note: Cakes can be made 3 days ahead and kept, layered between sheets of wax paper, in an airtight container at room temperature. Filling can be made 4 hours ahead and kept, covered, at room temperature.

85104-07

COOKIES & CANDIES

FIRST STATE-OWNED RESIDENCE

The Capitol Commission purchased a large tract of property east of Capitol Lake in August 1920. This purchase included the Hodoval home. That home was used as a Governors Residence until a new building was erected in 1936.

Governor W. H. McMaster was renting an apartment at the Saint Charles Hotel and declined to move into the new house. Instead, the state rented the new acquired house to Colonel Boyd Wales of the South Dakota National Guard.

The house was improved to make it usable as a Governors Residence. Some partitions were removed, a basement was added, and several porches were built. Governor Carl Gunderson and his family were the first family to occupy the new residence. Governors W. J. Bulow, Warren Green, and Tom Berry and their families also lived at this residence.

Governor Berry obtained a Works Progress Administration grant to build a new Governors Residence. The Berrys moved into an apartment at the St. Charles Hotel in October 1936. The old residence was sold to D. L. Kelley for $1,204. Kelley moved the house to the corner of Elizabeth Street and Euclid Avenue where it stands today.

TIDBITS

Florence M. Dexter Gubbrud was the chairperson
of the 1962 Easter Seals Campaign.

———

Borghild Boe was one of four sisters of Governor
Nils Boe. She served as his official hostess at important
occasions during her brother's two terms as governor.

———

Patricia Henley Farrar made her inaugural gown
of white brocade with a rhinestone buckle at the waist.

———

Patricia Pankey Kneip had eight young sons
while she lived in the Governors Residence.
She was active in their activities around Pierre.

———

The complete makeover of much of the
Capitol grounds and especially Hilgers Gulch was
through the initiative of Mary Dean Thom Janklow.

———

Mary Dean Thom Janklow initiated the
Pierre Petunia Project. She was one of the volunteers
who walked five miles to water the petunias.

———

Linda McCahren Mickelson was known as our
Centennial First Lady. She was involved in the
preparation and fundraising for celebrating
South Dakota's first 100 years in 1989.

———

Linda McCahren Mickelson started the First Lady Golf
Tournament in Pierre. Each year the proceeds from the
tournament were donated to a different charity.

———

Patricia Kilber Caldwell Miller is the only woman
to wed a sitting governor. She became First Lady on
July 4, 1993, at the Stagvig Church outside of Rapid City.
She made her wedding suit.

COOKIES & CANDY

Cookies

BANANA BARS

First Lady Patricia Farrar

2-³/₄ cups flour
1-¹/₄ cups sugar
1-¹/₄ tsp. baking powder
1-¹/₄ tsp. baking soda
¹/₂ tsp. salt

1-¹/₂ mashed ripe bananas
³/₄ cup butter, softened
2 eggs
2 tsp. vanilla

Combine all ingredients. Beat at low speed (2 - 3 minutes). Stir in 1 cup chocolate chips or chocolate chunks. Bake at 350° in greased and floured jellyroll pan for 25 minutes.

BANANA COOKIES

John Rounds

³/₄ cup shortening
³/₄ cup brown sugar
2 eggs
2 bananas, mashed
¹/₂ tsp. vanilla

¹/₄ tsp. salt
1 tsp. soda
2 cups flour (more may be
  needed)

Cream shortening and brown sugar, add eggs, vanilla and bananas. Beat well. Add soda and salt to flour, add to banana mixture. Drop by teaspoonful onto greased cookie sheet. Bake for 12 minutes at 350°.

Frosting:

6 tbls. brown sugar
4 tbls. butter

3 tbls. milk or cream
1 tsp. vanilla

Add powdered sugar to reach spreading consistency (about 2 cups).

Son of Governor M. Michael Rounds and First Lady Jean Rounds

BLONDE BROWNIES

Mary Miller

²/₃ cup butter, melted
2 cups brown sugar
2 eggs
1-½ tsp. vanilla
2 cups flour

1 tsp. baking powder
¼ tsp. soda
½ tsp. salt
chocolate chips

Cream butter, brown sugar, eggs, and vanilla. Combine flour, baking powder, soda, and salt; add to creamed mixture. Pour into greased 9 x 13 inch pan. Sprinkle with chocolate chips. Bake at 350° for 15-20 minutes.

Daughter-in-Law of Governor Walter Dale Miller

BROWN SUGAR GINGER CRISPS

Nicole Finke

1-½ cups flour
¾ tsp. baking powder
½ tsp. salt
2 sticks unsalted butter
   (softened)
1 cup packed light brown sugar

1 large egg yolk
1 tsp. vanilla
½ cup (3-oz.) finely chopped
   crystallized ginger
1 tsp. ground ginger

Sift together flour, baking powder, and salt. Beat together butter and brown sugar until fluffy-3 minutes on medium. Beat in yolk, vanilla, and ginger. Add flour mixture and mix on low speed until combined. Drop heaping tsp. of dough on ungreased cookie sheet. Bake 350° 13-15 minutes until golden brown on middle rack. Cool cookies on sheets or rack for 5 minutes. Transfer cookies to rack to cool completely. Store in airtight container (3 weeks).

Granddaughter of Governor Joe Foss

85104-07

BROWNIES

Dr. James Hansen
Former Governor's Cabinet

1-1/2 cups flour
1 tsp. salt
2 cups sugar
6 - 8 tbls. cocoa
2 tsp. vanilla

1 cup vegetable oil
4 eggs unbeaten
1/4 cup water
1/2 cup walnuts, chopped

Beat together until mixed. Stir in walnuts. Pour into greased and floured 11 x 15 inch pan. Bake at 350° in oven for 30 minutes. Do not overbake.

Frosting:

1/4 cup water
3 tbls. cocoa
18 marshmallows or 1 cup
  miniatures

2 tbls. margarine or butter

Cook in double-boiler or microwave oven until marshmallows are melted. Cool slightly, then beat enough powdered sugar until spreading consistency.

CARAMEL PIZZA BARS

Jean Blow
Governor's Staff

1 cup brown sugar
1 cup butter or margarine,
  softened
1-1/2 cups flour

1/2 tsp. baking soda
2 cups oatmeal (not the quick
  kind)

Mix all ingredients together and put into a 10 x 15 inch slightly greased pan. Bake 10-13 minutes at 350° or until lightly browned.

30 caramels
1 cup M&M candies
1 cup chocolate chips

3 squares white almond bark
1 - 2 tbls. vegetable oil

Melt caramels with 2 tbls. water and pour over crust. Mix the M&M's and chocolate chips together then sprinkle them onto the caramels. Melt the almond bark with the vegetable oil and drizzle all over.

CHERRY-CHOCOLATE DROP COOKIES

Gretchen Lord Anderson
Former Governor's Staff

$^1/_2$ cup shortening
1 cup brown sugar
1 egg, beaten
1 tsp. baking soda
3 tbls. Dutch cocoa (Droste's)
$^1/_2$ cup milk

1-$^3/_4$ cup flour
1 tsp. vanilla
$^1/_2$ tsp. salt
Hershey's cherry chocolate
 kisses

Mix together in order: shortening, brown sugar, egg, soda, cocoa, milk, flour, vanilla, and salt. Drop on greased sheet. Bake at 350° for 9 minutes. Top with cherry chocolate kiss and return to oven for 1 minute to set the kiss in the cookie.

CHOCOLATE BLOSSOMS

Deb Bowman
Governor's Cabinet

$^1/_2$ cup sugar
$^1/_2$ cup firmly packed brown
 sugar
$^1/_4$ cup unsweetened cocoa
$^1/_2$ cup shortening
$^1/_2$ cup butter or margarine,
 softened

1 tsp. vanilla
1 egg
1-$^3/_4$ cups all-purpose flour
$^1/_2$ tsp. salt
1 tsp. baking soda
48 Hershey Kisses
sugar

In a large bowl, combine $^1/_2$ cup sugar, brown sugar, cocoa, shortening and butter; beat until light and fluffy. Add vanilla and egg; blend well. Add flour, baking soda and salt. Cover with plastic wrap and refrigerate for 1 hour. Heat oven to 375°. Shape dough into 1 inch balls; roll in sugar. Place 2 inches apart on ungreased cookie sheet. Bake at 375° for 10-12 minutes or until set. Immediately top each cookie with a candy kiss, pressing down firmly so cookie cracks around edges. Remove from cookie sheets.

85104-07

CHOCOLATE CHIP & OATMEAL COOKIES

Linda Fridley
Governor's Staff

8 eggs
3 cups granulated sugar
3 packed cups brown sugar
4 cups Crisco
4 tsp. salt
4 tsp. vanilla

4 tsp. baking soda
4 tsp. hot water
8 cups oatmeal
6 cups flour
chocolate chips

Cream eggs, sugars, Crisco, and vanilla. Combine soda and hot water and add to flour, along with the salt. Add remaining ingredients. Mix well. Bake at 350° for 8-10 minutes.

CHOCOLATE CHIP BUTTERSCOTCH COOKIES

DeeAnn Rounds

2-1/4 cups all-purpose flour
1 tsp. baking soda ·
1 cup butter, softened
3/4 cup brown sugar, packed
1/4 cup white sugar
1 (3.4-oz.) pkg. instant
  butterscotch pudding mix

2 eggs
1 tsp. vanilla extract
1 cup butterscotch chips
1 cup semi-sweet chocolate
  chips

Preheat oven to 350°. Sift flour and baking soda together, set aside. In a large bowl, cream butter, brown sugar, and white sugar together. Add the instant pudding mix until blended. Stir in the eggs and vanilla. Add the flour mixture. Stir in the butterscotch and chocolate chips. Drop cookies by rounded spoonfuls onto an ungreased cookie sheet. Bake 10-12 minutes.

Sister-in-Law of Governor M. Michael Rounds

CHOCOLATE CHIP COOKIE CREAM CHEESE BARS

Tom Dravland
Governor's Cabinet

2 pkgs. chocolate chip cookie
  dough (1 pkg. softened at
  room temperature, other
  frozen)

2 (8-oz.) pkg. cream cheese
2 eggs
1/2 cup sugar
1 tsp. vanilla

In sprayed 9 x 13 inch pan, spread softened package of cookie dough (can warm in oven a few minutes to get it level). Next, beat until fluffy the cream cheese, sugar, eggs and vanilla. Spread over bottom layer of cookie dough. Slice small chunks of the frozen cookie dough and place on top of the cream cheese layer. Bake at 350° for 25-35 minutes.

CHOCOLATE CHIP SOFTIES

Donna Morlock
Former Governor's Staff

4 cups flour
1 cup butter
2 cups brown sugar
4 eggs
2 cups sour cream

2 tsp. vanilla
1 tsp. baking soda
1 tsp. salt
2 cups chocolate chips

Cream all ingredients, refrigerate 3 hours or better yet, overnight, for firm dough. Drop on cookie sheet and bake at 350° for 15 minutes. Makes a large batch.

CHOCOLATE CHOCOLATES

Ellen Javernick

¼ cup oil
2 cups sour cream
2 cups brown sugar
2 eggs
4 cups flour

3 squares melted chocolate
¾ tsp. soda
½ tsp. baking powder
½ tsp. salt
1 tsp. vanilla

Combine oil, sour cream, brown sugar, and eggs. Add melted chocolate, vanilla, flour, and remaining dry ingredients. Drop from tsp. onto cookie sheet. Bake at 375° about 12 minutes till firm.

Frosting:

1-½ cups sugar
2 squares melted chocolate

1 cup evaporated milk

Bring to a boil, then to softball stage when tested in cold water. Mix well and spread on cookie tops.

Granddaughter of Governor Harlan Bushfield

CHOCOLATE FROSTING FOR BROWNIES

Harla Jessop
Former Governor's Staff

1 cup sugar
3 tbls. butter

⅓ cup milk
6 oz. chocolate chips

Mix sugar, butter, and milk together and stir over medium heat. Bring to a boil one minute. Add chips and stir until completely melted.

250

CHOCOLATE KISS COOKIES

First Lady Jean Rounds

1 (14-oz.) can sweetened
  condensed milk
¾ cup peanut butter

1 tsp. vanilla
2 cups Bisquick
Hershey's Chocolate Kisses

Combine sweetened condensed milk, peanut butter, vanilla, and Bisquick. Roll dough into balls, and then roll in sugar. Bake 9-10 minutes at 350°. Remove from oven, and press Hershey's Kiss into center immediately.

CHOCOLATE PORCUPINE COOKIES (NO-BAKE COOKIES)

Patricia Van Gerpen
Former Governor's Cabinet

2 cups sugar
¼ cup cocoa
1-¼ sticks butter (or margarine)
½ cup milk

½ cup peanut butter
½ cup coconut
2 tsp. vanilla
3 cups quick quarter oats

Blend sugar, cocoa, and milk in a sauce pan or double-broiler on stove. Bring to a boil, then add butter and boil one minute. Add in this order: peanut butter, vanilla, coconut, and the oats. Mix together. Use an ice cream or similar size scoop to drop mixture in individual serving sizes onto wax paper. Cool well before serving.

CHOCOLATE REVEL BARS

Stacie Olson

1 cup butter
2 cups packed brown sugar
2 eggs
2 tsp. vanilla
3 cups quick-cooking rolled
   oats
2-1/2 cups all-purpose flour
1 tsp. baking soda

1 1/2 tsp. salt
1 (14-oz.) can sweetened
   condensed milk
1 (12-oz.) pkg. semi-sweet
   chocolate pieces (2 cups)
2 tbls. butter or margarine
1 cup chopped walnuts
2 tsp. vanilla

In large bowl cream together one cup butter and brown sugar till fluffy; beat in eggs and 2 tsp. vanilla. Stir together oats, flour, soda, and 1 tsp. of the salt; stir into creamed mixture till blended. Set aside. In heavy saucepan stir milk, chocolate, 2 tbls. butter and remaining 1/2 tsp. salt over low heat till smooth. Remove from heat, stir in nuts and 2 tsp. vanilla. Put 2/3 of the oat mixture into ungreased 15 1/2 x 10 1/2 x 1 inch baking pan. Spread chocolate mixture over oat layer; sprinkle with remaining oat mixture. Bake at 350° for 25 to 30 minutes. Cool - cut into bars.

Niece of Governor M. Michael Rounds

CHOCOLATE WALNUT CRUMB BARS

Deonne Bloomberg
Former Governor's Staff

1 cup softened butter
2 cups flour
1/2 cup sugar
1/4 tsp. salt
2 cups chocolate chips

1-1/4 cup sweetened condensed
   milk
1 tsp. vanilla
1 cup chopped walnuts

Beat butter, flour, sugar, and salt until crumbly. With floured fingers, press 2 cups of crumb mixture onto bottom of greased 9 x 13 inch pan. Reserve remaining mixture. Bake at 350° for 10 - 12 minutes or until edges are golden brown. Warm 1-1/2 cups chocolate chips and sweetened milk in small heavy sauce pan over low heat, stirring until smooth. Stir in vanilla. Spread over hot crust. Stir walnuts and remaining chocolate chips into reserved crumb mixture. Sprinkle over chocolate filling. Bake 25 - 30 minutes or until center is set. Cool in pan on wire rack.

85104-07

COOKIES FROM CAKE MIX

Bonnie Untereiner Bjork
Former Governor's Cabinet

½ cup vegetable oil
2 eggs
1 box regular cake mix (you
 pick the flavor)

¼ - ½ cup "morsels" (chocolate
 or peanut butter chips,
 chopped nuts or raisins)

Preheat oven to 350°. Mix vegetable oil and eggs with cake mix. DO NOT add water. Add "morsels", mix well. Then place the dough by the teaspoonful on an ungreased cookie sheet about 2 inches apart. Bake 8-10 minutes. Let cool.

DOUBLE CHOCOLATE COOKIES

Amber Taranto

2 eggs, beaten
½ cup milk
½ cup cooking oil
2 cups Bisquick mix

2 (4-½-oz.) pkgs. instant
 chocolate pudding mix
1 cup chocolate chips

Mix all ingredients and drop by spoonful on greased cookie sheet. Bake at 350° for 12 minutes. Can frost, if desired.

Frosting:

¼ cup butter
¼ cup milk

1 cup white sugar
½ cup chocolate chips

Bring butter, milk, and sugar to a rolling boil, boil 2 minutes and add ½ cup chocolate chips. Mix well, and frost cooled cookies.

Granddaughter of Governor Walter Dale Miller

FARMER'S BROWNIES

Lynnette M. Hauschild Eckert
Governor's Staff

¼ cup cocoa
¾ cup butter
1 tsp. baking soda
2 cups sugar
½ cup milk

1 tsp. vanilla
1 cup hot water
2-½ cups flour
½ tsp. salt
2 eggs, slightly beaten

Mix cocoa in hot water, add butter, let cool. Mix the baking soda, flour, salt together. Stir in cocoa mixture, beat in eggs. Beat in milk, then vanilla. Add nuts if desired. Spread onto buttered cookie sheet (10 x 15"). Bake at 375° for 20 minutes.

FUDGY PEANUT BUTTER BROWNIES

Katie Albers

1 pkg. fudgy brownie mix
1 cup peanut butter

1 cup light corn syrup
1 tsp. vanilla

Prepare brownie mix according to package instructions. While brownies cool, combine peanut butter, syrup, and vanilla in a saucepan. Stir constantly on low heat until smooth. Do not overcook. Pour over warm brownies and place in the refrigerator until chilled.

Granddaughter-in-Law of Governor Walter Dale Miller

GINGER COOKIES

Alan Vedvei

2 cups sugar
1-1/2 cups shortening
2 eggs
1/2 cup molasses

4 cups flour
4 tsp. soda
2 tsp. ginger
2 tsp. cinnamon

Beat well sugar, shortening, eggs, and molasses. In another bowl mix flour, soda, ginger and cinnamon. Add to sugar mixture and mix. Roll in balls and dip in sugar. Bake 10 minutes at 375°.

Brother of First Lady Jean Rounds

GRANDMA DOERING'S ENGLISH TOFFEE BARS

Deb Bowman
Governor's Cabinet

1 cup butter, softened
1 tsp. vanilla
1 cup brown sugar, packed
1-1/2 cup flour

1 egg yolk
6 Hershey milk chocolate bars
1/2 cup walnuts, chopped

Mix butter, vanilla, brown sugar, egg yolk, and flour together. Spread dough on ungreased large cookie sheet with a rolling pin. Bake at 350° 10-12 minutes or until light brown. Remove from oven and place Hershey bars on top to melt. Spread evenly. Sprinkle chopped walnuts on top. When cooled, cut into bars.

GRANDMA PAT'S SALTY NUT ROLL BARS

Brennan Bauer

3 cups flour
1-¹/₂ cups brown sugar
1 tsp. salt
1 cup butter, softened
¹/₂ cup white corn syrup

2 tbls. butter
1 tbls. water
6 oz. butterscotch chips
nuts (cashews or mixed)

Mix together the flour, brown sugar, salt, and softened butter. Pack into ungreased cookie sheet. Bake 10-12 minutes at 350°. Mix corn syrup, 2 tbls. butter, water and butterscotch chips, bring to a boil and boil for 2 minutes, stirring constantly. Cover baked crust with nuts, then pour caramel mixture over nuts. Bake 10-12 minutes at 350°. Cut while warm.

Grandson of Governor Walter Dale Miller

GRANDMA'S CHOCOLATE CHIP COOKIES

Justin Albers

1 cup brown sugar
³/₄ cup white sugar
1 cup Crisco
2 eggs
2 cups flour
1 (12-oz.) pkg. chocolate chips

1 tsp. baking soda
1 dash salt
1 tsp. vanilla
¹/₂ tsp. cinnamon
1 cup nuts

Cream together sugars, Crisco, eggs, and vanilla. Combine flour, baking soda, salt, and cinnamon; add to creamed mixture and mix well. Add chocolate chips and nuts - mix well. Bake on ungreased cookie sheet at 350° for approximately 10-12 minutes.

Grandson of Governor Walter Dale Miller

GRANDMA'S OATMEAL RAISIN BIG COOKIES

Governor Mike Rounds

$\frac{1}{2}$ cup raisins	2 cups all-purpose flour
$\frac{1}{3}$ cup water	1-$\frac{1}{4}$ cups oats (not instant)
$\frac{1}{2}$ cup vegetable shortening	2 tsp. baking soda
1 egg	$\frac{3}{4}$ tsp. cinnamon
1-$\frac{1}{2}$ cups dark brown sugar, packed	1 tsp. salt
1-$\frac{1}{2}$ tsp. vanilla	$\frac{1}{2}$ cup raisins

Preheat oven to 275°. Combine raisins with water in a food processor and blend on high speed for about 1 minute or until very smooth. Combine this raisin purée with the vegetable shortening, egg, brown sugar, and vanilla in a large bowl. Mix well with electric mixer until smooth. In a separate bowl, combine the flour with the oats, baking soda, cinnamon, and salt. Pour this dry mixture into the wet mixture and mix well until ingredients are incorporated. Mix in raisins. Roll 3 tbls. portions of the dough into a ball in your hands and press to $\frac{1}{2}$ inch flat on an ungreased baking sheet. Bake for 18-20 minutes. Be careful not to overcook, or the cookies will be not chewy. Store in a sealed container. Makes 16-18 cookies.

HEART ATTACK BROWNIES

First Lady Jean Rounds

1 cup sugar	1 (16-oz.) can Hershey's Syrup
$\frac{1}{2}$ cup margarine	1 cup flour
4 eggs	

Mix and spread in a greased and floured 10-$\frac{1}{2}$ x 15-$\frac{1}{2}$" pan. Bake 25 minutes at 350°.

$\frac{1}{2}$ cup margarine	1 tsp. mint extract
4 cups powdered sugar	few drops of red or green food coloring
4 tbls. milk	

Mix and spread on cooled brownies. Refrigerate 20 minutes.

$\frac{1}{2}$ cup margarine	1 (12-oz.) pkg. chocolate chips

Melt and let cool. Spread on brownies. Refrigerate. Before cutting, let set outside of refrigerator for awhile to keep top from cracking when cutting.

85104-07

HERSHEY SYRUP BROWNIES

Amber Taranto

4 eggs, beaten
1 cup flour
1 cup white sugar
1/2 cup butter or margarine

1 can Hershey's syrup (1-3/4 cups)
1 cup walnuts, optional

Combine all ingredients and spread into greased 10 x 13 inch pan. Bake at 350° for 25 minutes.

Frosting:

1/2 cup butter
1/2 cup milk

2 cups white sugar
1 cup chocolate chips

Put butter, milk, and sugar into sauce pan and bring to boil, boil for 2 minutes and add the chocolate chips. Cool until it thickens and spread on cool brownies.

Granddaughter of Governor Walter Dale Miller

JUBILEE JUMBLES

Shirley Jenssen
Former Governor's Staff

1/2 cup Crisco shortening
1 cup brown sugar
1/2 cup white sugar
2 eggs
1 cup undiluted evaporated milk

1 tsp. vanilla
2 3/4 cup flour
1/2 tsp. soda
1 tsp. salt
1 cup walnuts

Cream shortening, brown sugar, and white sugar. Add eggs, milk, and vanilla. Mix well. Add flour, soda, and salt to creamed mixture. Blend in nutmeats. Chill one hour. Bake 375° 8 - 10 minutes.

Frosting: Burnt Butter Glaze

2 tbls. butter
2 cups confectioners sugar

1/2 cup evaporated milk

Combine ingredients. Frost cooled cake.

KAROL'S CRAISIN COOKIES

Tanna Zabel
Governor's Staff

1 cup (2 sticks) softened
  margarine or butter
1-¼ cups firmly packed brown
  sugar
½ cup granulated sugar
2 eggs
2 tbls. milk
2 tsp. vanilla

1-¾ cup flour
1 tsp. baking soda
½ tsp. salt (optional)
2-½ cups Quaker Oats (quick or
  old fashioned, uncooked)
2 cups Craisins
1 cup chopped nuts (optional)

Heat oven to 375°. Beat margarine and sugars together until creamy.
Add eggs, milk, and vanilla, and beat well. Add combined flour, baking
soda, and salt, and mix well. Stir in oats, Craisins and nuts, and mix
well. Drop by rounded tablespoons onto on ungreased cookie sheet
and bake 9-10 minutes. Cool 1 minute on cookie sheet. Remove and
place on wire rack. This recipe makes approximately 5 dozen cookies. Enjoy!

KRINGLE

Helen Vedvei

2 cups sugar
1 cup Butter Flavored Crisco
2 eggs
2 cups buttermilk
2 tsp. soda

1 tsp. salt
2 tsp. baking powder
6 cups flour
2 tsp. vanilla

Cream sugar and shortening, add eggs and beat. Add buttermilk and
vanilla. Mix flour and spices and beat into mixture. Refrigerate several
hours or overnight. Roll on floured board to about ¼ inch thick and cut
with a doughnut cutter. Twist doughnut to look like an 8 and bake in a
450° oven on the middle shelf for 5 to 7 minutes. Kringle will be light
on top and only light brown on bottom. Kringle freeze well.

Mother of First Lady Jean Rounds

85104-07

MARBLE SQUARES

Mardell Davis
Governor's Staff

1 (8-oz.) pkg. cream cheese
2-1/3 cups sugar
3 eggs
3/4 cup water
1/2 cup butter
1-1/2 1 oz. squares of
  unsweetened chocolate

2 cups flour
1/2 cup sour cream
1 tsp. baking soda
1/2 tsp. salt
1 (6-oz.) pkg. semi-sweet
  chocolate pieces

Combine softened cream cheese and 1/3 cup sugar, mixing until well blended. Blend in one egg. In saucepan, combine water, butter and chocolate; bring to boil. Remove from heat. Add combined remaining sugar and flour; mix well. Blend in remaining two eggs, sour cream, baking soda and salt. Pour into greased and floured jellyroll pan. Spoon cream cheese mixture over chocolate batter. Cut through batter with knife several times for marble effect; sprinkle with chocolate pieces. Bake at 375° 25-30 minutes or until wooden pick inserted in center comes out clean. Cool. Cut in squares.

MILLION DOLLAR SUGAR COOKIES

First Lady June Foss

1 cup butter
1/2 cup granulated sugar
1/2 cup brown sugar
1 egg
1 tsp. vanilla

1 tsp. baking soda
1/2 tsp. salt
2 cups flour
1/2 cup finely chopped walnuts
  (optional)

Beat butter, granulated sugar, and brown sugar until fluffy. Beat in egg and vanilla. Add baking soda, salt, and flour - mix until combined. Add chopped walnuts. Roll teaspoon of dough into balls, roll in granulated sugar, place on greased baking sheet. Flatten cookie with bottom of a glass. Bake at 350° 10 to 15 minutes. They are meant to be crisp and golden brown. Makes 48 cookies - varies according to size you make them.

Note: Recipe submitted by Daughter Mary Joe Foss Finke

MOM'S BROWNIES

Joyce Rounds (1933 - 1987)

4 tbls. cocoa	4 eggs
1 cup butter or margarine	2 cups flour
2 cups sugar	

Melt cocoa and butter in a sauce pan over low heat; set aside. In a mixer, beat eggs and sugar. Blend in chocolate mixture and flour. Pour into greased jellyroll pan. Bake at 350° degrees for 25 minutes.

Frosting:

1/4 cup cocoa	1 cup sugar
1/4 cup butter or margarine	1/3 cup milk

Melt cocoa and butter in a saucepan over low heat. Add sugar and milk and heat slowly until sugar melts. Boil for 1 minute. Let cool slightly and beat until thickened. Spread on cooled brownies.

Mother of Governor M. Michael Rounds

MY MOM, JUNE HALVORSON'S, CHOCOLATE CHIP BARS

Harla Jessop
Former Governor's Staff

2 eggs	1-1/2 tsp. baking powder
1-1/2 cups brown sugar	1 tsp. salt
3/4 cup oil	1/2 cup chopped nuts
1 tsp. vanilla	1 cup chocolate chips
1-1/2 cup flour	

Mix eggs, sugar, oil, and vanilla with mixer. Add flour, baking powder, and salt. Stir until well mixed. Add nuts and chocolate chips. May eat plain or frost with favorite chocolate frosting.

NUT GOODIE BARS

Donna Morlock
Former Governor's Staff

1/2 cup butter	1/2 cup peanuts or chopped
1 (6-oz.) pkg. chocolate chips	walnuts
1 (6-oz.) pkg. butterscotch chips	4 cups miniature marshmallows
3/4 cup peanut butter	

Melt butter, chips, and peanut butter together, then add peanuts. Put marshmallows in bottom of buttered 9 x 13 inch pan. Pour the mixture over the marshmallows and keep in the refrigerator.

85104-07

O'HENRY BARS

First Lady Mary Dean Janklow

4 cups oatmeal (quick)
1 cup brown sugar, packed
3 tsp. vanilla
½ cup Karo white syrup
⅔ cup butter, melted (use salted)

1 (6-oz.) oz. pkg. chocolate chips
⅔ cup chunky peanut butter

Mix oatmeal, brown sugar, vanilla, and Karo syrup. Add melted butter, mix again, and put into well-greased 9 x 13 inch pan. Bake 12 minutes at 375°. Then let cool. Melt together the chocolate chips and chunky peanut butter, and spread over bars.

OATMEAL CHOCOLATE CHIP COOKIES

Mike Mueller
Former Governor's Staff

2 cups Crisco shortening
1-½ cups white sugar
1-½ cups brown sugar
1 tsp. salt
2 tsp. soda

1 - 2 cups chocolate chips
2 tsp. vanilla
4 eggs
3 cups flour
4 cups oatmeal

Cream together shortening, sugars, and vanilla until light. Add eggs. Add flour, soda, and salt. Stir in chocolate chips and oatmeal. Drop on cookie sheet, and bake at 350° for 10-15 minutes. Don't overbake. Makes 8 dozen.

ORANGE BROWNIES

Kelly Kneip

1-1/2 cups all-purpose flour
2 cups sugar
1 tsp. salt
1 cup (2 sticks) butter, softened

4 eggs
2 tsp. orange extract
1 tsp. grated orange zest

Preheat oven to 350°. Grease a 13 x 9 by 2 inch pan. In a mixing bowl, stir together flour, sugar, and salt. Add butter, eggs, orange extract, and orange zest and beat until well blended. Pour batter into prepared pan and bake for 30 minutes, or until light golden brown and set. Remove from oven and pierce top of entire cake with fork.

Glaze:

1 cup confectioners sugar
2 tbls. orange juice

1 tsp. grated orange zest

Combine all ingredients in a bowl, stirring until smooth. Pour glaze over cake. Cool cake and cut into squares.

Daughter-in-Law of Governor Richard Kneip

PAT'S "NANA" BARS

Karon Schaack
Former Governor's Cabinet

4 eggs
1-1/2 tsp. vanilla
2 cups white sugar
2-1/2 cups flour
1 tsp. salt
2 tsp. baking soda
3/4 cup canola oil

3/4 cup water (don't pour all in at once; you may not need the entire 3/4 c.)
3 mashed ripe bananas
1 cup chopped walnuts (optional)

Add vanilla to beaten eggs. Add sugar to egg mixture. Sift flour, salt, and soda together, and add to egg mixture. Add oil and mashed bananas. Now add water as you beat the ingredients together. Add just enough water to make a cake-like batter (not real thin). Pour evenly into prepared pan. Bake for 25-35 minutes. Use a toothpick to test for doneness.

Frosting:

1 (8-oz.) pkg. cream cheese, softened
1 stick of butter or margarine, softened

3-1/2 cups powdered sugar (may need a little more)
1-1/2 tsp. vanilla

Beat together with electric mixer until it has a smooth spreading consistency. Frosting makes enough for two jellyroll pans of bars.

85104-07

PEANUT BLOSSOMS

Georgiana Kauth (1901 - 1987)

1 cup white sugar
1 cup brown sugar, packed
1 cup butter or margarine,
  softened
1 cup peanut butter
2 large eggs
2 tsp. vanilla extract

3 cups all-purpose flour
½ tsp. salt
1-½ tsp. baking soda
¼ cup white sugar
48 chocolate kisses or stars,
  unwrapped

Preheat oven to 375°. Combine white sugar, brown sugar, butter, and peanut butter in large mixer bowl. Beat at medium speed until light and fluffy (1 to 2 minutes). Add eggs and vanilla. Continue beating until well mixed. Add flour, salt, and baking soda. Continue beating, scraping bowl often, until well mixed. Shape dough into 1-inch balls. (If dough is too soft, refrigerate 30 to 60 minutes.) Roll balls in the remaining ¼ cup white sugar. Place cookies 2 inches apart on ungreased cookie sheet. Bake for 8 to 10 minutes or until very lightly golden brown. Immediately press 1 chocolate kiss or star in center of each cookie. Bake another 30 seconds to 1 minute. Remove from oven and put cookies on wire racks to cool.

Grandmother of Governor M. Michael Rounds

PEANUT BUTTER CUP TEMPTATIONS

First Lady Jean Rounds

½ cup butter
½ cup peanut butter
½ cup sugar
½ cup brown sugar, packed
1 egg
1 tsp. vanilla

1-¼ cups flour
¾ tsp. baking soda
½ tsp. salt
1 pkg. miniature Reese's Peanut
  Butter Cups

Cream butter, peanut butter, and sugars. Beat in egg and vanilla; mix well. Sift dry ingredients and blend into mixture. Preheat oven to 350°. Shape batter in 1 inch balls; place in ungreased "miniature" muffin pans. Bake for 8-10 minutes. Remove from oven and press peanut butter cup in each until only top shows. Let set awhile before removing from tins. Makes 48-50 cookies. Great to freeze!

PEANUT BUTTER RICE KRISPIES BARS

First Lady Mary Dean Janklow

1 cup sugar
1 cup Karo syrup
1 cup peanut butter

5 cups Rice Krispies
1 cup butterscotch chips
1 cup chocolate chips

Heat sugar and Karo syrup together over low heat until sugar melts. Add peanut butter and Rice Krispies and mix together. Place in well-greased 9 x 13 inch cake pan. Melt together butterscotch chips and chocolate chips and pour over top of bars. Cool and cut into squares.

PECAN TASSIES

*Recipe Box at the
Governors Residence*

1 cup margarine
1 (8-oz.) pkg. cream cheese
2 cups flour

½ tsp. baking powder
½ tsp. salt

Mix well. Chill for 4 hours. Make balls the size of walnuts. Chill. Grease pan real well.

Filling:

2 cups pecans, chopped
3 eggs
2 cups brown sugar, packed

3 tbls. oleo
1 tbls. vanilla
⅛ tsp. salt

Sprinkle nuts in bottom. Add batter. Sprinkle with nuts again. Bake 15 minutes at 350° until golden. Let set a few minutes. Turn over and let set to dry bottom.

264

PUMPKIN COOKIES

Sandra Zinter
Governor's Cabinet

1 cup sugar
1 cup shortening
1 egg
1 cup pumpkin
1 tsp. vanilla

2 cups flour
1 tsp. baking powder
1 tsp. baking soda
1 tsp. cinnamon
½ tsp. salt

Cream together sugar, shortening, egg, pumpkin, and vanilla. Add to the creamed mixture the flour, baking powder, baking soda, cinnamon, and salt. Mix well. Drop on greased cookie sheet and bake at 350° for 10 - 12 minutes. When cooled, frost the cookie with the following frosting:

Frosting:

3 tbls. margarine
3 tbls. milk

3 tbls. brown sugar
1-¼ - 1-½ cups powdered sugar

Combine the three ingredients and cook until dissolved. Gradually add the powdered sugar. Beat until creamy. Add 1 tsp. vanilla. Spread on cooled cookies.

SOFT SUGAR COOKIES

Paige Bauer

1 cup butter (2 sticks), softened
1 cup oil
1 cup white sugar
1 cup powdered sugar
2 eggs

1 tsp. vanilla
4 cups flour
1 tsp. cream of tartar
1 tsp. soda
1 tsp. salt

Cream butter with oil. Add sugar and beat well. Add powdered sugar and beat well. Add eggs and vanilla; beat well. Add dry ingredients and mix well. Dough will be airy, light and fluffy. Drop by spoon or medium melon scoop, press with greased and sugared flat-bottomed glass. Bake at 350° for 8 - 10 minutes.

Granddaughter of Governor Walter Dale Miller

Note: Prior to baking, you can sprinkle with colored sugar or frost with cream cheese frosting. Store in airtight container for 2 - 3 weeks.

SPICED APPLE COOKIES

Nila Novotny
Governor's Staff

1 cup raisins
1/2 cup shortening
1-1/3 cups brown sugar, packed
1 egg
1/4 cup milk
2-1/3 cups flour
1 tsp. baking soda

1 tsp. cinnamon
1/2 tsp. salt
12 tsp. ground cloves
1/2 tsp. ground nutmeg
1 cup chopped walnuts
1 cup chopped, unpeeled apple

In saucepan, cover raisins with water and bring to boil. Remove from heat, cover and let stand 5 minutes. Drain. In mixing bowl, beat together shortening and brown sugar; beat in egg and milk. Stir together flour, baking soda, cinnamon, salt, cloves, and nutmeg and add to shortening mixture. Beat until well blended. Stir in nuts, apple and drained raisins. Drop by teaspoonfuls on to ungreased cookie sheet. 375° for 8 to 10 minutes.

SPRITZ COOKIES

Sheila Bonrud
Governor's Staff

2 cups butter
2 eggs
1 cup sugar

1 tsp. vanilla or almond extract
4 cups flour

Beat butter, eggs, and sugar until creamy. Add flour 2 cups at a time. Use cookie press to shape cookies. Bake at 375° degrees for 7 minutes. I double this recipe for Christmas cookies and use butter cream frosting recipe to frost. These will freeze well.

UNBAKED REESE BARS

Tim Reisch
Governor's Cabinet

1-1/2 cups peanut butter
4 cups powdered sugar

2 sticks margarine- melted
10 graham crackers-rolled fine

Mix peanut butter, powdered sugar, and crushed graham crackers together. Add melted butter and stir altogether. Pat into greased 9 x 13 inch pan. Frost with melted chocolate chips.

85104-07

Candy

BEST EVER CARAMELS

Pam Roberts
Governor's Staff

2 cups sugar
1 cup brown sugar
1 cup light corn syrup
1 cup heavy cream

1 cup milk
1 cup butter
1-½ tsp. vanilla

In a heavy saucepan, combine sugars, cream, milk, and butter. Cook slowly, stirring occasionally to soft ball stage - 248°. Remove from heat, stir in vanilla and pour onto a greased cookie sheet. Cool. When firm, turn out onto a board, cut in pieces, and wrap in waxed paper.

CANDIED NUTS

Recipe Box at the
Governors Residence

1-½ cups raw or roasted
  cashews, peanuts, whole
  almonds, and or pecan halves

½ cup sugar
2 tbls. butter
½ tsp. vanilla

Line a baking sheet with foil. Butter the foil; set baking sheet aside. In a heavy 10 inch skillet combine nuts, sugar, butter, and vanilla. Cook over medium high heat, shaking skillet occasionally till sugar begins to melt. Do not stir. Reduce heat to low; continue cooking till sugar is golden brown, stirring occasionally. Remove skillet from heat. Pour nut mixture onto the prepared baking sheet. Cool completely. Break into clusters. Store tightly covered. Makes about 10 oz. (12 servings).

CARAMEL CANDY

Ida Covey

1-¾ cups white syrup
2 cups white sugar

2 cups rich cream (divided)
½ cup butter

Place syrup, sugar, 1 cup cream, and butter in heavy pan and stir until it boils vigorously. Add 1 cup cream a little at a time. Boil until it forms a firm ball in cold water. Stir continually as it thickens. Pour into well buttered 9 x 13 inch pan.

Granddaughter-in-Law of Lieutenant Governor Hyatt Covey

Note: Recipe is one of First Lady Hyatt Covey's.

CARAMEL CEREAL TREATS

Bonnie Untereiner Bjork
Former Governor's Cabinet

5-6 cups mixed cereal (Chex or Crispix)
2 cups thin pretzels (broken up a little)

1-²/₃ cups dry roasted nuts (can use peanuts or cashews)

Mix together in a big bowl.

Topping:

1-¹/₃ cups sugar
1 cup margarine or butter

¹/₂ cup light corn syrup

Mix together in 2 quart pan. Cook, stirring constantly to soft ball stage. Take off burner and add 1 tsp. vanilla. Pour over cereal mix and stir quickly. Spread on buttered wax paper and break into pieces and cool.

CARAMELS

Courtney Albers

2 cups white sugar
1-³/₄ cups white syrup

¹/₂ cup butter
2 cups cream

Bring to boil the sugar, syrup, butter, and 1 cup cream. Then add the other 1 cup of cream and cook to firm ball stage. Pour in buttered pan. Cut into pieces and wrap.

Great-granddaughter of Governor Walter Dale Miller

CARAMELS (MICROWAVE)

Sheila Bonrud
Governor's Staff

1 cup butter
2-¹/₂ cup brown sugar
dash salt
1 cup Karo syrup

1 can Eagle Brand sweetened condensed milk
1 tsp. vanilla

Melt butter in a 2-qt. bowl for 1-¹/₂ minutes in the microwave. Add brown sugar and salt. Stir thoroughly. Stir in syrup and gradually add milk and vanilla. Cook on high for 7-¹/₂ minutes, stir and cook for 7-¹/₂ minutes more. Pour into 9 x 13 inch buttered pan. Cool and cut and wrap in wax paper. You need to use a large bowl so it does not boil over. Watch and stop and stir if it gets close to going over. These freeze well.

85104-07

FUDGE

Jeff Bloomberg
Governor's Cabinet

4-1/2 cups sugar
1 (12-oz.) can evaporated milk
1/2 lb. butter or margarine
1 tbls. vanilla

2 cups small marshmallows
1 (18-oz.) pkg. chocolate chips
chopped nuts

Bring sugar, butter, milk, and vanilla to a boil and boil exactly 11 minutes, stirring constantly. Take off the heat and add the marshmallows, chips, and nuts. Beat until dissolved and smooth. Pour into a well-buttered 9 x 13 inch pan and cool at room temperature. Cut into 24 pieces and wrap individually in plastic wrap.

MARSHMALLOW CANDY

Coen Bradley Caldwell

1 pkg. frozen big marshmallows
1 can Eagle Brand sweetened
 condensed milk

1 pkg. Kraft caramels
1/2 cup butter

Melt together the sweetened condensed milk, caramels, and butter. I melt these in the microwave, but you need to be careful and stir often as it burns easily. Roll frozen marshmallows in caramel sauce and then into toppings - our favorite is Rice Krispies, but other options are crushed nuts or coconut. Let them set on wax paper, and then they can be refrozen or stored in an airtight container.

Grandson of Governor Walter Dale Miller

MICROWAVE FUDGE

John Cooper
Former Governor's Cabinet

1 lb. powdered sugar
1/2 cup Hershey cocoa
1/4 lb. margarine

1/4 cup canned milk
1 tbls. vanilla
1/2 cup chopped nuts

Combine ingredients. "DO NOT STIR". Place in microwave on high, cook 2 minutes. Stir ingredients. Add 1 tbls. vanilla and nuts. Pour into dish and refrigerate.

PEOPLE'S PUPPY CHOW

*Recipe Box at the
Governors Residence*

1 (6-oz.) pkg. milk chocolate
  chips
1 (6-oz.) pkg. semi-sweet
  chocolate chips

1 cup peanut butter
1 stick margarine
1 box Crispix cereal
2 cups powdered sugar

Combine chips, peanut butter, and margarine, and melt over a low heat
or in the microwave. Pour over cereal; toss until coated. Place the
coated cereal in a paper bag and add powdered sugar, shake until
well coated.

PEPPERMINT STICK POPCORN BALLS

Robert Houck

1 cup popcorn, popped
1 tsp. salt
$\frac{1}{2}$ lb. marshmallows, cut fine (or
  may use miniature
  marshmallows)

$\frac{1}{2}$ lb. peppermint stick candy,
  ground
$\frac{1}{3}$ cup butter

Pop corn; place in a large pan. Shake pan so any un popped kernels
will go to the bottom. Transfer popped kernels to another pan. Melt,
butter and marshmallows and candy. Pour over popcorn. Make into
balls.

Nephew of Lieutenant Governor L. R. "Roy" Houck

POPCORN BALLS

*Recipe Box at the
Governors Residence*

16 qt. popped popcorn
4 cups sugar
1-$\frac{1}{3}$ cups white syrup

1 cup butter
1-$\frac{1}{4}$ tsp. salt
3 tsp. vanilla

Mix syrup, butter, sugar, and salt in a saucepan and cook to a soft
crack stage (275-280°). Add vanilla. Pour over popcorn and mix well.
Form into balls. This makes a crisp popcorn ball that won't stick to
your teeth.

85104-07

SALTED PEANUT CHEWS

Stacie Olson

1-1/2 cups flour
2/3 cup brown sugar
1/2 tsp. baking powder
1/2 tsp. salt

1/2 tsp. baking soda
1/2 cup butter or margarine
2 egg yolks
3 cups mini marshmallows

Combine flour, brown sugar, baking powder, salt, soda, butter, vanilla, and egg yolks. Press into ungreased 9 x 13 inch pan. Bake 12 - 15 minutes at 350° till light brown. Immediately sprinkle with marshmallows and bake 1-2 minutes. Cool while preparing topping.

Topping:

2/3 cup corn syrup
1/4 cup butter or margarine
2 tsp. vanilla
1 (12-oz.) pkg. peanut butter
  chips

2 cups Rice Krispies
2 cups salted peanuts

Heat corn syrup, butter, vanilla, and peanut butter chips in saucepan until chips melt. Remove from heat. Stir in Rice Krispies & peanuts. Pour over marshmallows. Let cool, then cut and serve.

Niece of Governor M. Michael Rounds

WHITE CHOCOLATE MIX

Monica Harding
Former Governor's Staff

1 (10-oz.) pkg. pretzels
5 cups Cheerios
5 cups cereal (Chex, Crispix, etc.)
2 cups salted peanuts

1 lb. M & M's
2 pkgs. white chocolate/vanilla chips
3 tbls. vegetable oil

Melt in microwave two packages white chocolate/vanilla chips and vegetable oil. Pour over dry ingredients, spread on wax paper.

Recipe Favorites

THIS & THAT

(Photo courtesy of the South Dakota Tourism)

2005 GOVERNORS RESIDENCE

This Governors Residence located at 119 North Washington Avenue was completed in June 2005. Measuring approximately 14,000 square feet, the two-story residence is poised peacefully on the shores of Capitol Lake. The residence serves as a private residence for the governor and his family. The private living quarters include a kitchen, living room, dining room, family room, and five family bedrooms. The grand dining room and the governor's private office include fireplaces accented with rock blasted from Crazy Horse Memorial in the Black Hills.

The public side of the Governors Residence includes a grand dining hall which will accommodate approximately 100 guests, a commercial kitchen and cooking facilities, greeting area, and two staterooms or guest quarters.

The exterior of the Governors Residence is adorned with field stone from near Miller, South Dakota, while other portions of the exterior feature copper flashing, specially cast concrete, South Dakota brick, and numerous roof adornments which add to the exterior appeal.

Thousands of South Dakotans and numerous corporations and companies from across the state contributed substantial amounts of money, products, and services to construct the new residence.

THIS & THAT

BREAD & BUTTER PICKLES

First Lady Jean Rounds

Slice cucumbers thin. Sprinkle pickling salt over them (1 tbls. per quart). Cover with water and let stand 4 hours or overnight. Drain and rinse with cold clear water. Heat quart of dark vinegar with 3-4 cups of sugar. Add 1 tsp. celery seed and 1 tsp. mustard seed, and one onion cut in rings. Bring vinegar, sugar, and spices to boil (not a hard boil). Add cucumbers and let simmer until the cucumbers are clear. Pack into hot jars and seal.

CHEESE PATTIES WITH SPANISH SAUCE

Luz Naasz
Residence Staff

½ lb. cheese, grated
½ cup chopped nuts
6 eggs, beaten
1 cup bread crumbs
1 onion, minced

Combine all ingredients. Fry patties in deep fat fryer (or frying pan). Cover with Spanish sauce and bake 1 hour in 350° oven. These can be frozen.

Spanish Sauce:

4 tbls. butter
1 green pepper, sliced
1 (3-oz.) can sliced mushrooms
1 tbls. honey
4 cups stewed tomatoes
1 (8-oz.) can tomato sauce

Sauté pepper and mushrooms in butter. Add tomatoes, tomato sauce, and honey (to cut acid taste). Let simmer. If desired, thicken with 2 tbls. cornstarch. Sauce may be made ahead and stored in refrigerator.

CHICKEN RUB

Recipe Box at the
Governors Residence

½ tsp. paprika
½ tsp. celery salt
½ tsp. oregano
½ tsp. poultry seasoning
1-½ cups flour

Combine ingredients. Use for chicken.

Note: This is Dottie Howe's rub for chicken.

CHOCOLATE FUDGE SAUCE

Rick Miller

2 cups white sugar
1 cup brown sugar
1 cup cream
½ cup white corn syrup

⅓ cup cocoa
½ cup butter
½ tsp. salt

Bring to a boil on the stove until soft ball stage. Do not stir very often as it will cause syrup to sugar. When cooked pour into a serving pitcher and let cool before serving.

Grandson of Governor Walter Dale Miller

CRANBERRY RELISH

Rick Albers

1 pkg. cranberries
2 oranges, chopped
2 apples, chopped

1 pkg. Cherry Jell-O
1 cup boiling water
2 cups sugar

Dissolve Jell-O in 1 cup boiling water. Combine with remaining ingredients.

Son-in-Law of Governor Walter Dale Miller

EASY PIZZA CRUST

Deb Bowman
Governor's Cabinet

1 cup warm water
1 pkg. yeast
1 tsp. salt

1 tsp. sugar
2 tbls. oil
2-½ cups flour

Mix water, sugar, and yeast together in large bowl. Add other ingredients and beat with a fork about 20 times. Let rest for 5-10 minutes. Spray pizza pan lightly with PAM or something similar. Spread dough in pizza pan and bake at 400° for 10 minutes or until slightly browned. Makes 1 large pizza.

85104-07

FREEZER TOMATO SAUCE

Steve Wegman
Former Governor's Staff

20 large tomatoes
4 large carrots, shredded
4 medium onions, chopped
½ cup chopped parsley

3 tbls. sugar
2 tbls. salt
¾ tsp. pepper

Wash, slip skins (blanch 30 seconds), core, and quarter tomatoes. Bring all ingredients to a boil, stirring frequently. Reduce heat and simmer 30 minutes. Cool and put 2 cups at a time in blender. Purée until thick, 30-40 seconds. Pour into freezer bags or containers, and freeze. Very good in hot dishes.

GINGER PLUM SAUCE

Recipe Box at the
Governors Residence

1 pt. plum jam
2 tbls. hot mustard (oriental)

1 tsp. ginger

Mix and heat on low heat. Serve in crock with pastry brush. More mustard or less can be used.

GRAMMA GEORGIANA'S BREAD-N-BUTTER PICKLES

Georgiana Kauth (1901 - 1987)

12-15 cucumbers
2 tbls. pickling salt
4 cups vinegar
4 cups sugar

1 tsp. celery seed
1 tsp. mustard seed
1 onion, sliced thin

Slice cucumbers very thin. Put in a large bowl and sprinkle with pickling salt. Cover with water and let stand overnight (at least 4 hours). Rinse with clear water and then drain. In a large sauce pan, bring vinegar, sugar, celery seed and mustard seed to soft boil. Add cucumbers and onion and stir mixture. Pack into hot, sterilized jars, leaving ¼ inch head space. Seal the jars. Process in boiling water for 10 minutes. Remove jars and set them on a towel away from drafts. Allow jars to cool undisturbed for 24 hours. Test by pressing in the center of each seal. It should not pop back up.

Grandmother of Governor M. Michael Rounds

HOLLANDAISE SAUCE

Recipe Box at the
Governors Residence

8 tbls. unsalted butter
3 egg yolks
2 tbls. fresh lemon juice

pinch cayenne pepper
salt and ground white pepper to
taste

Melt the butter in a small saucepan. Set it aside to cool to room temperature. Fill the bottom of a double boiler with water, and bring it almost to a boil. Then lower the heat so that the water is hot but not boiling. Mix the egg yolks and lemon juice together in the top of the double boiler. Then place the top over the bottom and whisk until smooth. Gradually whisk in the butter in a slow, steady stream. Add the cayenne, and salt and white pepper. Continue whisking until the sauce is thick. Serve immediately. Makes 1 cup.

Note: If the sauce should separate or curdle, add 1 ice cube and whisk briskly until it has melted. This will bring the sauce back together. Hollandaise, like mayonnaise, is an emulsion, but in this case, the egg yolks hold butter, not oil, in suspension. The trick here is to keep the egg yolks at a low, even heat as the melted butter is slowly added.

HOMEMADE NOODLES (FOR SOUP)

Connie Tveidt
Governor's Staff

3 eggs
6 tbls. milk

3 cups flour
2 tsp. salt

Beat eggs with fork in large bowl. Stir in milk. Stir in salt and about 2 cups of the flour. Work in the rest of the flour, kneading by hand if necessary. Use some of the flour to sprinkle on counter before rolling out dough to desired thickness with a rolling pin. Dry on the counter for 20-30 minutes. Use a pizza cutter to cut into the width of noodles you desire. Turn noodles over and spread on counter to dry for several hours. Drop into your favorite boiling broth with meat and vegetables. Boil 10 minutes before serving.

Note: Works great with chicken or turkey, carrots, celery, and spices.

85104-07

LIP-TAR

Patricia Mickelson Adam

½ tsp. mustard
½ tube anchovy paste
1 tsp. capers
2 buds of garlic, minced
2 (8-oz.) pkg. Philadelphia cream
  cheese

4 tsp. butter
2 onion juice
1 tsp. paprika

All ingredients should be at room temperature. Mix all ingredients together with an electric beater. Place in refrigerator for at least 2 hours before eating. Lip-Tar is very versatile. It is good when spread on red, yellow, and green peppers; on party crackers; and also good "stuffing" for celery as an hors d'oeuvre.

Daughter of Governor George T. Mickelson and Sister of Governor George S. Mickelson

Note: My mother, Madge Mickelson used this recipe especially during the holiday season when family and friends would gather.

MANGO SALSA

Karon Schaack
Former Governor's Cabinet

3 large mangoes, peeled and
  chopped into bite-sized cubes
1 lb. tomatillos, husked, rinsed,
  chopped
1 cup cilantro

2 tbls. minced fresh jalapeños
2 tbls. fresh lime juice
2 large garlic cloves, minced
2 cups chopped peeled fresh
  pineapple

Combine first six ingredients in a large bowl. (Can be made one day ahead. Cover; chill). One hour before serving time, add pineapple to salsa. Season to taste with salt and pepper. Let stand at least 1 hour to allow flavors to blend. Makes about 7 cups; we allow at least 1 cup per person.

Hint 1: If you can't get good fresh pineapple, this salsa is very good without it.

Hint 2: Mangoes become easier to use if you invest in the "mango splitter" made by OXO Good Grips. It comes with several good tips for removing the mango seed and cubing the fruit.

Hint 3: A curved Alaskan Ulu knife and bowl are very good for chopping fresh herbs such as cilantro.

Hint 4: Limes are juicier if microwaved about 10 - 15 seconds before squeezing out the juice!

NANCY'S FAVORITE PICKLES

First Lady Nancy Kneip Paprocki

16 cups sliced thin cucumbers
6 onions sliced thin
$1/3$ cup pickling salt
2 cups white vinegar

5 cups sugar
$1-1/2$ tsp. turmeric
$1-1/2$ tsp. celery seed
2 tbls. mustard seed

Combine cucumbers and onions. Add salt - cover with ice. Mix and let stand 3 hours, drain well. Combine remaining ingredients and pour over cucumbers. Heat to boiling stirring to combine well. Put in sterilized jars and seal. Makes 8 pints.

OYSTER CRACKERS

Corrie Holt

1 cup oil
1 tsp. dill
$1/2$ tsp. garlic

1 pkg. original dry ranch salad
dressing
2 (12-oz.) pkgs. oyster crackers

Mix all ingredients. Pour over the oyster crackers. Mix well and set aside for 1 hour. Enjoy.

Niece of First Lady Jean Rounds

PEPPER JELLY

Lori Shangreaux
Governor's Staff

$1/2$ cup chopped jalapeño
peppers (6 to 8)
1 cup chopped bell peppers (3
to 4)

2 tbls. hot red chilies
$6-1/2$ cups sugar
$1-1/2$ cups white wine vinegar
2 pouches Certo

Remove seeds from peppers and grind. Mix everything else but Certo. Bring to boil - boil 1 minute. Cool for 5 minutes, stirring constantly to prevent floating peppers. Add Certo - pour into hot jars and seal. Spread Triscuit crackers with cream cheese and spoon a dab of pepper jelly on top of cream cheese.

85104-07

PEPPY PECANS

Mary Joe Foss Finke

6 tbls. water
1 cup granulated sugar
2 tsp. salt

1 tsp. cayenne pepper
4 cups pecan halves

Combine water, sugar, salt, and cayenne pepper in large sauce pan. Cook and stir over medium heat until sugar dissolves. Bring to a boil and cook 2 minutes. Add pecans and stir until coated with mixture, about 1 minute. Transfer pecans to a large buttered baking sheet. Spread evenly in a single layer. Bake 350° until pecans are slightly brown, 13 to 15 minutes. Transfer to parchment paper, separating pecans. Cool completely. Store in airtight container for 1 week. May be frozen.

Daughter of Governor Joe Foss

Note: Great as a snack or use in salads.

PICANTE SAUCE

Steve Wegman
Former Governor's Staff

8 qts. chopped tomatoes
1 qt. chopped jalapeño peppers
2 qts. chopped onions
2 cans tomato soup
1 cup sugar

¼ cup vinegar
1 tbls. salt
1-½ tsp. garlic powder
½ cup cornstarch in water

Boil tomatoes and mash with potato masher. Add onions and peppers. Then add the tomato soup, sugar, vinegar, salt, and garlic powder. Boil well. Combine cornstarch and water to make a thickener. Add to tomato mixture. Fill jars and process 15 minutes in hot water bath.

PICKLED FISH

Charlie Vedvei

8 cups fish (northern or walleye pickle very well)

1 cup pickling salt to 4 cups water

Cut fish in bite size pieces, put in container, and cover with salt water. You may need more than one batch of salt water to cover fish. Refrigerate for 48 hours. Then drain and wash off salt. Cover fish with white vinegar and return to refrigerator for 24 hours. Remove fish from vinegar and put in small jars alternating a layer of fish and then a layer of onion.

Pickle juice:

1-3/4 cups sugar
1 tsp. whole allspice
1 tsp. pepper
4 bay leaves

1/2 tsp. whole cloves
2 tbls. mustard seed
2 cups white vinegar

Boil pickle juice ingredients together and when cool pour over fish in jars. May be eaten immediately but reaches peak in 4 to 5 days. Keeps well in refrigerator up to 6 weeks. You may need more than one batch of juice depending on how tightly your fish is packed in jars.

Brother of First Lady Jean Rounds

POTATO SALAD DRESSING

Recipe Box at the Governors Residence

3 oz. Italian dressing mix
mayonnaise
salt and pepper

mustard
pickles

Note: Ingredients for potato salad dressing from Dottie Howe.

PUMPKIN PIE SPICED NUTS

Patricia Mickelson Adam

1 tbls. homemade pumpkin pie
 spice
1 egg white
2 (12-oz.) cans salted mixed
 nuts

1 cup sugar
1 tsp. water

In large bowl, beat together egg white and 1 tsp. water. Add the salted, mixed nuts and toss to coat. Combine sugar and 1 tbls. pumpkin pie spice. Sprinkle over nuts, toss to coat. Spread nuts in a single layer in a greased 15 x 10 x 1 pan. Bake at 325° for about 20 minutes. Cool slightly in pan. Transfer to waxed paper to cool. Break into clumps. This recipe makes about 8 cups.

Homemade Pumpkin Pie Spice:

4 tsp. ground cinnamon
2 tsp. ground ginger

1 tsp. ground cloves
$\frac{1}{2}$ tsp. ground nutmeg

Store excess in tightly covered bottle.

Daughter of Governor George T. Mickelson and Sister of Governor George S. Mickelson

RHUBARB SAUCE

*Recipe Box at the
Governors Residence*

$\frac{1}{2}$-$\frac{3}{4}$ cup sugar
$\frac{1}{2}$ cup water
1 lb. rhubarb, cut into 1" pieces
 (4 cups)

ground cinnamon, if desired

Heat sugar and water to boiling in 2-quart saucepan, stirring occasionally. Stir in rhubarb; reduce heat to low. Simmer uncovered about 10 minutes, stirring occasionally, until rhubarb is tender and slightly transparent. Stir in cinnamon. Serve sauce warm or chilled. For Strawberry-Rhubarb Sauce, substitute 1 cup strawberries, cut in half, for 1 cup of the rhubarb. After simmering rhubarb, stir in strawberries; heat just to boiling.

SALMON MARINADE

Tim Reisch
Governor's Cabinet

lemon juice
soy sauce
water

1 tbls. brown sugar
1 tbls. garlic powder
Tabasco to taste

Mix equal parts of lemon juice, soy sauce, and water. Add sugar and spices. Marinade at least 2 hours. Spray pan, tear off gray meat. Add lemon and butter.

SALMON SAUCE

First Lady Nancy Kneip Paprocki

1 cup soy sauce
1 cup white sugar

1 tsp. crushed red pepper

Cook until thickened. Drizzle over salmon prepared anyway you like it.

SALSA

First Lady Jean Rounds

10 large tomatoes, peeled and
  chopped
2 onions, chopped
5-6 jalapeño peppers, chopped
4-5 salsa peppers, chopped

1 cup diced celery
1 tsp. salt
1 cup banana peppers, chopped
¾ cup vinegar
1 (46-oz.) can tomato juice

Combine in large kettle, and add:

1 tbls. pepper
2 tbls. oregano
2 tbls. basil

2 tbls. parsley
2 tbls. garlic
5-6 shakes Tabasco sauce

Simmer 45 minutes. Thicken with cornstarch if necessary. Can in hot jars. Process 15 minutes for pints, 25 minutes for quarts. Makes 9-11 pints.

85104-07

SPAGHETTI SAUCE

Susan Walker
Former Governor's Cabinet

1-½ lbs. ground beef
¼ lb. pork sausage
4 - 6 cloves garlic, chopped
⅓ cup olive oil
2 (15-oz.) cans tomato sauce
1 (6-oz.) cans mushrooms,
  undrained
1 tbls. parsley, dried or fresh
1 onion, chopped
3 stalks celery, chopped
¼ cup green pepper, chopped

1 tbls. salt
¼ tsp. pepper
1-½ tsp. chili powder
1 tbls. paprika
1 tsp. sugar
1 tsp. monosodium glutamate
½ tsp. oregano
½ tsp. basil
1 tsp. Worcestershire sauce
2 - 3 drops Tabasco sauce
sliced olives to serve on top

Mix garlic in meat and cook until done. Add remaining ingredients. Cook slowly 4 to 6 hours. Add tomato juice to thin if necessary.

SPICY PRETZELS

Catherine Sulzle
Former Governor's Staff

1 (12-oz.) bottle Orville
  Redenbacher Popcorn Oil
2 tbls. Mrs. Dash lemon pepper

1 pkg. dry ranch dressing
1 (20-oz.) bag pretzels

Mix popcorn oil, lemon pepper and ranch dressing in large bowl. Add pretzels. Stir occasionally until liquid is absorbed into pretzels.

THIN BUTTERMILK PANCAKES

Governor Nils A. Boe

2 eggs
1 cup flour
2 cups buttermilk

2 tsp. sugar
1 tsp. soda
¼ tsp. salt

Beat eggs thoroughly, add buttermilk. Sift together the dry ingredients and add to liquid mixture. Stir batter until well mixed. Cooks small-size cakes on heavy griddle. Servings depend on appetites.

THREE WAY DIP

Pam Roberts
Governor's Cabinet

2 cup cottage cheese
1 cup (4 oz.) bleu cheese
  (crumbled)
2 tbls. green onion (sliced)

2 tbls. lemon juice
1 tsp. Worcestershire sauce
1 cup sour cream

In a mixing bowl, combine cottage cheese and bleu cheese. Beat on highest speed until almost smooth. Add remaining ingredients and mix well. Chill and serve as dip with crackers and crisp vegetables, as a salad dressing, or on baked potatoes. Makes 4 cups.

WHITE SAUCE

Recipe Box at the
Governors Residence

2 tbls. margarine or butter
2 tbls. all-purpose flour
$\frac{1}{4}$ tsp. salt

$\frac{1}{8}$ tsp. pepper
1 cup milk

Melt margarine in 1-$\frac{1}{2}$ quart saucepan over low heat. Stir in flour, salt, and pepper. Cook over medium heat, stirring constantly, until mixture is smooth and bubbly; remove from heat. Gradually stir in milk. Heat to boiling, stirring constantly. Boil and stir 1 minute. Serve with vegetables, or use as a sauce in casseroles.

Recipe Favorites

85104-07

INDEX OF CONTRIBUTORS

- T -

- V -

- W -

- Z -

INDEX OF RECIPES

Brunches & Breakfasts

BREADS & ROLLS

DESSERTS

COOKIES & CANDY

Cookies

Candy

THIS & THAT

How to Order

Get additional copies of this cookbook by returning
an order form and your check or money order to:

**South Dakota Heritage Fund
900 Governors Drive
Pierre, SD 57501
(605) 773-3458
www.madeinsouthdakota.com**

Please send me _____ copies of **South Dakota's
Governors Residence Cookbook** at **$15.00** per copy and
$5.00 for shipping and handling per book. Enclosed is my
check or money order for $_____.

Mail Books To:

Name_____

Address _____

City _____ State _____ Zip _____

✂---

Please send me _____ copies of **South Dakota's
Governors Residence Cookbook** at **$15.00** per copy and
$5.00 for shipping and handling per book. Enclosed is my
check or money order for $_____.

Mail Books To:

Name_____

Address _____

City _____ State _____ Zip _____

85104-cb

PANTRY BASICS

A WELL-STOCKED PANTRY provides all the makings for a good meal. With the right ingredients, you can quickly create a variety of satisfying, delicious meals for family or guests. Keeping these items in stock also means avoiding extra trips to the grocery store, saving you time and money. Although everyone's pantry is different, there are basic items you should always have. Add other items according to your family's needs. For example, while some families consider chips, cereals and snacks as must-haves, others can't be without feta cheese and imported olives. Use these basic pantry suggestions as a handy reference list when creating your grocery list. Don't forget refrigerated items like milk, eggs, cheese and butter.

STAPLES

Baker's chocolate
Baking powder
Baking soda
Barbeque sauce
Bread crumbs (plain
  or seasoned)
Chocolate chips
Cocoa powder
Cornmeal
Cornstarch
Crackers
Flour
Honey
Ketchup
Lemon juice
Mayonnaise or salad
  dressing
Non-stick cooking
  spray
Nuts (almonds,
  pecans, walnuts)
Oatmeal
Oil (olive, vegetable)
Pancake baking mix
Pancake syrup
Peanut butter
Shortening
Sugar (granulated,
  brown, powdered)
Vinegar

PACKAGED/CANNED FOODS

Beans (canned, dry)
Broth (beef, chicken)
Cake mixes with frosting
Canned diced tomatoes
Canned fruit
Canned mushrooms
Canned soup
Canned tomato paste & sauce
Canned tuna & chicken
Cereal
Dried soup mix
Gelatin (flavored or plain)
Gravies
Jarred Salsa
Milk (evaporated,
  sweetened condensed)
Non-fat dry milk
Pastas
Rice (brown, white)
Spaghetti sauce

SPICES/SEASONINGS

Basil
Bay leaves
Black pepper
Bouillon cubes (beef,
  chicken)
Chives
Chili powder
Cinnamon
Mustard (dried, prepared)
Garlic powder or salt
Ginger
Nutmeg
Onion powder or salt
Oregano
Paprika
Parsley
Rosemary
Sage
Salt
Soy sauce
Tarragon
Thyme
Vanilla
Worcestershire sauce
Yeast

8-07

HERBS & SPICES

DRIED VS. FRESH. While dried herbs are convenient, they don't generally have the same purity of flavor as fresh herbs. Ensure dried herbs are still fresh by checking if they are green and not faded. Crush a few leaves to see if the aroma is still strong. Always store them in an air-tight container away from light and heat.

BASIL
Sweet, warm flavor with an aromatic odor. Use whole or ground. Good with lamb, fish, roast, stews, beef, vegetables, dressing and omelets.

BAY LEAVES
Pungent flavor. Use whole leaf but remove before serving. Good in vegetable dishes, seafood, stews and pickles.

CARAWAY
Spicy taste and aromatic smell. Use in cakes, breads, soups, cheese and sauerkraut.

CELERY SEED
Strong taste which resembles the vegetable. Can be used sparingly in pickles and chutney, meat and fish dishes, salads, bread, marinades, dressings and dips.

CHIVES
Sweet, mild flavor like that of onion. Excellent in salads, fish, soups and potatoes.

CILANTRO
Use fresh. Excellent in salads, fish, chicken, rice, beans and Mexican dishes.

CINNAMON
Sweet, pungent flavor. Widely used in many sweet baked goods, chocolate dishes, cheesecakes, pickles, chutneys and hot drinks.

CORIANDER
Mild, sweet, orangy flavor and available whole or ground. Common in curry powders and pickling spice and also used in chutney, meat dishes, casseroles, Greek-style dishes, apple pies and baked goods.

CURRY POWDER
Spices are combined to proper proportions to give a distinct flavor to meat, poultry, fish and vegetables.

DILL
Both seeds and leaves are flavorful. Leaves may be used as a garnish or cooked with fish, soup, dressings, potatoes and beans. Leaves or the whole plant may be used to flavor pickles.

FENNEL
Sweet, hot flavor. Both seeds and leaves are used. Use in small quantities in pies and baked goods. Leaves can be boiled with fish.

HERBS & SPICES

GINGER
A pungent root, this aromatic spice is sold fresh, dried or ground. Use in pickles, preserves, cakes, cookies, soups and meat dishes.

MARJORAM
May be used both dried or green. Use to flavor fish, poultry, omelets, lamb, stew, stuffing and tomato juice.

MINT
Aromatic with a cool flavor. Excellent in beverages, fish, lamb, cheese, soup, peas, carrots and fruit desserts.

NUTMEG
Whole or ground. Used in chicken and cream soups, cheese dishes, fish cakes, and with chicken and veal. Excellent in custards, milk puddings, pies and cakes.

OREGANO
Strong, aromatic odor. Use whole or ground in tomato juice, fish, eggs, pizza, omelets, chili, stew, gravy, poultry and vegetables.

PAPRIKA
A bright red pepper, this spice is used in meat, vegetables and soups or as a garnish for potatoes, salads or eggs.

PARSLEY
Best when used fresh, but can be used dried as a garnish or as a seasoning. Try in fish, omelets, soup, meat, stuffing and mixed greens.

ROSEMARY
Very aromatic. Can be used fresh or dried. Season fish, stuffing, beef, lamb, poultry, onions, eggs, bread and potatoes. Great in dressings.

SAFFRON
Aromatic, slightly bitter taste. Only a pinch needed to flavor and color dishes such as bouillabaisse, chicken soup, rice, paella, fish sauces, buns and cakes. Very expensive, so where a touch of color is needed, use turmeric instead, but the flavor will not be the same.

SAGE
Use fresh or dried. The flowers are sometimes used in salads. May be used in tomato juice, fish, omelets, beef, poultry, stuffing, cheese spreads and breads.

TARRAGON
Leaves have a pungent, hot taste. Use to flavor sauces, salads, fish, poultry, tomatoes, eggs, green beans, carrots and dressings.

THYME
Sprinkle leaves on fish or poultry before broiling or baking. Throw a few sprigs directly on coals shortly before meat is finished grilling.

TURMERIC
Aromatic, slightly bitter flavor. Should be used sparingly in curry powder and relishes and to color cakes and rice dishes.

Use 3 times more fresh herbs if substituting fresh for dried.

BAKING BREADS

HINTS FOR BAKING BREADS

- Kneading dough for 30 seconds after mixing improves the texture of baking powder biscuits.

- Instead of shortening, use cooking or salad oil in waffles and hot cakes.

- When bread is baking, a small dish of water in the oven will help keep the crust from hardening.

- Dip a spoon in hot water to measure shortening, butter, etc., and the fat will slip out more easily.

- Small amounts of leftover corn may be added to pancake batter for variety.

- To make bread crumbs, use the fine cutter of a food grinder and tie a large paper bag over the spout in order to prevent flying crumbs.

- When you are doing any sort of baking, you get better results if you remember to preheat your cookie sheet, muffin tins or cake pans.

3 RULES FOR USE OF LEAVENING AGENTS

1. In simple flour mixtures, use 2 teaspoons baking powder to leaven 1 cup flour. Reduce this amount 1/2 teaspoon for each egg used.

2. To 1 teaspoon soda, use 2 1/4 teaspoons cream of tartar, 2 cups freshly soured milk or 1 cup molasses.

3. To substitute soda and an acid for baking powder, divide the amount of baking powder by 4. Take that as your measure and add acid according to rule 2.

PROPORTIONS OF BAKING POWDER TO FLOUR

biscuits ....to 1 cup flour use 1 1/4 tsp. baking powder
cake with oil ....to 1 cup flour use 1 tsp. baking powder
muffins ....to 1 cup flour use 1 1/2 tsp. baking powder
popovers ....to 1 cup flour use 1 1/4 tsp. baking powder
waffles ....to 1 cup flour use 1 1/4 tsp. baking powder

PROPORTIONS OF LIQUID TO FLOUR

pour batter ....to 1 cup liquid use 1 cup flour
drop batter ....to 1 cup liquid use 2 to 2 1/2 cups flour
soft dough ....to 1 cup liquid use 3 to 3 1/2 cups flour
stiff dough ....to 1 cup liquid use 4 cups flour

TIME & TEMPERATURE CHART

Breads	Minutes	Temperature
biscuits	12 - 15	400° - 450°
cornbread	25 - 30	400° - 425°
gingerbread	40 - 50	350° - 370°
loaf	50 - 60	350° - 400°
nut bread	50 - 75	350°
popovers	30 - 40	425° - 450°
rolls	20 - 30	400° - 450°

BAKING DESSERTS

PERFECT COOKIES

Cookie dough that must be rolled is much easier to handle after it has been refrigerated for 10 to 30 minutes. This keeps the dough from sticking, even though it may be soft. If not done, the soft dough may require more flour and too much flour makes cookies hard and brittle. Place on a floured board only as much dough as can be easily managed. Flour the rolling pin slightly and roll lightly to desired thickness. Cut shapes close together and add trimmings to dough that needs to be rolled. Place pans or sheets in upper third of oven. Watch cookies carefully while baking in order to avoid burned edges. When sprinkling sugar on cookies, try putting it into a salt shaker in order to save time.

PERFECT PIES

- Pie crust will be better and easier to make if all the ingredients are cool.

- The lower crust should be placed in the pan so that it covers the surface smoothly. Air pockets beneath the surface will push the crust out of shape while baking.

- Folding the top crust over the lower crust before crimping will keep juices in the pie.

- When making custard pie, bake at a high temperature for about 10 minutes to prevent a soggy crust. Then finish baking at a low temperature.

- When making cream pie, sprinkle crust with powdered sugar in order to prevent it from becoming soggy.

PERFECT CAKES

- Fill cake pans two-thirds full and spread batter into corners and sides, leaving a slight hollow in the center.

- Cake is done when it shrinks from the sides of the pan or if it springs back when touched lightly with the finger.

- After removing a cake from the oven, place it on a rack for about 5 minutes. Then, the sides should be loosened and the cake turned out on a rack in order to finish cooling.

- Do not frost cakes until thoroughly cool.

- Icing will remain where you put it if you sprinkle cake with powdered sugar first.

TIME & TEMPERATURE CHART

Dessert	Time	Temperature
butter cake, layer	20-40 min.	380° - 400°
butter cake, loaf	40-60 min.	360° - 400°
cake, angel	50-60 min.	300° - 360°
cake, fruit	3-4 hrs.	275° - 325°
cake, sponge	40-60 min.	300° - 350°
cookies, molasses	18-20 min.	350° - 375°
cookies, thin	10-12 min.	380° - 390°
cream puffs	45-60 min.	300° - 350°
meringue	40-60 min.	250° - 300°
pie crust	20-40 min.	400° - 500°

VEGETABLES & FRUITS

COOKING TIME TABLE

Vegetable	Cooking Method	Time
artichokes	boiled	40 min.
	steamed	45-60 min.
asparagus tips	boiled	10-15 min.
beans, lima	boiled	20-40 min.
	steamed	60 min.
beans, string	boiled	15-35 min.
	steamed	60 min.
beets, old	boiled or steamed	1-2 hours.
beets, young with skin	boiled	30 min.
	steamed	60 min.
	baked	70-90 min.
broccoli, flowerets	boiled	5-10 min.
broccoli, stems	boiled	20-30 min.
brussels sprouts	boiled	20-30 min.
cabbage, chopped	boiled	10-20 min.
	steamed	25 min.
carrots, cut across	boiled	8-10 min.
	steamed	40 min.
cauliflower, flowerets	boiled	8-10 min.
cauliflower, stem down	boiled	20-30 min.
corn, green, tender	boiled	5-10 min.
	steamed	15 min.
	baked	20 min.
corn on the cob	boiled	8-10 min.
	steamed	15 min.
eggplant, whole	boiled	30 min.
	steamed	40 min.
	baked	45 min.
parsnips	boiled	25-40 min.
	steamed	60 min.
	baked	60-75 min.
peas, green	boiled or steamed	5-15 min.
potatoes	boiled	20-40 min.
	steamed	60 min.
	baked	45-60 min.
pumpkin or squash	boiled	20-40 min.
	steamed	45 min.
	baked	60 min.
tomatoes	boiled	5-15 min.
turnips	boiled	25-40 min.

DRYING TIME TABLE

Fruit	Sugar or Honey	Cooking Time
apricots	1/4 c. for each cup of fruit	about 40 min.
figs	1 T. for each cup of fruit	about 30 min.
peaches	1/4 c. for each cup of fruit	about 45 min.
prunes	2 T. for each cup of fruit	about 45 min.

VEGETABLES & FRUITS

BUYING FRESH VEGETABLES

Artichokes: Look for compact, tightly closed heads with green, clean-looking leaves. Avoid those with leaves that are brown or separated.

Asparagus: Stalks should be tender and firm; tips should be close and compact. Choose the stalks with very little white; they are more tender. Use asparagus soon because it toughens quickly.

Beans, Snap: Those with small seeds inside the pods are best. Avoid beans with dry-looking pods.

Broccoli, Brussels Sprouts and Cauliflower: Flower clusters on broccoli and cauliflower should be tight and close together. Brussels sprouts should be firm and compact. Smudgy, dirty spots may indicate pests or disease.

Cabbage and Head Lettuce: Choose heads that are heavy for their size. Avoid cabbage with worm holes and lettuce with discoloration or soft rot.

Cucumbers: Choose long, slender cucumbers for best quality. May be dark or medium green, but yellow ones are undesirable.

Mushrooms: Caps should be closed around the stems. Avoid black or brown gills.

Peas and Lima Beans: Select pods that are well-filled but not bulging. Avoid dried, spotted, yellow or limp pods.

BUYING FRESH FRUITS

Bananas: Skin should be free of bruises and black or brown spots. Purchase them slightly green and allow them to ripen at room temperature.

Berries: Select plump, solid berries with good color. Avoid stained containers which indicate wet or leaky berries. Berries with clinging caps, such as blackberries and raspberries, may be unripe. Strawberries without caps may be overripe.

Melons: In cantaloupes, thick, close netting on the rind indicates best quality. Cantaloupes are ripe when the stem scar is smooth and the space between the netting is yellow or yellow-green. They are best when fully ripe with fruity odor.

Honeydews are ripe when rind has creamy to yellowish color and velvety texture. Immature honeydews are whitish-green.

Ripe watermelons have some yellow color on one side. If melons are white or pale green on one side, they are not ripe.

Oranges, Grapefruit and Lemons: Choose those heavy for their size. Smoother, thinner skins usually indicate more juice. Most skin markings do not affect quality. Oranges with a slight greenish tinge may be just as ripe as fully colored ones. Light or greenish-yellow lemons are more tart than deep yellow ones. Avoid citrus fruits showing withered, sunken or soft areas.

NAPKIN FOLDING

FOR BEST RESULTS, use well-starched linen napkins if possible. For more complicated folds, 24-inch napkins work best. Practice the folds with newspapers. Children will have fun decorating the table once they learn these attractive folds!

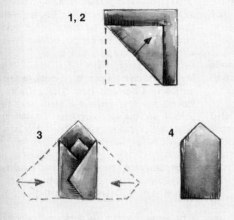

SHIELD

Easy fold. Elegant with monogram in corner.

Instructions:
1. Fold into quarter size. If monogrammed, ornate corner should face down.
2. Turn up folded corner three-quarters.
3. Overlap right side and left side points.
4. Turn over; adjust sides so they are even, single point in center.
5. Place point up or down on plate, or left of plate.

ROSETTE

Elegant on plate.

Instructions:
1. Fold left and right edges to center, leaving 1/2" opening along center.
2. Pleat firmly from top edge to bottom edge. Sharpen edges with hot iron.
3. Pinch center together. If necessary, use small piece of pipe cleaner to secure and top with single flower.
4. Spread out rosette.

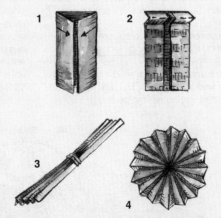

NAPKIN FOLDING

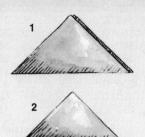

CANDLE

Easy to do; can be decorated.

Instructions:
1. Fold into triangle, point at top.
2. Turn lower edge up 1".
3. Turn over, folded edge down.
4. Roll tightly from left to right.
5. Tuck in corner. Stand upright.

FAN

Pretty in napkin ring or on plate.

Instructions:
1. Fold top and bottom edges to center.
2. Fold top and bottom edges to center a second time.
3. Pleat firmly from the left edge. Sharpen edges with hot iron.
4. Spread out fan. Balance flat folds of each side on table. Well-starched napkins will hold shape.

LILY

Effective and pretty on table.

Instructions:
1. Fold napkin into quarters.
2. Fold into triangle, closed corner to open points.
3. Turn two points over to other side. (Two points are on either side of closed point.)
4. Pleat.
5. Place closed end in glass. Pull down two points on each side and shape.

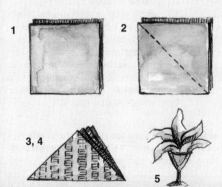

MEASUREMENTS & SUBSTITUTIONS

MEASUREMENTS

a pinch	1/8 teaspoon or less
3 teaspoons	1 tablespoon
4 tablespoons	1/4 cup
8 tablespoons	1/2 cup
12 tablespoons	3/4 cup
16 tablespoons	1 cup
2 cups	1 pint
4 cups	1 quart
4 quarts	1 gallon
8 quarts	1 peck
4 pecks	1 bushel
16 ounces	1 pound
32 ounces	1 quart
1 ounce liquid	2 tablespoons
8 ounces liquid	1 cup

Use standard measuring spoons and cups. All measurements are level.

C° TO F° CONVERSION

120° C	250° F
140° C	275° F
150° C	300° F
160° C	325° F
180° C	350° F
190° C	375° F
200° C	400° F
220° C	425° F
230° C	450° F

Temperature conversions are estimates.

SUBSTITUTIONS

Ingredient	Quantity	Substitute
baking powder	1 teaspoon	1/4 tsp. baking soda plus 1/2 tsp. cream of tartar
chocolate	1 square (1 oz.)	3 or 4 T. cocoa plus 1 T. butter
cornstarch	1 tablespoon	2 T. flour or 2 tsp. quick-cooking tapioca
cracker crumbs	3/4 cup	1 c. bread crumbs
dates	1 lb.	1 1/2 c. dates, pitted and cut
dry mustard	1 teaspoon	1 T. prepared mustard
flour, self-rising	1 cup	1 c. all-purpose flour, 1/2 tsp. salt, and 1 tsp. baking powder
herbs, fresh	1 tablespoon	1 tsp. dried herbs
ketchup or chili sauce	1 cup	1 c. tomato sauce plus 1/2 c. sugar and 2 T. vinegar (for use in cooking)
milk, sour	1 cup	1 T. lemon juice or vinegar plus sweet milk to make 1 c. (let stand 5 minutes)
whole	1 cup	1/2 c. evaporated milk plus 1/2 c. water
min. marshmallows	10	1 lg. marshmallow
onion, fresh	1 small	1 T. instant minced onion, rehydrated
sugar, brown	1/2 cup	2 T. molasses in 1/2 c. granulated sugar
powdered	1 cup	1 c. granulated sugar plus 1 tsp. cornstarch
tomato juice	1 cup	1/2 c. tomato sauce plus 1/2 c. water

When substituting cocoa for chocolate in cakes, the amount of flour must be reduced. Brown and white sugars usually can be interchanged.

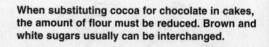

EQUIVALENCY CHART

Food	Quantity	Yield
apple	1 medium	1 cup
banana, mashed	1 medium	1/3 cup
bread	1 1/2 slices	1 cup soft crumbs
bread	1 slice	1/4 cup fine, dry crumbs
butter	1 stick or 1/4 pound	1/2 cup
cheese, American, cubed	1 pound	2 2/3 cups
American, grated	1 pound	5 cups
cream cheese	3-ounce package	6 2/3 tablespoons
chocolate, bitter	1 square	1 ounce
cocoa	1 pound	4 cups
coconut	1 1/2 pound package	2 2/3 cups
coffee, ground	1 pound	5 cups
cornmeal	1 pound	3 cups
cornstarch	1 pound	3 cups
crackers, graham	14 squares	1 cup fine crumbs
saltine	28 crackers	1 cup fine crumbs
egg	4-5 whole	1 cup
whites	8-10	1 cup
yolks	10-12	1 cup
evaporated milk	1 cup	3 cups whipped
flour, cake, sifted	1 pound	4 1/2 cups
rye	1 pound	5 cups
white, sifted	1 pound	4 cups
white, unsifted	1 pound	3 3/4 cups
gelatin, flavored	3 1/4 ounces	1/2 cup
unflavored	1/4 ounce	1 tablespoon
lemon	1 medium	3 tablespoon juice
marshmallows	16	1/4 pound
noodles, cooked	8-ounce package	7 cups
uncooked	4 ounces (1 1/2 cups)	2-3 cups cooked
macaroni, cooked	8-ounce package	6 cups
macaroni, uncooked	4 ounces (1 1/4 cups)	2 1/4 cups cooked
spaghetti, uncooked	7 ounces	4 cups cooked
nuts, chopped	1/4 pound	1 cup
almonds	1 pound	3 1/2 cups
walnuts, broken	1 pound	3 cups
walnuts, unshelled	1 pound	1 1/2 to 1 3/4 cups
onion	1 medium	1/2 cup
orange	3-4 medium	1 cup juice
raisins	1 pound	3 1/2 cups
rice, brown	1 cup	4 cups cooked
converted	1 cup	3 1/2 cups cooked
regular	1 cup	3 cups cooked
wild	1 cup	4 cups cooked
sugar, brown	1 pound	2 1/2 cups
powdered	1 pound	3 1/2 cups
white	1 pound	2 cups
vanilla wafers	22	1 cup fine crumbs
zwieback, crumbled	4	1 cups

FOOD QUANTITIES

FOR LARGE SERVINGS

	25 Servings	50 Servings	100 Servings
Beverages:			
coffee	1/2 pound and 1 1/2 gallons water	1 pound and 3 gallons water	2 pounds and 6 gallons water
lemonade	10-15 lemons and 1 1/2 gallons water	20-30 lemons and 3 gallons water	40-60 lemons and 6 gallons water
tea	1/12 pound and 1 1/2 gallons water	1/6 pound and 3 gallons water	1/3 pound and 6 gallons water
Desserts:			
layered cake	1 12" cake	3 10" cakes	6 10" cakes
sheet cake	1 10" x 12" cake	1 12" x 20" cake	2 12" x 20" cakes
watermelon	37 1/2 pounds	75 pounds	150 pounds
whipping cream	3/4 pint	1 1/2 to 2 pints	3-4 pints
Ice cream:			
brick	3 1/4 quarts	6 1/2 quarts	13 quarts
bulk	2 1/4 quarts	4 1/2 quarts or 1 1/4 gallons	9 quarts or 2 1/2 gallons
Meat, poultry or fish:			
fish	13 pounds	25 pounds	50 pounds
fish, fillets or steak	7 1/2 pounds	15 pounds	30 pounds
hamburger	9 pounds	18 pounds	35 pounds
turkey or chicken	13 pounds	25 to 35 pounds	50 to 75 pounds
wieners (beef)	6 1/2 pounds	13 pounds	25 pounds
Salads, casseroles:			
baked beans	3/4 gallon	1 1/4 gallons	2 1/2 gallons
jello salad	3/4 gallon	1 1/4 gallons	2 1/2 gallons
potato salad	4 1/4 quarts	2 1/4 gallons	4 1/2 gallons
scalloped potatoes	4 1/2 quarts or 1 12" x 20" pan	9 quarts or 2 1/4 gallons	18 quarts 4 1/2 gallons
spaghetti	1 1/4 gallons	2 1/2 gallons	5 gallons
Sandwiches:			
bread	50 slices or 3 1-pound loaves	100 slices or 6 1-pound loaves	200 slices or 12 1-pound loaves
butter	1/2 pound	1 pound	2 pounds
lettuce	1 1/2 heads	3 heads	6 heads
mayonnaise	1 cup	2 cups	4 cups
mixed filling			
meat, eggs, fish	1 1/2 quarts	3 quarts	6 quarts
jam, jelly	1 quart	2 quarts	4 quarts

QUICK FIXES

PRACTICALLY EVERYONE has experienced that dreadful moment in the kitchen when a recipe failed and dinner guests have arrived. Perhaps a failed timer, distraction or a missing or mismeasured ingredient is to blame. These handy tips can save the day!

Acidic foods – Sometimes a tomato-based sauce will become too acidic. Add baking soda, one teaspoon at a time, to the sauce. Use sugar as a sweeter alternative.

Burnt food on pots and pans – Allow the pan to cool on its own. Remove as much of the food as possible. Fill with hot water and add a capful of liquid fabric softener to the pot; let it stand for a few hours. You'll have an easier time removing the burnt food.

Chocolate seizes – Chocolate can seize (turn course and grainy) when it comes into contact with water. Place seized chocolate in a metal bowl over a large saucepan with an inch of simmering water in it. Over medium heat, slowly whisk in warm heavy cream. Use 1/4 cup cream to 4 ounces of chocolate. The chocolate will melt and become smooth.

Forgot to thaw whipped topping – Thaw in microwave for 1 minute on the defrost setting. Stir to blend well. Do not over thaw!

Hands smell like garlic or onion – Rinse hands under cold water while rubbing them with a large stainless steel spoon.

Hard brown sugar – Place in a paper bag and microwave for a few seconds, or place hard chunks in a food processor.

Jello too hard – Heat on a low microwave power setting for a very short time.

Lumpy gravy or sauce – Use a blender, food processor or simply strain.

No tomato juice – Mix 1/2 cup ketchup with 1/2 cup water.

Out of honey – Substitute 1 1/4 cups sugar dissolved in 1 cup water.

Overcooked sweet potatoes or carrots – Softened sweet potatoes and carrots make a wonderful soufflé with the addition of eggs and sugar. Consult your favorite cookbook for a good soufflé recipe. Overcooked sweet potatoes can also be used as pie filling.

Sandwich bread is stale – Toast or microwave bread briefly. Otherwise, turn it into breadcrumbs. Bread exposed to light and heat will hasten its demise, so consider using a bread box.

Soup, sauce, gravy too thin – Add 1 tablespoon of flour to hot soup, sauce or gravy. Whisk well (to avoid lumps) while the mixture is boiling. Repeat if necessary.

Sticky rice – Rinse rice with warm water.

Stew or soup is greasy – Refrigerate and remove grease once it congeals. Another trick is to lay cold lettuce leaves over the hot stew for about 10 seconds and then remove. Repeat as necessary.

Too salty – Add a little sugar and vinegar. For soups or sauces, add a raw peeled potato.

Too sweet – Add a little vinegar or lemon juice.

Undercooked cakes and cookies – Serve over vanilla ice cream. You can also layer pieces of cake or cookies with whipped cream and fresh fruit to form a dessert parfait. Crumbled cookies also make an excellent ice cream or cream pie topping.

COUNTING CALORIES

BEVERAGES

apple juice, 6 oz.	90
coffee (black)	0
cola, 12 oz.	115
cranberry juice, 6 oz.	115
ginger ale, 12 oz.	115
grape juice, (prepared from frozen concentrate), 6 oz.	142
lemonade, (prepared from frozen concentrate), 6 oz.	85
milk, protein fortified, 1 c.	105
skim, 1 c.	90
whole, 1 c.	160
orange juice, 6 oz.	85
pineapple juice, unsweetened, 6 oz.	95
root beer, 12 oz.	150
tonic (quinine water) 12 oz.	132

BREADS

cornbread, 1 sm. square	130
dumplings, 1 med.	70
French toast, 1 slice	135
melba toast, 1 slice	25
muffins, blueberry, 1 muffin	110
bran, 1 muffin	106
corn, 1 muffin	125
English, 1 muffin	280
pancakes, 1 (4-in.)	60
pumpernickel, 1 slice	75
rye, 1 slice	60
waffle, 1	216
white, 1 slice	60-70
whole wheat, 1 slice	55-65

CEREALS

cornflakes, 1 c.	105
cream of wheat, 1 c.	120
oatmeal, 1 c.	148
rice flakes, 1 c.	105
shredded wheat, 1 biscuit	100
sugar krisps, 3/4 c.	110

CRACKERS

graham, 1 cracker	15-30
rye crisp, 1 cracker	35
saltine, 1 cracker	17-20
wheat thins, 1 cracker	9

DAIRY PRODUCTS

butter or margarine, 1 T.	100
cheese, American, 1 oz.	100
camembert, 1 oz.	85
cheddar, 1 oz.	115
cottage cheese, 1 oz.	30
mozzarella, 1 oz.	90
parmesan, 1 oz.	130
ricotta, 1 oz.	50
roquefort, 1 oz.	105
Swiss, 1 oz.	105
cream, light, 1 T.	30
heavy, 1 T.	55
sour, 1 T.	45
hot chocolate, with milk, 1 c.	277
milk chocolate, 1 oz.	145-155
yogurt	
made w/ whole milk, 1 c.	150-165
made w/ skimmed milk, 1 c.	125

EGGS

fried, 1 lg.	100
poached or boiled, 1 lg.	75-80
scrambled or in omelet, 1 lg.	110-130

FISH AND SEAFOOD

bass, 4 oz.	105
salmon, broiled or baked, 3 oz.	155
sardines, canned in oil, 3 oz.	170
trout, fried, 3 1/2 oz.	220
tuna, in oil, 3 oz.	170
in water, 3 oz.	110

COUNTING CALORIES

FRUITS

apple, 1 med. 80-100
applesauce, sweetened, 1/2 c. 90-115
   unsweetened, 1/2 c. 50
banana, 1 med. 85
blueberries, 1/2 c. 45
cantaloupe, 1/2 c. 24
cherries (pitted), raw, 1/2 c. 40
grapefruit, 1/2 med. 55
grapes, 1/2 c. 35-55
honeydew, 1/2 c. 55
mango, 1 med. 90
orange, 1 med. 65-75
peach, 1 med. 35
pear, 1 med. 60-100
pineapple, fresh, 1/2 c. 40
   canned in syrup, 1/2 c. 95
plum, 1 med. 30
strawberries, fresh, 1/2 c. 30
   frozen and sweetened, 1/2 c. ..120-140
tangerine, 1 lg. 39
watermelon, 1/2 c. 42

MEAT AND POULTRY

beef, ground (lean), 3 oz. 185
   roast, 3 oz. 185
chicken, broiled, 3 oz. 115
lamb chop (lean), 3 oz. 175-200
steak, sirloin, 3 oz. 175
   tenderloin, 3 oz. 174
   top round, 3 oz. 162
turkey, dark meat, 3 oz. 175
   white meat, 3 oz. 150
veal, cutlet, 3 oz. 156
   roast, 3 oz. 76

NUTS

almonds, 2 T. 105
cashews, 2 T. 100
peanuts, 2 T. 105
peanut butter, 1 T. 95
pecans, 2 T. 95
pistachios, 2 T. 92
walnuts, 2 T. 80

PASTA

macaroni or spaghetti,
   cooked, 3/4 c. 115

SALAD DRESSINGS

blue cheese, 1 T. 70
French, 1 T. 65
Italian, 1 T. 80
mayonnaise, 1 T. 100
olive oil, 1 T. 124
Russian, 1 T. 70
salad oil, 1 T. 120

SOUPS

bean, 1 c. 130-180
beef noodle, 1 c. 70
bouillon and consomme, 1 c. 30
chicken noodle, 1 c. 65
chicken with rice, 1 c. 50
minestrone, 1 c. 80-150
split pea, 1 c. 145-170
tomato with milk, 1 c. 170
vegetable, 1 c. 80-100

VEGETABLES

asparagus, 1 c. 35
broccoli, cooked, 1/2 c. 25
cabbage, cooked, 1/2 c. 15-20
carrots, cooked, 1/2 c. 25-30
cauliflower, 1/2 c. 10-15
corn (kernels), 1/2 c. 70
green beans, 1 c. 30
lettuce, shredded, 1/2 c. 5
mushrooms, canned, 1/2 c. 20
onions, cooked, 1/2 c. 30
peas, cooked, 1/2 c. 60
potato, baked, 1 med. 90
   chips, 8-10 100
   mashed, w/milk & butter, 1 c. ..200-300
spinach, 1 c. 40
tomato, raw, 1 med. 25
   cooked, 1/2 c. 30

COOKING TERMS

Au gratin: Topped with crumbs and/or cheese and browned in oven or under broiler.

Au jus: Served in its own juices.

Baste: To moisten foods during cooking with pan drippings or special sauce in order to add flavor and prevent drying.

Bisque: A thick cream soup.

Blanch: To immerse in rapidly boiling water and allow to cook slightly.

Cream: To soften a fat, especially butter, by beating it at room temperature. Butter and sugar are often creamed together, making a smooth, soft paste.

Crimp: To seal the edges of a two-crust pie either by pinching them at intervals with the fingers or by pressing them together with the tines of a fork.

Crudites: An assortment of raw vegetables (i.e. carrots, broccoli, celery, mushrooms) that is served as an hors d'oeuvre, often accompanied by a dip.

Degrease: To remove fat from the surface of stews, soups or stock. Usually cooled in the refrigerator so that fat hardens and is easily removed.

Dredge: To coat lightly with flour, corn-meal, etc.

Entree: The main course.

Fold: To incorporate a delicate substance, such as whipped cream or beaten egg whites, into another substance without releasing air bubbles. A spatula is used to gently bring part of the mixture from the bottom of the bowl to the top. The process is repeated, while slowly rotating the bowl, until the ingredients are thoroughly blended.

Glaze: To cover with a glossy coating, such as a melted and somewhat diluted jelly for fruit desserts.

Julienne: To cut or slice vegetables, fruits or cheeses into match-shaped slivers.

Marinate: To allow food to stand in a liquid in order to tenderize or to add flavor.

Meuniére: Dredged with flour and sautéed in butter.

Mince: To chop food into very small pieces.

Parboil: To boil until partially cooked; to blanch. Usually final cooking in a sea-soned sauce follows this procedure.

Pare: To remove the outermost skin of a fruit or vegetable.

Poach: To cook gently in hot liquid kept just below the boiling point.

Purée: To mash foods by hand by rubbing through a sieve or food mill, or by whirling in a blender or food processor until per-fectly smooth.

Refresh: To run cold water over food that has been parboiled in order to stop the cooking process quickly.

Sauté: To cook and/or brown food in a small quantity of hot shortening.

Scald: To heat to just below the boiling point, when tiny bubbles appear at the edge of the saucepan.

Simmer: To cook in liquid just below the boiling point. The surface of the liquid should be barely moving, broken from time to time by slowly rising bubbles.

Steep: To let food stand in hot liquid in order to extract or to enhance flavor, like tea in hot water or poached fruit in syrup.

Toss: To combine ingredients with a re-peated lifting motion.

Whip: To beat rapidly in order to incorpo-rate air and produce expansion, as in heavy cream or egg whites.